MAISON
JANSEN

20TH CENTURY DECORATORS SERIES

JANSEN

MITCHELL OWENS, SERIES EDITOR

JANSEN

JAMES ARCHER ABBOTT

ACANTHUS PRESS

NEW YORK : 2006

ACANTHUS PRESS, LLC
48 West 22nd Street
New York, New York 10010
www.acanthuspress.com
212.414.0108

Library of Congress Cataloging-in-Publication Data
Abbott, James A. (James Archer), 1963-
Jansen / James Archer Abbott ; edited by Mitchell Owens ;
   p. cm.
Includes bibliographical references and index.
ISBN 0-926494-33-3 (alk. paper)
1. Maison Jansen (Firm)--Catalogs. 2. Interior decoration--France--History--19th century--Catalogs. 3. Interior
decoration--France--History--20th century--Catalogs. 4. Maison Jansen (Firm)--History. I. Owens, Mitchell. II.
Jansen, Jean-Henri, 1854-1928. III. Maison Jansen (Firm) IV. Title.
NK2049.Z9J362 2006
747'.8880922--dc22
                    2005030968

THIS BOOK IS DEDICATED TO: BRIGITTE BOUDIN DE LAAGE DE MEUX (1939-2004),
KEEPER OF THE FLAME; THOMAS HILLS COOK, APPRECIATOR OF BEAUTIFUL THINGS;
AND JONATHAN ALBERT MCINTYRE, REALIST.

FRONTISPIECE: View of the grand staircase, residence of Solveig and Francis Francis Jr., Château Solveig,
Gland, Switzerland.

Printed in China

CONTENTS

INTRODUCTION

ATRONIZED BY QUEENS AND MILLIONAIRES, CAPTAINS OF INDUSTRY, leaders of international society, and the occasional dictator, Maison Jansen was the most famous and influential interior-decorating firm of the 20th century. Although long associated with an elite block of buildings on rue Royale in Paris, near the Ritz Hotel and the restaurant Maxim's, the firm had a global reputation almost from its founding in 1880.

Jansen initially promoted contemporary design—including the heavily tufted Turkish style and the restrained Japanism of the 1880s—and continued to do so throughout its existence. But in response to political and social influences within France, the firm adopted an 18th-century revival aesthetic that became its calling card. Later, Jansen added the early-19th-century imperialistic design vocabulary created for Napoleon Bonaparte, a resurrection that appealed to modern "emperors" (kings, shahs, and presidents) who sought the firm's guidance throughout the 20th century.

By the time Jean-Henri Jansen (1854–1928) founded the company in the early years of France's Third Republic, Jansen and its now largely forgotten contemporaries—among them Jules Allard et Fils, E. Delmas, Mercier Frères, A. Gouverneur, and Duveen Brothers—had redefined the profession of decorator. The best designers operated not as servants but as social equals: dinner partners or weekend guests who maintained a keen eye for architecture, design, and antiques. Jansen never decorated a house for a client, noted one employee; the firm's staff "instead assisted the individual . . . [This] is why you rarely see a period credit assigned to a Jansen interior . . . We merely aided . . . It was not proper for one to overshadow the client."[1]

Embedded in the foundation of Jansen's reputation were talented artists, designers, and businessmen. Some of them, frustratingly, are known only by their surnames; others have a more visible established history. During its existence, Jansen employed Leon Amar, Roger Bengue, Léon Bénouville, Carlos Ortiz-Cabrera, Michel Camus, Albert Cazes, Francis Chaillou, Delavigne, Pierre Deshays, Dietrich, Harold Eberhard, Oliver Ford, André Gignoux, Paul Heuclin, Michel Ignazi, René Joubert, Arthur Kouwenhoven, Victor Lehmann, Henri Leris, Claude Mandron, Paul Manno, Leo Monte, Poubelle, J. Regnault, Serge Robin, Pierre-Marie

9 RUE ROYALE, C. 1922

Rudelle, Henri Samuel, Gaston Schwartz, Jean Travers, Pierre Valéry, and Vandries. Its most important employees were Stéphane Boudin (1888–1967) and Pierre Delbée (1900–1974), two of the most influential tastemakers of the 20th century. Boudin ruled Jansen from 1936 to 1961, as its president, and his name was virtually interchangeable with the firm's. He established the recognizable Jansen look: a skillful and seemingly impossible melding of 18th-century French palace historicism, 1920s Hollywood theatrics, and country house subtleties.

The firm's extraordinary ateliers, or workshops, produced magnificent woodwork, furniture, and metalwork—and also restored antiques—for the company's projects. It was an unrivaled group of talents. Gilt bronze, mirrored glass, forged iron, lacquer, Lucite,

and many other materials, natural and manmade, were used to make both one-of-a-kind and limited-production pieces, most of them intended for a specific client's house or for purchase through the many incarnations of the Jansen boutique. The firm's best-known creations included gilt-bronze occasional tables topped with sheets of mirror and an oblong dining table mounted on castors, its gunmetal legs ornamented with rings of brass to mimic bamboo.

Jansen's clients also relied on the firm to provide 18th-century furniture and art objects. The rue Royale headquarters was the site of the company's first antiques gallery, but at least one other followed by 1920. From these galleries came richly veneered writing tables by Jean-Henri Riesener (1734–1806), rare sets of tapestries from the workshop of Gaspard van der Borght,

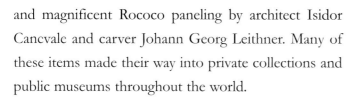

DISPLAY WINDOW AT 9 RUE ROYALE, C. 1922, REPRESENTING A
LOUIS XVI SALON

9 RUE ROYALE, C. 1970

and magnificent Rococo paneling by architect Isidor Cancvale and carver Johann Georg Leithner. Many of these items made their way into private collections and public museums throughout the world.

After its defeat by Germany in 1871, France eagerly sought a sense of security, along with validity as a new republic. Napoleon III had gone into exile in England, and the French nation rebelled against a continuation of monarchical rule. Ironically, its cultural and civic leaders adopted an aesthetic that looked back to the 18th-century Bourbon kings.

Jean-Henri Jansen, like many other artists, decorators, and antique dealers of the time, soon offered furniture and room schemes representative of the kingly Rococo and monarchical classicism that also heralded a newfound nationalism. This embrace of the past

brought about a new appreciation for the decorative arts in general. By 1887, two similar yet sometimes disagreeing organizations—the Union Centrale des Beaux-Arts Appliqués à l'Industrie and the Société du Musée des Arts Décoratifs—merged to establish the Union Central des Arts Décoratifs, the eventual sponsor of a national Musée des Arts Décoratifs. Supported by collectors, gallery owners, and manufacturers, this institution celebrated the applied arts. Collections of historic cabinetwork, metalwork, textiles, glass, and ceramics were assembled as a physical reference for designers and manufacturers—an encyclopedic homage to the artistry of France. Maison Jansen, as did other, similar enterprises, both supported this endeavor and benefited from its celebration of antique styles. The appetite for the historic became

JEAN-HENRI JANSEN, THE COMPANY'S FOUNDER, c. 1920

the crest of the Spanish royal house was emblazoned on the firm's letterhead even after the latter king was sent into exile in 1931.

Maison Jansen's success warranted a move in 1885 to larger, more prestigious quarters at 9 rue Royale, between the fashionable rue de Rivoli and the Place de la Madeleine.[2] Behind a Louis XV facade designed by Ange-Jacques Gabriel (1698–1782), the architect of the Petit Trianon, the five-story, four-bay building had been constructed in 1758 by architect Louis Le Tellier. Using the large expanses of two later street-level windows, Jean-Henri became adept at promoting the highly fashionable historical styles of 18th-century France in changing vignettes; his "skill and attention to detail . . . were new to Paris."[3] Some of these displays consisted of simple arrangements of Sèvres vases and ormolu clocks, and others were more ambitious room settings. Illuminated by the glow of gas streetlamps, these elegant displays became destinations for strolling couples and potential clients.

Within its first decade, Maison Jansen became one of Europe's leading design houses, in no small measure because of Jean-Henri Jansen's masterful promotional skills, which included participation in the important exhibition venues. One of the firm's earliest acknowledgments was a silver medal at the 1883 Amsterdam exposition, which emphasized the political and military importance of colonial empires. Along with re-creations of Dutch East Indies villages were displays by other empire-building nations. France was given the largest space, and Jansen, only three years in existence, was among the chosen exhibitors. Jansen's interpretation of 18th-century royal taste reinforced France's unrivaled domination of the aesthetic world.

Similar recognition came at Paris' Exposition Universelle in 1889, where Jansen received another

well ensconced in France, and Jean-Henri Jansen was dedicated to its satisfaction.

Little is known about Jean-Henri Jansen (1854–1928), reportedly a native of the Netherlands. (It is possible that he was born Jan-Hendrik or Johannes Hendrickus.) Only 25 or 26 when he founded his firm in 1880, he probably had worked for a decorating or architecture firm, one that offered the kind of expert training and rarified client contacts that led to his quick professional ascent. During or soon after the 1883 International Colonial Exposition in Amsterdam, for example, Maison Jansen began its long history as a decorator to royalty with commissions for William III of the Netherlands and Alfonso XII of Spain. Alfonso XII and his posthumous son and heir, Alfonso XIII, were among Maison Jansen's important patrons, and silver medal. During this fair, the firm executed special themes for its nearby windows on rue Royale. The firm's presentations apparently led Leopold II of the Belgians to commission Jansen to restore Château de Laeken, an 18th-century residence of the royal family, soon after it was badly damaged by fire on New Year's Day 1890. This project became the firm's longest commission, with work extending into the 1960s.

Jansen was known across the Atlantic by this time, its interpretations of 18th-century rooms having captured the attention of Americans such as the architect Ogden Codman Jr. (1863–1951). He admired the firm's espousal of historicism and incorporated some of its decorative accessories in projects such as the private rooms of The Breakers, built in Newport, Rhode Island, between 1893 and 1895 by railroad heir Cornelius Vanderbilt.[4] A history of Jansen published in 1971 noted that the names Rockefeller, Gould, and Goelet were listed among its important early U.S. clients. By the 1920s, Jansen's influence extended to the American heartland through the design of a suite of rooms for cosmetics manufacturer Carl Week's wife, Edith, in the couple's Des Moines, Iowa mansion, Salisbury House.

The firm did not completely abandon contemporary design, however. Although it celebrated the achievements of the 18th century, it continued to promote new fashions. For this purpose, Jean-Henri acquired neighboring 6 rue Royale, where Madame de Staël had lived during the Directoire period. The building's marquee changed to reflect each new trend; in an 1897 photograph of 6 rue Royale it reads, "modern styles," in an Art Nouveau typeface. Jansen embraced the fluid, asymmetrical vocabulary of that briefly fashionable movement. At the Exposition Universelle in 1900, the firm exhibited a fire screen, chairs, and paneling, cre-

ated in collaboration with sculptor Jean Escoula (1851–1911) and the artist and designer Eugène Martial Simas (1862–?), that rivaled the work of movement's promoter, Louis Majorelle (1859–1926).[5]

Presumably around 1900, Jean-Henri Jansen established a separate gallery for the presentation and sale of mostly 18th-century furniture and objects at 9 rue Royale. It "contain[ed] what furnished the palaces . . . of Queen Catherine de Medici and the boudoirs of the agitated years where philosophers prepared for the Revolution inside the mezzanine retreats of Madame de Pompadour."[6] This endeavor was a great success, and it led to the creation of a New York City gallery in October 1915.[7] Jansen, Inc., as it was called, opened at 25 West 54th Street.[8] Seven years later, a writer observed, "The Jansen firm is the first among antiquaires of the world."[9]

The definition of *antique* during the early decades of the 20th century differed from the very specific meaning now accepted by decorators, art dealers, and collectors. Antique was as much a style for emulation, if not exact reproduction, as it was a qualifier of age. Jansen promoted an appreciation for the exquisite craftsmanship of the 18th century while developing the skills necessary to replicate period pieces. Indeed, although pre-Revolutionary furniture by ébénistes Jean-Henri Riesener and George Jacob (1739–1814) was sold to appreciative collectors, it was also copied. In the early years, these reproductions were often assigned to outside artisans, such as Joseph Emmanuel Zwiener (1849–c.1900), Henry Dasson (1825–1896), and François Linke (1855–1946). By 1900, Jansen's expanded ateliers could match the work of Paris' finest furniture makers. "In bringing together this entire body of professionals," observed one visitor to Jansen's workrooms, "it becomes possible to give to

ABOVE AND TOP: BEDROOM OF EDITH WEEKS, SALISBURY HOUSE, DES MOINES, IOWA, 1927

CHAISE LONGUE, C. 1900

the workmanship a focus, unusual accommodations, and assurance [of] perfection otherwise unknown."[10]

The workrooms, originally located on rue Pergolèse, in the 16th arrondissement, presumably started as a warehouse for the receipt and distribution of works commissioned from independent artisans. In or around 1900, Jansen acquired a larger complex on rue Saint-Sabin, near the Bastille, which served the firm for nearly 80 years. The complex became a five-story, nearly 40,000-square-foot facility, at its peak employing between 500 and 700 people, mostly men.

Maison Jansen, encouraged by its already long list of South American patrons, opened its first satellite office in Argentina, in 1905. Buenos Aires was recognized as European in sophistication, and thanks to Beaux-Arts-trained architects, its streets were lined with mansions inspired by the still highly fashionable taste of 18th-century French monarchs. So successful was Jansen's Buenos Aires enterprise—some of the firm's best antiques were shipped here for clients such as the German armaments king Fritz Mandl—that by 1938 the firm oversaw the interior decoration of a new luxury oceanliner scheduled for the French–Argentine route, the *Pasteur*.[11]

The existence of satellite offices enhanced the firm's reputation as an international tastemaker, but it also posed some problems. Office administrators were to serve the firm's clients, but without overshadowing Jean-Henri Jansen and his successors as the firm's arbiters of taste. This in itself proved a continual challenge. Billing was usually directed from the smaller office, but sometimes invoices were submitted from

LOUIS-XV-STYLE ROCKING CHAIR FOR THE CUBAN MARKET

Paris, causing confusion for both the client and Jansen's staff. Other complications involved actual furniture and the production of carved paneling. The Paris ateliers usually supplied the majority of specially commissioned woodwork and furniture. However, the Buenos Aries office at 5 calle Florida used Argentinean craftspeople, especially during World War I, when contact with the Paris office and shipment of decorative elements from France became difficult.

Between 1905 and 1922, additional offices followed in Havana, Cairo, Alexandria, and London. For Cuban clients, all new furniture and paneling was made from native woods, mainly mahogany, shipped to the Paris ateliers as raw lumber and returned in historically inspired forms. (Native woods were less susceptible to insect infestations and climate-induced rot.) Of the antiques that found their way to Cuba, careful

consideration was given to methods of controlling interior humidity levels, an intriguingly sophisticated concern for the time period. Such efforts on the part of preservation were demonstrated time and again in Havana, particularly in the Petit Trianon–inspired residence of Countess de Revilla de Camargo. For the countess and other Cuban clients, the island's hot, humid climate often dictated modifications to the popular historicism espoused by Jansen; electric fans were integrated into Rococo-style ceilings, and a breeze-inducing rocking chair occasionally emulated a Louis XV fauteuil. By the 1930s, the formality of the French ancien régime was gradually replaced with a more casual mix of 18th-century monarchical design and 20th-century modernism. In the area of preservation, Jansen was eventually recognized as an important source for the restoration of non-French architecture and decorative objects; in the 1940s, the firm helped to restore the interior of a 16th-century Spanish-built church, Iglesia Mayor de San Juan Bautista de los Remedios.

French historical taste entered the Egyptian national aesthetic with the opening of the Suez Canal in 1869, and by the first decades of the 20th century, Jansen had opened offices at 1 rue Baehler in Cairo and 58 rue Fouad I in Alexandria. Considered "the most sought after buildings," they were perfectly positioned to enhance Jansen's presence in Egypt, being adjacent to "the leading boutiques," banks, and consulates.[12] The firm is recorded as having provided decorating services to fashion-conscious King Farouk and other members of his family, such as his uncle Cherif Sabry, as well as the Cattauis and Baharis banking families.[13] From its Alexandria and Cairo offices, Jansen handled everything from the creation of elegant rooms to housekeeping services during off-season retreats by the royal family and the Anglo- and Franco-Egyptian elite.

PRIVATE STUDY OF EDWARD VII AT BUCKINGHAM PALACE, C. 1910

The London office was less well known. Opened at around the same time as the Argentinean and Egyptian offices, Jansen, Ltd., as it was called, concentrated almost exclusively on a vocabulary blending Louis XV and XVI with the designs of 18th-century British tastemakers William Kent and Robert Adam. Before the opening of the London office, Maison Jansen purportedly provided decorating services to Edward VII at Buckingham Palace, sometime during the king's 1901–10 reign.[14] After World War II, Jansen was located at 102 George Street, off Portman Square. For most of the 1950s, the interior designer Oliver Ford (1925–1992), who at one time worked for Queen Elizabeth (the Queen Mother), served as director of this office. At this time, letterhead for the firm recorded "Jansen of Paris, Ltd.," emphasizing the French origin and, presumably, French concentration

of the firm's work.[15] By 1915, with most of Europe at war, Jean-Henri Jansen, then in his 60s, was concerned about the future of his global enterprise. "I would imagine Monsieur Jansen saw that he could not go on forever . . . certainly not as long as his great design house [would]," said onetime Jansen employee Claude Mandron.[16] The founder purportedly approached Stéphane Boudin, a 35-year-old salesman in his family's trimmings firm, and asked him to join the business in the early 1920s. Accounts of this proposal differ. One has Boudin solicited by Jansen during a showing of the latest Boudin trimmings; Jean-Henri Jansen's appreciation of the younger man's eye for detail and proportion was apparently noted. However, according to Boudin's daughter, Brigitte Boudin de Laage de Meux, the arrangement was more an agreement between Jean-Henri Jansen and her grandfather Alexandre

ALEXANDRE BOUDIN, FATHER OF STÉPHANE, AND FOUNDER OF
THE TRIMMINGS BUSINESS THAT BORE HIS NAME

Boudin, who were longtime friends. "Jansen approached my grandfather with a proposition," de Laage said. "Since you have two sons to succeed you, and I have none, won't you spare me one for the future of Jansen?"[17]

There probably was also a financial incentive for Boudin's induction into the firm. Ambitious expansion of the Jansen ateliers and the services they provided in the years just prior to World War I left the firm with little liquid capital. Added to this fact was the economic devastation of the war, as well as the Third Republic's attempt to defray the costs of battle with the implementation of an income tax in 1917. By 1920, Jean-Henri Jansen needed investors.[18] The Boudin family probably had funds that could secure the firm's survival. Gaston Schwartz and a man known only as Vandries also joined Jean-Henri Jansen in business at this time, becoming partners in or soon after 1920. Vandries is associated with the ateliers, and he apparently administered all aspects of production and restoration work for the firm; he may have risen through the ranks of the workshops. Although some historians have assessed the Paris-born Gaston Schwartz's name and his presumed religious faith of Judaism as evidence of his role as businessman or financial backer, he was in fact a designer, and one who espoused a burgeoning European modernism.

Following the incorporation of this partnership, a number of talented designers were brought into the firm. In 1925, at the age of 21, Henri Samuel was hired, purportedly as Boudin's assistant; among his clients was the American publisher William Randolph Hearst. Samuel left the firm in 1934 to join Ramsay, a Jansen competitor. An equally talented designer named Pierre Delbée joined Maison Jansen in the late 1920s, possibly 1930. He took the theatrics of interior design to a new level, even designing sets for stage productions such as the Madeleine Renaud/Jean-Louis Barrault 1956 production of Molière's *Le Misanthrope*. Delbée's marriage to Suzy Lazard, reportedly a member of the family that owned the French investment firm Lazard Frères et Cie, likely also provided Maison Jansen with introductions to many important clients.[19]

Jean-Henri Jansen died on September 21, 1928. His share of the enterprise was probably divided equally among his three younger partners, whose names—in the order of Schwartz, Vandries, and Boudin—were added to the firm's letterhead. Schwartz, the new president, led the firm's way in contemporary design, while Vandries administered the ateliers and Boudin guided the more traditional, 18th-century-focused arm of the design house. Schwartz's elevation to the presidency assuredly had much to do with the climate of French decorative arts and design. He was well ensconced in the modernism of the 1925 Exposition Internationale des Arts Décoratifs et Industriels Modernes held in Paris, which refuted adherence to traditional design and thus had been the first international exposition since Jansen's founding not to include representations of the firm's trademark historical work. In the postwar era, Europeans were encouraged to look toward the future, not the past. Thus, Schwartz appeared the most qualified to lead the firm forward.

Under Schwartz, Jansen continued to expand and opened offices in New York and Prague. Jansen, Inc., launched in 1934 at 1 East 57th Street and Fifth Avenue, was actually an expanded version of the Jansen gallery opened nearly 20 years before on West 54th Street. This larger enterprise, located in the New York Trust Company Building, included a new gallery of antique furniture, a design studio, and offices, which was administered by interior decorator Francis Chaillou.

The Prague office seems to have been short-lived and likely did not produce independent work, being more for the general supervision of Paris-born designs installed in Eastern European countries, such as the decoration of Prince Regent Paul of Yugoslavia's Beli Dvor (White Palace), in the Belgrade suburb of Dedinje.

Like Boudin, Schwartz was best known by his last name alone. Schwartz's contributions to the firm have gone largely undocumented, however. Presumably it was the modern-minded Schwartz who refreshed the Jansen design vocabulary by incorporating mirrored glass and molded crystal into the firm's more dominant repertoire of 18th-century paneling and furniture. The low lacquer tables that also became part of a Jansen aes-

thetic at this time should be credited to Schwartz, as record suggests that the better-known Boudin remained much more the traditionalist until later in the 1930s.

These and other contemporary features were brought together at Château Solveig in Gland, Switzerland, a 1935 project credited to Schwartz.[20] Executed for an Anglo-American millionaire and his wife, this astounding residence—with dramatic recessed lighting, chartreuse-colored lacquered walls, and glass balustrades—is uncharacteristic of Jansen's work of the early 20th century. It epitomized French modernism.

Another example of Jansen modernism was found in New York's new 47-story Waldorf-Astoria Hotel, which opened in 1931. Jansen was selected to design the reincarnation of Peacock Alley, a corridor that had become a promenade for America's social elite in the original Waldorf-Astoria of the 1890s. Large planes of polished French burled walnut, framed by red marble pilasters, divided the walls in a minimalist manner uncommon to American hotels at the time. Furnishings consisted of delicate upholstered club chairs, open-armed loveseats, and mirror-topped coffee tables, all neatly arranged in conversation groupings along the sides of a broad central pathway. Like Château Solveig's interiors, the new Peacock Alley reflected European modernism, although this American interpretation was a bit more conservative in its overall composition.

Traditional interiors continued to have an enthusiastic appreciation among the majority of Jansen's private clients, such as Lady Baillie, Lady Honor and Henry Channon, Nancy and Ronald Tree, and Katherine and Theodore A. Havemeyer. Although some of these commissions came from existing patrons of the firm or self-established art connoisseurs seeking sympathetic backdrops for their collections, others were for people new to a social or political stage and in need of validation via a tried-and-true formula that included pedigree and provenance.

To this end, and with Schwartz and Vandries' support, Boudin negotiated the purchase and removal of a number of circa-1770 paneled rooms from Paar Palace in Vienna, before its demolition in the 1930s. This acquisition was a coup for Maison Jansen, for the paneling was among the finest examples of the Rococo period, having been designed by French-born architect Isidor Canevale and ornamented by Austrian sculptor Johann Georg Leithner. Boudin used these architectural remnants in a number of key projects. Beautifully carved pine panels from two of the rooms, retaining much of their original pale blue pigment, were sent to Sir Philip Sassoon, the English art connoisseur, for his London residence at 25 Park Lane.[21] Other interior features were later included in the Paris houses of Bolivian tin-mining heirs Antenor Patino and his brother-in-law Jorge Ortiz Linares. An oak parquet floor from Paar Palace was incorporated in Boudin's inspired evocation of an 18th-century German mirrored room for the Henry Channons' London house, 5 Belgrave Square.

While working for Nancy and Ronald Tree at their country residence, Ditchley, Boudin met Russell Page (1906–1985), a young landscape architect planning the formal gardens. Kindred spirits with regard to their admiration for proportion and balance, Page and Boudin formed a near partnership for the next 30 years. "Knowing his own field so well," wrote Page of Boudin, "he could understand the complications and possibilities of garden design without any specialized knowledge."[22] The duo worked together on a number of properties, including Château du Vert Bois in northern France for Anne and Albert Prouvost, director of the newspaper *Paris Soir,* and Château de

Mivoisin, the country house of textile manufacturer Marcel Boussac and his wife, Fanny.

In the realm of country houses, Boudin is perhaps best known for his decades of work at Leeds Castle, near Maidstone, Kent, England. In 1933 he met the castle's owner, Olive, Lady Baillie, granddaughter of the American multimillionaire William C. Whitney, and assisted with the decoration of her London residence on Grosvenor Square.[23] Boudin's greatest creations for Lady Baillie included an exceptional Louis XV–style bedchamber with patinated blue paneling and a banquette-lined library modeled on the designs of 17th-century French architect Daniel Marot. Lady Baillie, more than any other patron of the pre–World War II era, directed new customers to the Jansen firm.

A variation of this partnership was enjoyed by Lady Mendl, née Elsie de Wolfe. The American actress turned decorator employed Jansen to assist with the decoration of Villa Trianon in Versailles, France, and the relationship later developed symbiotic aspects. Boudin directed certain choice pieces of furniture and art objects to Lady Mendl's attention and also provided design services for projects such as Mendl's celebrated Circus Ball of 1938, and she reciprocated by securing new patrons and taking some professional credit (and presumably commissions) for resulting interiors. Columnist Janet Flanner noted that the "European houses [de Wolfe] decorated, through the collaboration of Jansen of Paris, include the magnificent Vaucresson country residence of the banker, Fritz Mannheimer."[24] Boudin likely had an extensive hand in some of the houses—notably, Villa Le Noviciat—that Lady Mendl reportedly decorated for Paul-Louis Weiller, a French aeronautics industrialist, just as it is certain that she was involved in Boudin's decoration of Château de La Cröe for the Duke and Duchess of Windsor.

In 1935, Maison Jansen began cultivating a relationship with the Prince of Wales, the future Edward VIII. Boudin was invited to meet with the prince, whose friends included established clients Sir Philip Sassoon and Chips Channon.[25] Intending to discuss plans to redecorate part of St. James's Palace in London, Boudin arrived at the royal residence early, but his appointment was delayed. The Frenchman fell asleep waiting, only to be woken by the prince asking, "I'm impressing you, aren't I?" Boudin gained enough composure to respond with, "It is always a great honor to work for a king."[26] The decorator's flattering slip of the tongue was proved true a year later, when the prince acceded to the British throne and Jansen began plans to refurbish the private quarters of Buckingham Palace. Little is known of this commission or of the project for St. James's Palace.[27] Presumably the redecoration of Buckingham Palace never extended beyond planning, for only 11 months after ascending to the throne, on December 10, 1936, the king abdicated for the woman he loved, American divorcée Wallis Simpson.

That same year, Boudin succeeded Schwartz as president of Jansen. This change in leadership may have had something to do with the firm's stronger association with historically inspired interiors. However, Boudin's concentrated approach to business was probably viewed as a better fit in overseeing the firm. "Jansen would fail," he later summarized in consideration of his eventual retirement or demise, "because no one would be as strict as I am."[28] His nephew Claude Mandron agreed, remembering in 1999 how Boudin "would proclaim to a new draftsman or designer—no matter what their experience—that 'you don't know how to work . . . [but] you will learn how [through me].'"[29] This strong approach helped rein in and unify the Jansen staff, restoring a reputation for precision

MAQUETTE OF TENT ROOM FOR LADY MENDL'S CIRCUS BALL OF 1938

and cohesiveness that had apparently waned somewhat under Schwartz. Boudin "was in charge."[30]

Stéphane Boudin was a man of extremes. He was a master decorator who never learned to draw. He was not born a member of the world's elite, yet he became one through dictating much of what was fashionable for nearly five decades, from the 1920s through the mid-1960s. He had a gift for translating the personalities and ambitions of near-iconic figures to a vocabulary of silks, mirrors, and pedigreed woodwork.

Stéphane Jules Léon Boudin was born October 28, 1888, in Paris, the second child and elder son of Alexandre Boudin and his wife, Victoire Gautier.[31] Alexandre oversaw a family trimmings business that was founded in the second half of the 19th century. Well versed in the burgeoning field of interior design,

HÔTEL DE GOUTHIÈRE, HEADQUARTERS OF THE BOUDIN FAMILY'S TRIMMINGS BUSINESS

the Boudins supplied products to the great decorating houses that arose after the Franco-Prussian War, including that of Jean-Henri Jansen. (The Boudin firm supplied intricate trimmings to restorations of palaces and châteaux throughout the late 19th and 20th centuries, including those at Versailles. This long association later led to a mistaken claim of Stéphane Boudin's involvement, through Jansen, with the ongoing preservation of the royal palaces at Versailles.)

Boudin was educated to the modern-day high school level at the distinguished Collège de Juilly and joined his father in business upon graduation. He volunteered for military service in 1915 and fought in the Battle of Verdun the following year. Later serving in Siberia, he was promoted to lieutenant and honorably discharged in September 1919. Then 30 years old, Boudin returned to Hôtel Gouthière, the family's business headquarters, only to find himself somewhat frustrated by the limited responsibilities that lay before him. The opportunity to join Maison Jansen "awakened in him a sense of ambition."[32] Many years later, he described to client Jayne Wrightsman that his greatest lesson in design was learned early and not without some professional pain. "Asked to decorate a house for an Englishman who was planning a return to London after many years abroad, Boudin set about decorating it from drawing room to bedrooms to study. When the gentleman arrived, the house was a complete failure. Boudin vowed never again to decorate for someone without first seeing how he lives

STÉPHANE JULES LÉON BOUDIN, 1919

within the rooms . . . how he uses each one."[33] Through this costly lesson, Boudin adopted Jean-Henri Jansen's approach of investing in clients' lives, A onetime director of Jansen, Inc., Paul Manno, remembers when he and Boudin counseled the wife of an important client, listening to her tearful description of the marital abuses she had to endure. "We stayed with her, talking her out of the momentary threat to leave the marriage."[34]

Boudin compartmentalized his own existence, however. Few knew his wife, Marie Léontine Geneviève Prévost, whom he married in January 1921. By all accounts their marriage was close but somewhat formal. "She was," recalled a family member, "a very serious woman, once in love with a soldier who did not

make it back from the [first world] war."[35] After accepting Boudin's proposal, this handsome woman never craved a large house, extensive travel, or imposing jewelry like most of her husband's clients; she was their antithesis.[36] Even the mistress Boudin maintained for many years—and for whom Lady Baillie secured a deathbed visit through Boudin's wife—was described as "surprisingly unassuming."[37]

The Boudins had one child, Brigitte, who was adopted in 1939, shortly after her birth. The product of an extramarital affair of her father's, Brigitte Boudin was devoted to her father and her adoptive mother, as well as to Maison Jansen.[38] When she became older, she accompanied Boudin to South America and the United States, meeting many of his famous clients and experiencing much of the social extravagances of Manhattan, Palm Beach, and Buenos Aires.

Boudin's own residences were simplistic compared to the fantastic creations he designed for others. Granted, there were exquisite objects, ranging from a handsome ormolu-adorned bureau plat to a fine group of 19th-century drawings by Eugène Boudin, but all were simply arranged against discreet painted walls and unostentatious carpets.[39] For the windows, Boudin avoided the luxurious fringes and braids considered family hallmarks and which he was so passionate about obtaining for his clients. Even his country houses—La Chatellerie on the Seine and Rochebonne in the Loire Valley—were treated in a simplistic manner.[40] Artist and Boudin friend Etienne Drian definitively captured his modesty and work ethic by portraying the decorator with his back toward the viewer, seated in an austere Charles X chair at a neatly organized Louis XVI writing table before a window hung with cotton voile.[41] The simplicity and restrained orderliness of the scene well defined

Boudin and were evident in his administration of Jansen. His staff understood that Boudin "didn't want to be disappointed."[42] According to employee and former collaborator Albert Ernandez, "when he said he wanted something in one or two days, he expected it to be done in that time . . . [He was] very strict."[43]

Boudin's tenure as president of Jansen has been accorded near-mythical status by historians. At first, it seems hard to believe that one man could have overseen all of the projects attributed to Maison Jansen from the 1930s through the early 1960s, but he did just that. With the exception of the war years, when the headquarters and satellite offices were unable to communicate with one another, Boudin was at least familiar with each commission. He worked closely with Poubelle, an artist who supervised Jansen's design studio.[44] Boudin worried about the future of design as early as the mid-1930s, fearing that modernism would alienate the importance of basic skills and familiarity with traditional orders and vocabularies. "With his schedule," remembers Ernandez, "he was [to spend] almost every night with the young artists on the top floor of 9 rue Royale, overseeing what they had accomplished during the day. He noted what was right—and what was not right—with each project."[45]

Boudin employed artists to travel about Europe to study and draw architectural details of the 17th, 18th, and 19th centuries. These drawings were photostatted and bound in large volumes, measuring approximately 18 by 24 inches, and catalogued as a continuing series under the heading "Collection Jansen, Ornaments de Style." These volumes were added to Jansen's encyclopedic collection of photographs, objets d'art, and architecture. With published books, drawings, and a museum-quality collection of furniture and textiles, the archive was considered one of the most important design resources in the world.

Its reputation burnished by high-profile clients such as Coco Chanel, Helena Rubinstein, and the Duke and Duchess of Windsor, Maison Jansen took a lead role in the representation of French taste at the 1939–40 World's Fair in New York. A resurgence of French nationalism—reminiscent of the political climate of Jansen's earliest years—was evident on the eve of World War II and well suited to an exhibition of nonmodern fine and decorative arts, which the firm helped to organize. The catalogue to the exhibition, "Five Centuries of French History Mirrored in Five Centuries of French Art," noted how "the forward-looking mind can never afford to ignore the past."[46]

The firm designed and supervised the installation of two of the 11 main galleries. The first of these was the rather formulaic Henry IV Room, which featured early-17th-century carved oak paneling from the residence of French explorer Marion de Fresne (1724–1772), along with treasures such as Philippe de Champagne's portrait of Cardinal de Richelieu from the Musée de Versailles and Simon Vouet's allegorical portrait of Louis XIII from the Louvre. The space chronicled the history of France in the late 16th and early 17th centuries.

Jansen's second gallery was the Marie-Antoinette Boudoir, and it proved to be more in keeping with the theatrical expectations of an international exposition. By its association with Louis XVI's Austrian-born queen—and the romanticism such a connection conjured—the room became a dreamlike draw for women and young girls. Against historic paneling (white and gilt boiserie, part of the treasures salvaged from Vienna's Paar Palace by Boudin), Jansen created a fairytale hideaway with a lady's writing desk, a small marquetry-adorned bookcase, silk-upholstered armchairs, and a portrait of the French queen.

BEDROOM FOR THE PARIS HOUSE OF COSMETICS MANUFACTURER HELENA RUBINSTEIN, 1937

The fair closed on October 27, 1940. With Europe at war and France occupied by Germany, Jansen lost contact with its foreign offices. Clients who had approved projects or sent antiques to the firm's ateliers for restoration abandoned their great châteaux and townhouses; some escaped to other countries, while others were interred in Nazi concentration camps.

Within hours of Germany's occupation of Paris on June 14, 1940, Nazi officials arrived at the doors of 9 rue Royale. Countless works of art were confiscated without any type of monetary compensation, and others were inquired for. Boudin assured the protection of some important pieces by rotating them through the Jansen workshops, which had also taken on the task of making camouflage netting. Eighteenth-century commodes and bergères went through an endless cycle of restoration, regilding, and reupholstery in a process secretly heralded within the firm as defiance of the Nazis.[47]

Maison Jansen and its employees demonstrated other acts of careful rebellion. Just prior to the arrival of the German army, Boudin ordered the removal of the plumbing from Marcel Boussac's Château de Mivoisin, one hundred miles south of Paris. According to future client C. Z. Guest, Boudin "found a wonderfully perverse way of annoying Hitler's air minister, Hermann Goering, on his way to Maxim's next door to Jansen. . . . Boudin would put a figure of the British lion in Jansen's window . . . Goering came in one day and said, 'The British lion will not be roaring much longer.' Of course, it was the time of nightly German air raids on London."[48]

The firm remained open for the duration of the four-year occupation, fulfilling limited orders for French clients while attending to those of the Nazi government. Following the German directive to have Paris appear unchanged during the occupation, Jansen actually increased its visibility through additional window displays. "Hermès, deprived of leather, is lending its shop windows to the antique dealer, Jansen," observed the historian and novelist Alfred Fabre-Luce.[49] Arranged under the supervision of the occupying forces, these new window displays included, among the Louis XV commodes and ormolu clocks, small signs stating that none of the objects shown were available for purchase.

Although its details have never been recorded, Maison Jansen created a paneled room for Adolf Hitler. Not known to be a connoisseur of French decorative arts, Hitler presumably allowed the commission to be initiated by someone else, possibly Goering. The paneling was probably designed in either the Louis XVI or Empire style, vocabularies complementary to the Third Reich's restrained Neoclassicism. Made in Jansen's ateliers, this paneling was never delivered; its completion came too near to the end of the war.[50]

So strong was the German affinity for the Jansen taste that Boudin was asked to oversee the design of reception rooms for the Bank of Germany's headquarters in Berlin. Boudin took this opportunity to ask for the release of some imprisoned employees, explaining that the work could be completed only with these craftsmen. The Nazis agreed to release the prisoners and have them waiting for Boudin when he arrived in Berlin. Traveling with messages from the various families of his former artisans, the decorator was disappointed when he was greeted by a group of Frenchmen none of whom were the familiar and skilled workers he had requested. The Nazi officials explained that the task of tracking down Jansen's imprisoned employees had been too daunting and that he must accomplish the work with the people before him. Recognizing that the

ABOVE AND RIGHT: COCO CHANEL'S PARIS APARTMENT, 1930S

lives of these men were in danger, Boudin guided them through the unfamiliar tasks of assembling paneling and plasterwork, installing draperies, and hanging works of art. He then returned to Paris with disappointing news for the families of the Jansen workers; he distributed messages to the relatives of the men he had found in Berlin and who were later returned to their prisons.[51]

Jansen's satellite offices in Buenos Aires, Cairo, and Alexandria apparently remained open through the war, although there are no known surviving records of their output. The New York office stayed open under Francis Chaillou, designing mostly apartments for a range of clients, including the American fashion entrepreneur Hattie Carnegie and the socialite Ava Ribblesdale.

With the Normandy invasion of June 6, 1944, and the defeat of the Third Reich a year later, Europe was left damaged and smoldering, and Boudin, like many of his contemporaries, saw the future of his firm tied to millionaires in the United States. Although many of Jansen's prewar clients had been Americans, Boudin ensured that the main concentration of the firm was directed to garnering new clients in New York City, Washington, and Palm Beach. In his personal life, too, Boudin embraced anything American. He acquired a Packard convertible for driving around Paris and encouraged his daughter, Brigitte, to communicate with him in English whenever possible, whether in letters or conversation.[52]

The first years after the war were difficult. Employees had been incarcerated by the Germans, among them Poubelle. Boudin's was now the sole name associated with the firm. What became of Boudin's partners Vandries and Schwartz—whether they were incarcerated or had sold their interests in Maison Jansen prior to the outbreak of war—is not known. Pierre Delbée remained, taking on greater responsibilities in the administration of the Jansen enterprise, and perhaps bought into a partnership agreement. He became the heir apparent for the firm's leadership.

Boudin's first objective was reunification of the satellite offices with the Paris headquarters. His personal papers contain records of frequent trips to South America, and his daughter recalled his need to replace people in the Buenos Aires office.[53] New York posed a similar problem, as Chaillou had demonstrated great autonomy and personal success during the war years and resented Boudin's reestablishment of the Paris office as final authority. A resolution to this situation was years away, but Boudin increased the number of trips he made to the United States, to regain control of Jansen, Inc. During these trips he oversaw work for new clients, such as Francophile art collector and real estate businessman Robert Goelet and his wife, Roberta, in New York City and Newport; stockbroker George Tyson and his wife, Marguerite, in Washington, D.C.; and the president of the New York Central Railroad, Robert R. Young, and his wife, Anita, in New York City and Palm Beach.

In 1944, Boudin also addressed a personal concern for the future of interior design in postwar France. Mourning the loss of some of his most talented colleagues through imprisonment and battle and fearing an abandonment of the teaching of historical styles in general, he committed Jansen to the sponsorship of what would become known as the Ecole Camondo.

Here the evolution of design and the understanding of proportion and balance were taught to a new generation of tastemakers by designers and artisans, including staff from Jansen. Eventually this stellar program encompassed contemporary vocabularies, as well as architecture.

Maison Jansen also re-implemented some of the marketing strategies of the prewar years, among them the use of existing clients to attract new commissions. The best-recognized clients were the Duke and Duchess of Windsor, who sought Jansen's help in reopening their Paris house at 24 boulevard Suchet after the war. Boudin became reacquainted with the duchess, then much more secure in her position, and he carefully promoted their buying trips to London, New York, and Paris. In 1952, Boudin helped in the negotiation of the sale of his friend Etienne Drian's country house, a former mill in the Chevreuse Valley, to the Windsors, securing for the couple the first house they owned together. Moulin de la Tuilerie, as the small complex of buildings was known, was reinterpreted by Boudin, the staff of Jansen, and Boudin's kindred spirit, landscape architect Russell Page, as a romantic fantasy on the level of Queen Marie Antoinette's famous Le Hameau de la Reine at Versailles. In place of an idealized dairy, Boudin and Page created lively interior and exterior distractions for the enthusiastic royal gardener and his far-from-domestic wife. The Frenchman's exaggerated palette of colors and patterns, and Page's picturesque design of bubbling streams and color-saturated beds of dahlias and other somewhat garish flowers, greatly enhanced the increasingly admired Windsor style.

Soon after the completion of Moulin de la Tuilerie, Boudin aided the Windsors in the establishment of a

New York apartment of Roberta and Robert Goelet

dramatic Paris residence in the Bois de Boulogne that had previously been the house of General Charles de Gaulle. Like Lady Baillie and Lady Mendl, the duchess began promoting Jansen to friends such as C. Z. and Winston Guest of New York, a highly social couple who became two of Jansen's greatest American patrons of the 1950s and 1960s. As a reward for each new social star directed to 9 rue Royale, she attained constant access to Boudin and his talented staff. Jansen-affiliated trompe l'oeil artist Pierre-Marie Rudelle painted portraits of the Windsors' pugs, retaining a couple of incomplete panels featuring empty velvet-cushioned pedestals for whenever a portrait of a new dog was requested.

The English-born Pamela Churchill also became a valued client of Jansen at this time. The former daughter-in-law of Winston Churchill commissioned Jansen to decorate a number of residences she shared with her lover, the Italian automotive heir Gianni Agnelli. La Leopolda on the French Riviera was the grandest. Designed by Ogden Codman Jr, this great mountaintop villa was given a tentlike dining room reminiscent of Napoleon's consul chamber at Malmaison and a redefinition of its expansive terrace as an outdoor drawing room.

At the rue Royale headquarters, Cora Caetani, an Italian-American wine heiress and fashion authority, took over the management of the Jansen boutique.[54] She took the boutique's marketing to an elegant new level, traveling globally to find unique and innovative frames, candlesticks, tables, rugs, and so forth. The inventory was eclectic, perhaps reflecting postwar globalism. Caetani's personal style further enhanced the exclusivity of the Jansen name.

In the United States, Americans were becoming enamored with the Windsor taste and French period

UPPER TERRACE OF LA LEOPOLDA, 1952

decorative arts; the cyclical exchange between the coveting of English and French antiques was gradually moving once again to the tastes of the Bourbons in the late 1940s and early 1950s. Among the progenitors of this revival were Baroness Renée de Becker and Baron Erich von Goldschmidt-Rothschild.[55] Through entertaining in their expansive apartment at 820 Fifth Avenue, and canny sales of some of their furnishings, the glamorous pair provided basic introductions to ormolu-mounted furniture, Sèvres porcelains, and Aubusson tapestries. Among their pupils was Jayne Wrightsman, wife of oilman Charles B. Wrightsman. She demonstrated an unrivaled acumen, and the baron and baroness encouraged her appetite for knowledge through an introduction to Boudin.

Jayne and Charles Wrightsman took a lead role in the postwar history of Maison Jansen, by this time known as Jansen, S.A. "It was the Wrightsmans who contributed greatly to Boudin's American triumph."[56] Befriended by National Gallery of Art director John Walker, and subsequently by internationally recognized art historian Bernard Berenson, they assembled an impressive collection of Old Master paintings, some

Impressionist works, and a small number of equally fine drawings. Where they made their mark, and where Jayne Wrightsman came into her own as a true expert, was in the area of 18th-century French decorative arts. "She had in her," wrote John Walker, "a spark ready to burst into flame, an instinctive love of beauty, and innate good taste."[57] Boudin became her personal tutor, taking her on tours of furniture galleries and museums, introducing her to fellow collectors and curators. He aided in the transformation of the Wrightsmans' 28-room residence in Palm Beach and led the way in the fine-tuning of the Wrightsmans' New York apartment.[58] And when the Wrightsmans became interested in legacy and the transfer of some of their collection to an American museum, Boudin guided them in creating their Jansen-designed galleries within the Metropolitan Museum of Art.

Jayne Wrightsman considered Boudin a close friend. She spent hours with him at 9 rue Royale, and when Boudin traveled to America, he almost always included a few days with the Wrightsmans in Palm Beach or New York. Jayne Wrightsman directed business to Jansen, insisting that jeweler Harry Winston use the firm for the remodeling of his newly purchased Fifth Avenue building. She also introduced to Jansen new clients such as Anne Ford, the first wife of automotive king Henry Ford II, and Jacqueline Kennedy.

In November 1958, Boudin dismissed Chaillou as head of the New York office and appointed Paul Manno, who had started as an office boy in 1937, as his replacement. Boudin liked Manno and felt that he could rely on him completely. By this time, Jansen, Inc., was one of only two remaining satellite offices. The Buenos Aires endeavor presumably closed during the reign of Evita and Juan Perón, a casualty of the couple's rebellion against the established social elite of

JAYNE WRIGHTSMAN IN THE MAIN SALON OF HER NEW YORK APARTMENT AT 820 FIFTH AVENUE, C. 1960

Argentina. The Egyptian offices closed possibly during World War II or certainly by the time of King Farouk's abdication in 1952. As for the Havana studio, it is presumed that this did not remain a staffed entity in or around 1940, although an independent architect or designer may have collaborated with the staffs of the New York and Paris offices on Cuban commissions.

In May 1954, Boudin wrote to his daughter, Brigitte: "Here is the first letter that I have written on the 'Jansen at London's' stationery!"[59] Today, this letter proves particularly important, as it lists only three addresses for the company at the time: "Jansen S.A. 9 rue Royale, Paris"; "Jansen, Inc., 1 East 57th Street, New York"; and "Jansen of Paris, Ltd., 102 George Street, Portman Square, London." Whether a continuation of the earlier-recorded London office or a new attempt to establish a physical presence in the British capital, this studio would not last through the end of the decade. By the time of Manno's official appointment to the directorship of the New York office at the beginning of 1959, Oliver Ford, the director of the London branch, was preparing to open his own decorating firm. Jansen, Ltd., was subsequently relocated to St. Swithin's House, Walbrook, London, and headed by a gentleman named W. D. White. Later addresses were listed as "7 Duke Street" and then "137 Victoria Street." This last location was typed over an earlier letterhead on a bill for Lady Baillie, dated April 27, 1967. Presumably the post-Ford incarnations of Jansen, Ltd., involved limited representation negotiated with an independent designer.

This streamlining of Jansen's global organization did not accompany financial worries. On the contrary, Jansen was fulfilling commissions of a number equal to that of the mid-1930s, its golden years. Instead, dependable air travel made multiple offices unnecessary, as Paris-based designers and installers could be at nearly any location within a day. Also, the majority of special-order materials for projects—paneling, ironwork, furniture—was still being made within the rue Saint-Sabin ateliers and not regional workrooms. There was little need to continue the antiquated satellite system, but in the media the firm continued to promote its network of offices as if it still existed.

Jansen continued to be a global business. Boudin renewed the firm's relationship with the Belgian royal family following King Leopold III's return to Belgium in 1950. Even with the monarch's forced abdication in favor of his young son Baudouin, Leopold and his second wife, Princess Lilian, remained residents of the royal palace at Laeken. As it had since 1890, Jansen led the decoration and freshening of the palace's state rooms, and the aging Boudin began to call the seemingly endless commission his "swan song."[60] But it wasn't the end of his career at all. In the late 1950s, the 70-year-old Boudin began another project for the Belgian royal couple, Domaine d'Argenteuil, near Waterloo.

Boudin's soon-to-be successor, Delbée, was already working with a new roster of clients, including Shah Mohamed Reza Pahlavi of Iran, Tunisian president Habib Bourguiba, Greek shipping tycoon Aristotle Onassis, Onassis' former brother-in-law Stavros Niarchos, and the trendsetting celebrity hairdresser Alexandre de Paris. In visual contrast to the slender, reserved Boudin, Delbée was flamboyant and overweight. As the avenue Foch apartment he shared with his wife, Suzy, suggested, he was an eclectic collector and appreciator of the most luxurious art objects, materials, and finishes. His eye was much more varied than Boudin's. His mix of inlaid-ebony trompe l'oeil doors against distressed Louis XV–style paneling revealed an ability to embrace both modernistic design and Jansen's historical styles. As had been the case with Boudin, Delbée's personal domain indicated his intended direction for the firm.

At the presidential palace in Carthage, Tunisia, Delbée created a symbolic cabinet room with specially woven, nationalistic-patterned Genoa velvet-upholstered walls; bracket-suspended busts of famous Tunisians Hannibal, St. Augustine, Ibn Khaldun, and Jugurtha; and Napoleonic-style parcel-gilt chairs dressed in regal yellow silk that had been trimmed with elaborate gilt military braid. The finishes were crisp, not distressed, and the contrasts of color were strong. He also created a private theater for the palace; inspired by the 18th-century royal theater at Versailles, the oval room included modern lighting and sound, carefully

ABOVE AND TOP: BARONESS RENÉE DE BECKER'S SALON IN HER NEW YORK APARTMENT

STÉPHANE BOUDIN IN 1961, THE YEAR HE RETIRED AS PRESIDENT OF JANSEN

hidden behind marbleized balustrades, velvet-adorned balconies, and a trompe l'oeil sky.

Boudin scheduled his retirement for the end of 1961. His motivations were never stated, although his health was becoming an issue. Jayne Wrightsman remembered walking back to the Hotel Pierre after discussing ongoing plans for the Metropolitan Museum of Art when "Boudin fell into a tree along the sidewalk, in pain from what he described as a severe migraine headache."[61] His strength had been declining, but he did accept one more commission, for the newly elected president of the United States, John F. Kennedy.

The White House commission, made possible through Wrightsman's careful tutoring of her protégée and friend Jacqueline Kennedy, was one of Jansen's greatest works. Much of what Boudin accomplished at the White House could be classified as an encapsulation or synopsis of his life's work, a visual autobiography. For the oak-paneled State Dining Room and knotty-pine Vermeil Room, he resurrected paint schemes created years before for Lady Baillie. His controversial tentlike treatment of the oval Blue Room evidenced his lifelong affinity for German design sources. His constant concern for the interior version of landscape vistas, the view from one room to another, no doubt reflected the exchange of ideas that had grown through friendship with Russell Page.

Capitalizing on the word-of-mouth praise of Jansen's role in the Kennedy White House restoration and maintaining an illustrious list of clients, the New York office was highly profitable during this period. More literal in its translation of 18th-century French taste than it had been under Chaillou, the office adhered to a conservative, Boudin-dictated vocabulary through the directorship of Paul Manno. Impeccably dressed in tailored suits and chauffeured in a company car, Manno attended to each client in a distinguished and formal manner, over lunch, dinner, or the occasional weekend retreat to a newly acquired country house that required the firm's attention. In the seventh-floor office at 1 East 57th Street that consisted of a small gallery of choice French antiques with studio and offices beyond, Manno relied on his talented staff, including designers Arthur Bennett Kouwenhoven and Harold Eberhard. Parsons-trained, these men maintained their own coterie of clients. The gifted yet quiet Leo Monte and Roger Bengue produced elevation drawings and miniature room models that allowed clients to scrutinize every aspect of a proposed scheme. With administrative help provided by Madame Casse, the office followed the model established 30 years before.

But this stability was to change. Recognizing a rising fashion for informality in interior design, and encouraged by the more contemporary vision sought by Delbée, Manno partnered with Pamela (Churchill) Hayward to propose a reorganization of Jansen, Inc. Retaining the existing design studio and gallery, the new configuration centered on an independently operated American version of Jansen's famous Paris boutique, as redefined by Cora Caetani. The New York endeavor duplicated the aristocratic Caetani look, with affordable and not-so-affordable decorative ornaments of varying styles from around the world. Partially owned and overseen by Hayward, the boutique was meant to increase Jansen's visibility and profitability.

In late summer 1963, Jansen, Inc., moved to new quarters at 42 East 57th Street that included a street-level retail space for the boutique, a second floor for the design studio, and a basement storage area. Patrons now entered an eclectic bazaar offering inexpensive lacquerware ashtrays, elaborate gilt-bronze console tables, Louis XVI–style bouillotte lamps, and contemporary Lucite picture frames. The formerly exclusive Jansen now became accessible to a mainstream audience, and the boutique proved a great success. All concerned— Hayward, Manno, and Jansen, S.A.—shared in the profits. Not everyone was impressed with the arrangement. Established clients of Jansen, Inc., "did not like having to pass through the boutique to reach the designers," remembered Kouwenhoven. "The organization of the space did not encourage business, as it compromised the cachet of Jansen as one of the world's great design houses."[62]

The popularity of the New York boutique, however, led to the creation of similar boutiques in Milan, Rome, São Paulo, and Buenos Aires.[63] Presumably established as franchises that could offer some independent design

TROMPE-L'OEIL ARTIST PIERRE-MARIE RUDELLE WORKING ON PANELS COMMISSIONED BY FIRST LADY JACQUELINE KENNEDY

services, these shops or galleries resurrected of Jansen's global identity without great investment by the rue Royale headquarters. Brigitte Boudin de Laage de Meux and her husband opened the last of these independent boutiques in Geneva, Switzerland, in 1972.

This redirection for Jansen was no doubt encouraged by changes in the decorating world. The design aesthetic of the mid-1960s reflected the energy and spontaneity of a new generation of decorators and designers, as well as a change in how people lived. Under Delbée's leadership, the Paris office further adjusted to such changes, even entering into commercial design for hotels and restaurants, such as Le Maschere, a dining room at the Grand Hotel in Rome. Designers who fluidly melded many styles soon rose in the ranks. Cuban-born Carlos Ortiz-Cabrera, for example, combined materials such as informal rattan, paisley-printed cottons, and plastics

PAUL MANNO, DIRECTOR OF JANSEN, INC., FROM 1959 TO 1967

with more traditional silks, mahogany, and marble, proving himself a great talent in Paris and becoming a favorite of Delbée.

In New York, even with the celebrated boutique, Jansen, Inc., retained a more staid, conservative image. Some clients still sought the taste of the last Bourbons, but they were gradually moving over to other firms, such as Parish-Hadley, where Sister Parish's sensitivity to history was complemented by Albert Hadley's sophisticated modern minimalism. When CBS chairman William S. Paley and his wife, Babe, switched from Jansen, Inc., to Parish-Hadley in the middle of renovating their Manhattan apartment, Delbée was no doubt concerned. Boudin had begun the project, but his failing health had limited his access. And Babe Paley, never relying exclusively on one decorator or firm, had seemingly moved on from the purely historical as a

backdrop for her stylish lifestyle. When Henry Ford II dismissed Jansen, Inc., Delbée began plans for his own reorganization of the New York office. Manno's traditional ways, so tied to those of Boudin right down to the dependence on Katzenbach and Warren's booklet of muted and antiquated plainground papers as a design color range, were not in keeping with Delbée's desire to update the Jansen image and its offerings, and Manno left in early 1967.[64] Delbée briefly contemplated dividing the directorship between Kouwenhoven and Eberhard, but the former was unable to master the French language.[65] Instead, the favored Ortiz-Cabrera was brought over from Paris to head Jansen, Inc.

Manno's departure was followed with the closing of the Manhattan boutique, as Pamela Hayward was tiring of running the enterprise. She also no doubt missed Manno, who moved on to briefly represent the prestigious art gallery Wildenstein and Company. At or about this time, Leo Monte retired as head draftsman. An additional loss came with the departure of Kouwenhoven. Having gone to see the influential Jane Engelhard (the widow of 1930s Boudin–de Wolfe client Fritz Mannheimer) on his own, he was angrily fired by Ortiz-Cabrera, who was still settling in; Kouwenhoven immediately went into business with Jansen client Carroll de Portago in a decorating firm called Bennett-Portago, Inc., before establishing his own design studio.

By October 1967, when Ortiz-Cabrera sent a conciliatory note to the Boudin family following the decorator's death, Jansen, Inc., had moved to 25 East 55th Street. Soon afterward, Harold Eberhard left to form his own concern, continuing to work for the Wrightsmans.

Leon Amar, a talented designer born in Morocco, joined the firm, enhancing the modern-design capabilities of the office. Within less than a year, Jansen, Inc., had

MAQUETTE OF JANSEN'S DOUBLE-HEIGHT LIVING ROOM FOR THE NEW YORK RESIDENCE OF DRUE AND HENRY J. HEINZ II, C. 1963

gone from an almost exclusive espousal of 18th-century taste to a concentration on contemporary design.

In the new headquarters, Ortiz-Cabrera demonstrated economy while promoting innovative design. The walls were covered in overlapping panels of brown butcher paper, which provided a "wonderful, energetic look," remembered Amar. "He was a genius in the way he could take very little and make it come across as something so magnificent."[66] Added to this simple scheme were faux-wood doors, trimmed in black lacquer, with gold fittings. The furniture was more traditional, but spare in quantity, with Louis XVI–style chairs and a fabric-lined bookcase serving as the main grouping. The mix "was chic for that time because no

one dared to take such chances . . . that's what made Carlos so great."[67]

This transformation was no doubt to Delbée's liking. Unfortunately, it was accompanied by a dramatic reduction in clients. Those that remained true to Jansen included connoisseur and art patron Ailsa Mellon Bruce, a banking heiress whose drawn-out commission ended with her 1969 death; the completed apartment, which included a dining room with "paneling" made of upholstered silk trimmed with various decorative tapes, was never photographed nor celebrated to the benefit of Ortiz-Cabrera and Jansen, Inc.[68]

The unfortunate reality was that the New York office had sacrificed the style for which it was best known to

VIGNETTE DESIGNED FOR THE WASHINGTON ANTIQUES SHOW, 1963

enter a much more competitive and unfamiliar field, and it soon proved no longer profitable. When viewed as a cost drain to the Paris headquarters, the New York office closed its doors. However, Carlos Ortiz-Cabrera continued to use the name Jansen, Inc., representing the Paris office out of his Manhattan apartment until at least 1974.[69]

Jansen, S.A., was once again facing financial worries. Delbée's near-decade-long leadership had allowed for the expansion of the firm's offerings, but it also had proven careless in its planning and monitoring of expenditures. By the late 1960s, Jansen had sold 6 rue Royale and consolidated its galleries and offices within 9 rue Royale.[70] The firm's largest and most ambitious commission—a multiday celebration of the 2,500th anniversary of the Persian Empire, scheduled for October 1971—was a couple of years away, and it was in danger of not becoming a reality. Delbée had been working with the Shah of Iran on this project since the early 1960s, when money was plentiful, but the firm's lowered financial standing put the signing of the final contracts in doubt.[71] Fearing the loss of a commission,

PAMELA AND LELAND HAYWARD'S NEW YORK LIVING ROOM, WATERCOLOR C. 1965

Delbée negotiated an "alliance" with Maison Deshays-Leleu of Paris in 1969; Leleu had been a family-owned design house, dedicated almost exclusively to modernistic luxury residential interiors, when businessman Pierre Deshays bought it in 1967.[72]

This merger altered the succession of Jansen's leadership. Boudin had hoped his nephew, Claude Mandron, would take the presidency following Pierre Delbée's eventual retirement. Delbée had presumably agreed to such a plan, or was at least considering it, when the merger with Maison Deshays-Leleu occurred. The new

company included the transfer of leadership to Deshays in 1971, when the house also was recognized as Leleu-Jansen. Mandron resigned in 1972, taking with him some of the firm's most important clients.

The hope for Jansen's salvation through the Iranian celebration went unrealized. In the political climate of the time, with student protests of racism, poverty, and military escalations occurring throughout the Western world, the shah of Iran's regal, seemingly self-promoting celebration with silk-festooned tents, gilt-adorned parades, and elaborate banquets showed

THE MASCHERE RESTAURANT IN ROME'S GRAND HOTEL AS DECORATED BY JANSEN, C. 1965

poorly in media coverage. Jansen was applauded as its planner, but the pomposity of the event overshadowed the expertise and level of detail offered by the firm, making its employment by other, perhaps more scrutinized leaders impossible. As if this were not enough of a setback, portions of the monies paid by the shah—presumably through Swiss bank accounts—did not reach the coffers of Jansen, S.A.[73]

Accompanying the Iranian celebration was a book on the history of Jansen that, for many, was as much an embarrassment as the ill-timed Iranian pageant. The brainchild of Ortiz-Cabrera, according to designer Leon Amar, the handsome publication was intended to be a celebration of the firm's future—a wise strategy in the marketing of a talented design house. Although the book celebrated Jansen, it included a highly editorialized history of the firm. Through the negation of much of Jansen's past, the firm's overall accomplishments were assigned to the careers and vision of recently retired president Delbée

New York apartment decorated by Leon Amar

PIERRE DESHAYS, SUCCESSOR TO PIERRE DELBÉE AS
PRESIDENT OF JANSEN, S.A.

and his immediate successor, Deshays; the accomplishments of Jean-Henri Jansen, Schwartz, and Boudin were downplayed, with Boudin not even receiving acknowledgment in the credits for illustrated rooms he had personally decorated.

Soon after the shah's celebration, Deshays introduced a line of Jansen-designed furniture, which was made available to designers throughout the world. Marketed as JC or the Jansen Collections, the line of cabinets, tables, writing desks, and chairs was promoted as "exclusives Jansen." Ranging from Louis XV, XVI, and Directoire standards to more contemporary confections, such as the Persepolis Pouf—a stool or seat made of two or three stacked cushions, upholstered in leather or fabric—the collection offered luxurious custom finishes, ranging from white, black, and navy blue lacquer to imitation malachite, ivory-veneer, and mahogany with ormolu mounts. One of the more suc-

cessful designs was the "Royal Table with 'Leaf-Work' Decoration," an ingenious extension dining table that easily could be reduced to a demilune console.

The need for this line was explained in an orchestrated interview with Deshays that accompanied its launch. He said: "Several decades ago we worked on mansions . . . today we do five bedroom apartments. A new class of consumers has been born. This class demands beauty, sophistication, but also accessibility. It is for this class that we have created the Jansen Collection."[74] When asked whether he was afraid that the firm would subsequently be viewed as a furniture maker, as opposed to a decorating house, Deshays responded: "Our reputation guarantees to our clients that we will not make mistakes of taste. We do not direct to our clients anything that we do not stand behind. It would not be in our collection . . . be it selected by us, or made by us, it always needs to fit the [Jansen] décor."[75]

Deshays's effort to tailor Jansen, S.A., into a more mainstream design firm was not as successful as he had initially hoped. The Jansen Collections sold well at first, but inevitably the designs were copied and sold much more affordably by others. By the mid-1970s, Jansen of Paris focused almost exclusively on modern design. Eventually, the designer Serge Robin took over the contemporary design department and secured the highest level of quality. New furniture designers were celebrated within the ground-floor galleries of rue Royale. Representative of this program was the work of artists and designers Elizabeth Garouste and Mattia Bonetti, known as The New Barbarians. They unveiled their first collection at Jansen in 1981. Garouste, a theater and costume designer, and Bonetti, a photographer and sculptor, produced avant-garde designs, somewhat reminiscent of the naturalistic Art Nouveau

LOUIS XVI-STYLE DESK FROM THE JANSEN COLLECTIONS, A PRODUCT LINE LAUNCHED IN 1972
BY PIERRE DESHAYS

taste espoused by Jansen at 6 rue Royale nearly a century before. Some of these installations were met with great enthusiasm, but the days of Jansen ruling as one of the premier houses was gone.

With Jansen continuing to face financial difficulties, the firm made the decision to divest itself from its ambitious but underused ateliers. Sold in 1979 to long-time Jansen staff members and brothers Albert and Paul Ernandez, the workshops were reincorporated under the name L.O.R.D. and presumably moved at this time to smaller quarters at 10 rue de Toul. This business proved independently successful with a resurgence of interest in traditional decor and faux finishes in the mid-1980s. Among its greatest commissions was the restora-

tion of Maison Jansen's original 1950s work for the Duke and Duchess of Windsor's Bois de Boulogne villa, which was acquired through lease in 1986 by Mohammed Al Fayed, the owner of Harrods. Boudin's nephew and former Maison Jansen designer Claude Mandron joined L.O.R.D. artisans in this restoration, which was greatly celebrated by the press. A parallel rediscovery of Jansen—tied in part to the Windsor project—led the Ernandez brothers to change the name of the workshops to Ateliers Jansen in 1996. Although this nod to its past attracted some new clients, the workshops went out of business in 2000. As for Jansen itself, Deshays sold the company to Monsieur and Madame Gambert de Loche in the early 1980s. Its

JANSEN'S ATELIERS, C. 1978

last president was Edouard Dana, who closed the doors of 9 rue Royale in 1989. The famous address subsequently became the flagship gallery for silver manufacturer Christofle.

When Maison Jansen began its existence in the late 19th century, its celebration of the tastes of Louis XV and XVI was a response to the great changes France experienced through the Franco-Prussian War and its aftermath. This romantic reclamation of past eras, which included many more firms and talents than Jansen, protected, if only symbolically, a still-healing nation from the uncertainties of a new century. Like America's own Colonial Revival movement of the same period, France's emulation of long-ago monarchs and their celebrated aesthetic achievements provided a safe haven against an unknown future. That is how it began.

But Maison Jansen's offerings became more than restatements of the past. Through the ambition of Jean-Henri Jansen, the firm bridged the historical with the contemporary, subsequently adding the scholarship of the antiquaire and the accessibility afforded by a global network of offices. Especially crucial to its development and stature were the ateliers, which had no true rival. The rue Royale firm became iconic in the annals of decorative arts history through its sheer size and extraordinary expertise.

Maison Jansen's success was tied to its initial audience, society's elite. This association lasted through the 1930s, but just as one war had created the initial appetite for luxury, the harsh realities of World War II gradually changed the aesthetic needs of Jansen clientele. The great country houses of England and France disappeared, and decorative tastes entered a more democratic sphere. Even with an expanded American market, Jansen faced a gradual decline. Whether it could have withstood such a fall from favor cannot be known. But its closing became inevitable when its overseers dismissed what it did best for the opportunity to compete in what others did better.

JANSEN

1890–c. 1965

CHÂTEAU DE LAEKEN

THE HOME OF THE BELGIAN ROYAL FAMILY, CHÂTEAU DE LAEKEN IS a classically symmetrical, domed palace that stands in a suburban park, about three miles from the center of Brussels. Stéphane Boudin later referred to the château as his swan song, but other important projects actually followed.[1] The firm's work at Laeken was, however, considered a major component of Jansen's reputation. All known published histories and press releases produced by Maison Jansen from the early 20th century to its closing in the late 1980s listed the royal residence as one of its most celebrated efforts. The inclusion of the coat of arms of the Belgian monarchy on the firm's letterhead, alongside those of Spain and the Netherlands, honored this distinction, in the manner of a royal warrant.

Built between 1782 and 1784, on the foundation of an earlier house, the château was designed by the French architect Charles de Wailly for Albert, Duke von Sachsen-Teschen, who was governor of the Netherlands, and his wife, an Austrian archduchess; Belgium was part of the then-Austrian-ruled Dutch nation.[2] By 1804, France had seized control of the region, and Napoleon ordered the building purchased for France and decorated with grand furniture representative of his reign.[3] When the French emperor was defeated at Waterloo in 1815, Château de Laeken became a residence of King William I of the Netherlands.

OPPOSITE: DRAWING ROOM, C. 1965

GREAT HALL FOLLOWING THE JANUARY 1, 1890, FIRE

Following the announcement of Belgium's independence in 1830, it became one of the homes of the first king of the Belgians, Leopold I. It did not become the Belgian royal family's primary residence until 1935, when Leopold III (after the death of his first wife, Queen Astrid) and his children moved from nearby Château de Stuyvenberg.[4] State entertaining continued to be held at the royal palace in the center of Brussels.

On the evening of January 1, 1890, when King Leopold II and Queen Marie Henriette were holding a New Year's reception at the royal palace, the château caught fire; the cause was reported to be either a defective stove or overheated boilers. The entire interior was gutted and the central dome destroyed, and a governess was suffocated when she ran back in a vain attempt to save some of the family's valuables. "At 10 p.m. the palace had the appearance of a huge furnace, and there came from it constant crashes and volcanic bursts of flame and sparks as portions of timber, stone, or masses of debris fell into the fire," a contemporary news account reported. "The heat was so great as to prevent the approach of the small fire brigade, which at best could have done but little."[5] Almost everything was lost: Gobelin tapestries, masterworks of silver, the library with its thousands of rare books.

Garden facade, c. 1965

EMPIRE SOFA FOR A RECEPTION ROOM

A strong nationalist, Leopold II recognized the house's historical importance and initiated a complete reconstruction of his favorite home, a building once called the "Versailles of the Belgian Court."[6] Charles-Louis Girault, a French architect later famous for designing much of the 1900 Exposition Universelle in Paris, including the Grand Palais, oversaw the rebuilding, which included some reconfiguration of the original floor plan and the addition of two wings.[7] Jean-Henri Jansen, presumably well acquainted with Girault, secured the main contract for the refurbishing of the royal residence, now twice its original size, with schemes based on Louis XVI and Napoleonic design vocabularies. The company's recognized work for the monarchs of Spain and the Netherlands surely attracted the king of the Belgians, who wanted the rebuilt château to be "one of the most palatial royal abodes on the Continent."[8]

Maison Jansen remained involved with Château de Laeken throughout the 20th century. Given the firm's close association with the Belgian royal family, it appears that after Leopold II's death in 1909, Jansen was called on to execute schemes for the interiors of the château for the new king, Albert I. Shortly before his death, Leopold II reportedly sold most of the contents of Laeken, to prevent his daughters from inheriting anything valuable and to raise money to provide independent fortunes for his two young sons by Blanche Delacroix, a former courtesan he married four days before he died.[9] In 1950, when King

Formal dining room as redecorated by Boudin for Leopold III and Princess Lilian in the 1950s

Leopold III and his second wife, Princess Lilian, returned to Belgium, Jansen and Stéphane Boudin were employed to reestablish the grandeur that had been worn away by the war and German occupation. Even after the king's 1951 abdication in favor of his son Baudoin, Boudin continued with the redecoration of the state rooms and private quarters, first in association with Princess Lilian, and later with King Baudoin's wife, Queen Fabiola.

Because the château served as the personal backdrop for the king, great attention was given to ceremony. For the formal dining room, Boudin chose a favorite palette of water green and ivory, which he had used previously in the decoration of Lady Baillie's dining room at Leeds Castle. The late-19th-century paneling was glazed in shades of off-white, with the soft green color inserted as the background for large panels of classically inspired plasterwork. At the room's four windows, the Frenchman placed panels of unlined ivory silk, which were tied back in the day but drawn in the evening. These hangings were topped with shirred valances trimmed with contrasting decorative tape. Parcel-gilt Empire-style side chairs were covered in similar silk woven with a pattern of golden bees long associated with Napoleon. When not placed around the banquet table (an item that was removed when the room hosted levées or other large gatherings that did not require a dinner), these chairs were arranged against the long walls of the room, in two rows facing its center. This formal configuration, almost like that of an audience chamber, opened up the central panel of the large Aubusson-style carpet, with cerise, ivory, and gold garlands, bouquets, and anthemia.

For the long gallery, Boudin called on the restraint he typically exercised in similar spaces reserved for processionals and ceremonies. As he did for the Duke and Duchess of Windsor at Château de La Cröe, Lady Baillie at Leeds Castle, and later the Kennedys at the White House, Boudin restricted the furnishings to mostly pier and console tables. Three large Empire-style chandeliers, possibly manufactured in the Jansen ateliers, dominated the central space, illuminating larger-than-life royal portraits, including a painting of Napoleon draped in ermine-trimmed robes.

For the salon, a dramatic space that was easily the most elegant in the royal residence, Boudin derived his palette from the vibrant reds of the 18th-century French tapestries that hung on the white and gilt walls. Regal red damask was selected for the upholstery of a four-panel screen, gilded chairs, and curule-base stools that stood about the room. The Louis XVI and Empire mahogany tables were placed along the walls to counter the visual weight of the vast tapestries. A delicate Louis XVI gueridon was positioned in the center of the magnificent red and gold Savonnerie carpet, around which were drawn a few gilt chairs.

Though it was given to the Belgian state by Leopold II in 1900, along with other royal homes, Château de Laeken remains the private residence of the Belgian royal family.

HALL ON THE STATE FLOOR, 1965

Count and Countess de Revilla de Camargo

STANDING ON A CORNER OF 17TH AND E STREETS IN THE HAVANA neighborhood of Vedado, the Revilla de Camargo mansion is one of the most elegant in Cuba, a prime example of the aristocratic French taste that prevailed among the Latin American rich in the 1920s as a result of the still-popular turn-of-the-century Beaux Arts movement. It was built between 1924 and 1927 by sugar millionaire José Gómez Mena, who eventually gave the house and its furnishings to his only child, Lillian, around 1936, when she married Alfonso Gerónimo Fanjul y Estrada. Wishing instead to live in an exclusive country-club suburb outside of Havana, Lillian de Fanjul gave the house, in turn, to her father's sister María Luisa and her husband, Agapito de la Cagiga Aparicio, a Spanish-born lumber magnate who was created a count in 1927 by King Alfonso XIII. The architects were P. Virad and M. Destuque, a French team that participated in the post–World War I restorations of Versailles and the Petit Trianon; construction of the house was supervised by Adrian Macia, a Cuban architect and civil engineer.

In addition to hiring French architects, José Gómez Mena and his first wife, the former Olga Seglie, commissioned Jansen's Paris and Havana offices to oversee the decoration of the house. According to the couple's grandson José "Pepe" Fanjul, after they divorced in the mid 1930s and Gómez Mena quickly remarried and moved to another palatial home with his new

OPPOSITE: DETAIL, ENTRANCE HALL

wife, the French antique furnishings remained in the Vedado house. Most of the paintings, however, particularly an impressive cache of works by the Spanish impressionist Joaquin Sorolla y Bastida, went with him.

Daughter of a family that built one of the largest sugar-refining fortunes in the country, María Luisa de Revilla de Camargo (1880–1963) was well ensconced in the art world of not only Cuba, but also North America and Europe. She was known for her collection of 18th-century art, which went well with the furniture by Jean-Henri Riesener, Nicolas Largillière, and Léonard Boudin with which her father had furnished his Havana mansion. Among the ancien-régime artists the countess brought in to underscore the 18th-century atmosphere of the Jansen interiors were Jean-Marc Nattier, Nicolas Largillière, and Hubert Robert.

Her niece María Luisa Vivez y Gómez Mena was equally invested in the arts, having founded the Havana gallery El Prado, nurtured the careers of native painters and sculptors, and assisted Alfred H. Barr Jr., founding member and first director of New York's Museum of Modern Art, with the acquisition of works by Latin American artists. Bedecked in actual laurel leaves at a dinner given in honor of Barr in her aunt's marble dining room, the younger María Luisa was described by art patron Edgar Kaufmann Jr. as "surrealism alive."[1]

Reflecting their position at the top of Havana's social order, the residence of the Revillas de Camargo was designed for entertaining. Vedado, the neighborhood in which the house was located, had become increasingly fashionable after Cuba declared its independence from Spain in 1902, the year the count and countess were married.

By the time the couple, who married in 1902, took possession of the house–they spent only three months each year in Havana, preferring to live most of the time in a Jansen-decorated hotel suite in Paris–Vedado's shaded streets were lined with the palatial residences of Cuba's major industrialists.

Beyond the columned portico of the house was a two-story marble entrance hall crowned by a patinated bronze balustrade that ended in the curves of a waterfall staircase. At the foot of the stairs was a formal seating area consisting of Louis XIV–style sofa and chairs upholstered in damask, marble pedestals holding aloft rock crystal and gilt-bronze torchères, and a low red and gilt lacquer table. Reigning from above was a landscape by the 18th-century artist Hubert Robert. Another Robert canvas was placed against the opposing wall, above a magnificent Louis XV ormolu-mounted bureau plat.

The main salon opened off the hall and was lined with elaborate gilt and ivory Louis XV paneling, some of which dated to the 18th century; the remainder was created in Jansen's Paris workrooms and shipped to Cuba for installation. Four rock crystal and gilt chandeliers were suspended from the ceiling, but not down the center of the room, as would be expected. Instead, curiously, one chandelier was centered along each wall, a lighting plan echoed in the Bois de Boulogne library of Jansen's later clients the Duke and Duchess of Windsor. The Italian white marble floor was almost completely covered by a 19th-century Savonnerie carpet of ivory, gold, and pink. Grouped throughout the room were Louis XV fauteuils and canapés upholstered in velvet, silk damask, and antique tapestries. In the center of the room stood a fine gilded Louis XIV table with marble top, on which were displayed French and Chinese porcelains. Opposite the fireplace, between the windows, was displayed a portrait of the countess above an exceptional ormolu- and marquetry-adorned 18th-century commode.

FRONT FACADE

Decorated in shades of amber, green, and white, the marble dining room was inspired by the Queen's Guards' Room at Versailles, one of the suite that made up the private quarters of Marie Antoinette. In a candlelighted atmosphere, guests were seated in cane-back Louis XV–style side chairs placed around a richly veneered mahogany oval table or, for large dinners, a massive banqueting table. Gilt bronze trophies representing musical instruments adorned the walls above the doors and in the corners, and a handsome 18th-century tapestry of a pastoral scene served as the central focus.

Less-formal gatherings took place in the long gallery, which was furnished with white upholstered chairs and sofas, red lacquer tables, and green lamps. A modern green carpet with large white lilies and red ribbons united the two main seating areas. Colorful tropical plants were displayed in green lattice-lined recesses that also featured a Jansen design staple of the period: 18th-century Meissen birds perched on randomly mounted

MAIN SALON

VIEW OF THE MAIN SALON SHOWING A PORTRAIT OF THE COUNTESS

DINING ROOM

LONG GALLERY

brackets. Outside the long gallery, on a terrace, Jansen continued the lattice theme in a Baroque-style trompe l'oeil backdrop for a Rococo garden fountain. Dramatically lighted at night, this stage was used for special dinners and musical entertainment.

In 1961, two years after the Cuban Revolution, María Luisa de Revilla de Camargo, now a widow, reportedly left the island to spend the winter in Palm Beach. Before her departure, however, she took the unusual precaution of hiding some of her most important treasures in a secret room in her cellar, as well as behind newly constructed walls elsewhere in the house. Some of these paintings and art objects were discovered within months of her departure, including paintings by Goya and Murillo and a number of important examples of gold and silver flatware. These were seized by the Cuban government, which claimed that the countess had abandoned the house. (Other items took

GARDEN, FEATURING TROMPE-L'OEIL BACKDROP

decades to locate. Five large 18th-century paintings were found behind the living room walls during a 2003 renovation of the mansion.)

The quality of the collection led the government of Fidel Castro to secure the residence as a museum. On July 24, 1964, the mansion opened as the National Museum of Decorative Arts, which it remains today. Its collection of 18th-century French decorative arts is considered one of the most important in the Americas.

Nancy and Ronald Tree

DITCHLEY PARK, ENSTONE

CHIPPING NORTON, OXFORDSHIRE, ENGLAND

B UILT IN 1722, DITCHLEY PARK EPITOMIZES THE GREAT ENGLISH country house, with a three-part Georgian plan assigned to James Gibbs, Henry Filcroft, and the great William Kent. The estate holds an equally impressive place in English history, spanning an association with Elizabeth I to service as the wartime retreat of Prime Minister Winston Churchill and his cabinet. Nancy and Ronald Tree acquired the house in 1933 from the executors of the 17th Viscount Dillon, and soon after, it became a showplace of creative design both inside and out. Here the highly creative Trees—most notably Nancy, who gained renown in later years as Nancy Lancaster, the owner of the London decorating company Sibyl Colefax & John Fowler—explored aesthetics on a grand scale, working with landscape designers Russell Page and Geoffrey Jellicoe on the exterior and Stéphane Boudin of Jansen on the interior.

The Trees, who married in 1920, were among the cream of Anglo-American society. The former Nancy Perkins (1897–1994) was born into an energetic Virginia family that included her namesake aunt Lady Astor, a politician and hostess who famously told Winston Churchill that if he were her husband, she would put poison in his coffee.1 One of her uncles was the American illustrator Charles Dana Gibson, and another was the British society architect Paul Phipps, who worked with Boudin on the renovation of a house for another couple with

OPPOSITE: GREAT HALL

EXTERIOR, EARLY 1930S

Anglo-American connections, Audrey and Peter Pleydell-Bouverie. As for Ronald Tree (1897–1976), he was a half-English grandson of the Chicago department store founder Marshall Field and the stepson of the British naval hero Admiral Lord Beatty.[2] Mr. and Mrs. Tree were a handsome duo and greatly admired, their social position further heightened after Ronald Tree was elected to Parliament.

Though Nancy Tree used the services of several designers and workrooms in the creation of Ditchley's interiors, Jansen's contributions were numerous and highly evident. She saw the house initially as "very beautiful, particularly as it hadn't been touched for a century, but it was not at all my type of house. It was much too grand and formal."[3] Jansen had decorated far

larger palaces and châteaux than the 40-room Ditchley, and the firm's decorators were adept in the creation of livable yet historically sympathetic interiors. This approach must have appealed to the young society matron, who was still some years away from demonstrating her own confidence and expertise as an influential tastemaker.

For the house's highly ornamented Kent-designed great hall, Boudin and Tree cleared the accumulations of furniture left by more than 300 years of residency by the Dillon and Lee families to create a theatrical but comfortable living space. They defined a central seating area before the large fireplace, which they framed with an ormolu-mounted Louis XV–style bureau plat and an eight-panel, Venetian-style painted screen. Such visual

Tapestry Room

anchors as the writing table and screen, and their respective placements, were characteristic of Boudin's work and were later duplicated for other clients, including the Duchess of Windsor. Further delineating the room was a large classical carpet, with a blue and yellow border of anthemia and laurel wreaths on a red ground. The brightness of the carpet contrasted greatly with the walls, which were painted a light water green, a favored color of the Frenchman. When a professional decorator in her own right, Nancy Tree recalled years later that Boudin "had the most extraordinary good taste and understood about color."[4] The green also softened the large room, somewhat reducing the formality of the architecture—pedimented doorways, Neoclassical reliefs, and monumental painted ceiling—while lightening the overall space.

An equally dramatic remodeling occurred in the Tapestry Room. Boudin and the Trees stripped the space of its antique Flemish wallcoverings, thereby allowing a sympathetic rearrangement of existing 18th-century giltwood architectural details that had formerly been relegated to the corners of the room. Against a newly installed background of muted, almost yellow-pink silk damask—it was originally a bold red fabric of Victorian vintage, which Nancy Tree recalled Boudin telling her to purchase because the quality was good and then showing her how to bleach it pink—Boudin rearranged the flora- and Chinese-inspired moldings, adding to them additional gilt details such as a multi-tiered shelf for the display of fine porcelains. Again, Boudin was borrowing from his already-established Rococo vocabulary, which became even more celebrated upon the completion of Jansen's parallel decoration of Chips Channon's London dining room. The central seating area in front of the pedimented mantelpiece included painted fauteuils, small lacquered tables,

and a loveseat backed by another French writing desk. The colors were restrained, appearing almost faded by age, a distressed impression that Boudin and Tree both favored. The decorator also presumably designed the gilt-and-ivory-colored low bookcases, as they were reminiscent of examples made for the Yellow Drawing Room at Leeds Castle for Lady Baillie. Indeed, this interior for the Trees reflected other aspects of that better-known room, from the wall treatment to the sizable Chinese porcelain birds guarding the mantelshelf.

Jansen's mark could be seen in other rooms at Ditchley. For the salon, Boudin provided an 18th-century design for an expandable table that was manufactured for the Trees, presumably in the Paris ateliers. "I had it copied," Nancy Lancaster later said, "and a cloth made to fit the several sizes we would need." Busts of blackamoors, a staple of Jansen interiors of the time, were positioned on either side of the door leading to the garden. Boudin also found the "perfect rug . . . in Paris . . . [an] Aubusson with faded gray, green and blue vines and flowers in geometric patterns."[5]

The Blue and White Bedroom on the second floor of the house demonstrated simplicity in composition. Though the walls were left a neutral off-white, the windows were hung with a blue-and-white printed antique fabric, trimmed with a dual-color fringe. The English-manufactured French-style bed was draped with the same fabric, with a new solid-blue silk skirt of drawn swags. Between the windows stood a dressing table draped in white cotton, topped by a tassel-adorned series of matching swags. The overall composition of this space is looked upon as an early representation of Nancy Lancaster's relaxed but elegant design vocabulary, but it is equally in keeping with Boudin's designs for similar rooms. The flat, scalloped valances, straight-falling drapery panels, and

SALON

LIBRARY

upholstered dressing table all are strikingly similar to respective elements in the Queens' Sitting Room in the White House.

The Yellow Bedroom, which was used by Winston Churchill during the war, also displayed aspects of Boudin's vocabulary. The headcloth of the great English bed incorporated elaborate Baroque patterning through the application of decorative tapes. This level of finish was characteristic of Boudin, whose family's passementerie business made the majority of trimmings that were used in Jansen commissions.[6] The dec-

orative-tape trimming also was reminiscent of his more prolific work at Leeds.

Ditchley played an important role in the evolution of Boudin's reputation as a decorator, although his work there has been given little attention. Nancy Lancaster promoted the humble story of the Frenchman starting as a salesman of trimmings and eventually rising through the ranks of Maison Jansen; he was, however, a partner in the firm from the time he joined the company. In her later years, she described Boudin as more of a contractor than a designer or major contributor to

BLUE AND WHITE BEDROOM

the interiors of her country house.[7] Surviving renderings of the Trees' rooms, however, reveal too many similarities to parallel Boudin projects for his role to have been simply a supplier of goods. Also, he was recognized at the time as much more than a purveyor of fabric samples: he counted Prince Paul of Yugoslavia, the Prince of Wales, and Lady Baillie in his list of clients. The limited credit he received for his efforts at Ditchley may have resulted from Nancy Lancaster's decision to downplay his role as the years passed, but it also was very much in keeping with the Jansen belief that a decorator should never overshadow the client.[8]

After the Trees divorced in 1947, Ditchley Park and many of its contents were sold in 1949 to the seventh Earl of Wilton.[9] Four years later, the house was sold to Sir David Wills, a philanthropist, who turned it into the headquarters of the Ditchley Foundation, which conducts conferences on international cooperation.[10]

Prince Regent Paul and
Princess Olga of Yugoslavia

BELI DVOR

BULEVAR MIRA, BELGRADE, YUGOSLAVIA

THE DECORATION OF BELI DVOR, A PALLADIAN-INSPIRED MANSION, was among a number of royal commissions undertaken by Jansen in the 1930s, although this particular project has largely been forgotten. Although not involved with the initial design of the palace, the construction of which began in August 1934, Stéphane Boudin was soon brought in to advise on the interior architecture and decoration by Prince Regent Paul of Yugoslavia (1893–1976), a great Anglophile, who assuredly became acquainted with the work of Jansen—and Boudin—through his devoted friendship with Chips Channon, an Oxford classmate, British member of Parliament, and celebrated Jansen client. The selection of a French decorating firm might have seemed particularly odd considering Prince Paul's affinity for aristocratic English decoration and lifestyle.[1] However, Jansen's status as the fashionable choice by key players in 1930s London society—including the Prince of Wales (who was a cousin by marriage of the Yugoslavian prince regent), Nancy and Ronald Tree, Sir Adrian and Lady Baillie, and Channon and his wife, Lady Honor—made the firm's selection almost inevitable.

Located within the royal compound outside Belgrade, Beli Dvor was commissioned by King Alexander I and Queen Marie, a former princess of Romania, as a private residence for them and their young sons, Crown Prince Peter (the future King Peter and the

OPPOSITE: VIEW TO THE MAIN SALON FROM THE DINING ROOM

Main salon

DINING ROOM

VIEW THROUGH SECOND FLOOR SITTING ROOM

princes Tomislav and Andrej.[2] Architect Aleksandar Djordjevich (1890–?) designed the house as a neo-Georgian interpretation of Andrea Palladio's Villa Emo at Fanzolo, Italy. When the king was assassinated in Marseilles in October 1934, the plans for the royal ascension, as well as those for the yet-to-be-completed palace, were drastically changed. Beli Dvor became the official residence of Prince Paul, a cousin of the dead monarch, who was appointed regent on behalf of the young crown prince. He lived there with his wife, the former Princess Olga of Greece and Denmark (1903–1997), and their children, Alexander, Nikola, and Elizabeth.

The ground or main floor of the palace was centered on a skylighted two-story hall with black and white marble floor, arched galleries, and patinated bronze and iron balustrade. This grand interior was highly restrained in its ornamentation; the stone-colored walls and plain plaster ceiling were unadorned, much in keeping with Boudin's preference for minimalism in such spaces. Perhaps this intentional restraint—carried over into other rooms—led Chips Channon, an occasional houseguest, to define Beli Dvor as "the perfect house: it is too exquisite to be a Palace, for Palaces usually are hideous."[3]

The decoration of the main salon of Beli Dvor incorporated features befitting a great English country house of the second half of the 18th century. Ionic fluted pilasters defined ivory-colored wall panels and framed three arched windows that led to formal flower gardens. Two Adam-style, urn-form crystal chandeliers were suspended from the ceiling, and four matching sconces were installed on the room's long walls. To this near-period background, Boudin added a mélange of contemporary and antique furniture, including a colorful 18th-century classically inspired carpet with Prince of Wales plumage, interlaced strapwork, and a thick border of gold trompe l'oeil gadroon. Before a subdued white marble mantelpiece with miniature Ionic pilasters stood four serpentine-back club chairs and a similarly shaped sofa, all neatly upholstered in pale silk damask, as if to highlight instead the room's collection of delicate late-18th-century parcel-gilt chairs, tilt-top tea tables, and a number of George III mahogany shield-back armchairs. Large Chinese polychrome porcelain urns flanked the fireplace, and another pair of lesser size was positioned on matching mid-18th-century Chippendale mahogany gaming tables between the windows. A characteristic representation of Jansen modernism was a low table veneered in mirrored glass, on which was displayed an array of

SOUTHWEST SALON

PRINCESS OLGA'S BEDROOM

SECOND FLOOR SITTING ROOM

smoking equipage and other small finery. "Lying about," Channon observed on a visit to Beli Dvor, "there are many of my presents, a [English Paul de] Lamerie gilt coffee pot, always used; snuff boxes; a silver seal box I sent out this Christmas."[4]

Like the main salon, the dining room was reminiscent of interiors in an English country house. Rectangular in form and reflective of similarly sized 18th-century rooms designed by rivals Robert Adam and James Wyatt, it was symmetrically defined with highly polished mahogany doors capped by classically inspired carved entablatures and hemmed by elegantly tapering Etruscan-order columns. Between the two tripartite Palladian windows of the long exterior wall hung a large Savonnerie tapestry whose great ovoid central panel represented reclining figures partaking of wine. An oval looking glass was suspended on the opposing wall, above a white marble mantelpiece adorned with porcelain garniture. At the far end of the room, framed by service doors, was a recessed arched niche, used by the prince regent to display an extensive mid-18th-century Sèvres dinner service ornamented with colorful bouquets; it was purportedly made for Madame Du Barry, the principal mistress of Louis XV. As in true 18th-century English banqueting halls, there was no chandelier; instead, lighting came from crystal wall sconces and from candelabra placed on the mahogany extension table; there were also a quartet of Adam silver candlesticks that Channon gave to the prince regent in 1935.[5] Mahogany shield-back chairs, demilune side tables, and a serpentine-form hunt-board all adhered to the espousals of Georgian tastemakers Thomas Sheraton and George Hepplewhite.

A nearby sitting room allowed for the inclusion of some regional classicism along with the predominating English-born examples. Against a backdrop that featured another large Palladian window, an Irish multicolored Classical marble mantelpiece, and an English crystal chandelier, Boudin arranged a suite of early-19th-century Russian brass-inlaid chairs and similarly ornamented classically inspired tables; these possibly were family heirlooms, acquired either through the prince regent's marriage to Princess Olga, whose mother was a Romanov grand duchess, or through his Russian mother, Princess Aurora Demidoff. Although the general furniture arrangement continued the previously described restraint of the residence's decor, the composition was less successful than in other rooms, possibly because of differences in scale and proportion between Western and Eastern European interpretations of classicism.

Princess Olga's bedroom, however, revealed an almost Hollywood-inspired modernity that included a silk damask-covered king-sized bed raised on a dais. Similar to Jansen treatments devised for Helena Rubinstein's Paris bedroom and Sunny Francis' bedroom at Château Solveig, the raised bed read as a throne against an otherwise monochromatic and unadorned backdrop; the room's color is unrecorded, but it probably was an ivory or oyster hue, a shade that predominated the wallcovering and upholstery selections. The pair of modern club chairs positioned at the foot of the bed was the room's only evidence of texture or pattern, with the sides of the otherwise plain silk seats and back cushions exhibiting a delicate treatment reminiscent of smocking. Straight-falling drapery panels of matching silk were ornamented with a vine-patterned woven tape. A modern mirrored commode and similarly treated low table presumably came from the Jansen ateliers. Also characteristic of the rue Royale firm was the voile-draped dressing table placed in one corner, similar to confections made

BEDROOM

for Nancy Tree, Lady Baillie, and other female clients throughout the 1930s.

Beli Dvor served as the stylish backdrop of Prince Regent Paul's short reign, which ended with his agreement to sign the Tripartite Pact—the formal agreement uniting Nazi Germany, Fascist Italy, and Japan in war— on March 25, 1941. Two days later, a coup d'état ensued, led by his cousin Crown Prince Peter, who was supported by government officials desiring to align Yugoslavia with England. Yet even after Paul's down-

fall, the country adhered to the unpopular pact, in fear of German invasion. Hitler's forces eventually attacked nonetheless, leading to the exile of the royal family, including Prince Paul, his wife, and his children, whom the British kept under house arrest in Africa for the duration of the war.

At war's end, Beli Dvor became the official residence of President Josip Broz Tito, and in 2000 the house was returned to the pretender to the throne, Crown Prince Alexander II of Serbia and Yugoslavia.

Solveig and Francis Francis Jr.

CHÂTEAU SOLVEIG

GLAND, SWITZERLAND

THIS MODERN COUNTRY HOUSE IS ONE OF THE RARE DOCUMENTED examples of the work of the decorator Gaston Schwartz, who became president of Jansen upon Jean-Henri Jansen's death in 1928. Schwartz embraced the modernism espoused by the Exposition Internationale des Arts Décoratifs et Industriels Modernes, held in Paris in 1925, and he apparently was the person who promoted forward design concepts at Jansen, such as mirrored glass veneering of traditional commodes, coffee tables, and paneling, actions that redefined the firm's otherwise historically based, staid design vocabulary.

A large house whose interiors had been conceived in a notably advanced style, Château Solveig was an important commission for Maison Jansen, and it was promoted among the firm's satellite offices as an example for emulation. To the New York office's director, Francis Chaillou, Schwartz sent a detailed description of the house's most important rooms.[1] The staff translated his survey of the Francis commission under the title "These Beautiful Modern Rooms in The Château de [sic] Solveig in Switzerland were Decorated by Jansen of Paris."[2]

The glamorous modernism of this sprawling house reflected the youth and vitality of its owners. Educated in his father's native England, and a grandson of a founder of Standard Oil, Francis Francis (1906–1982) was forced to resign from the Royal Horse Guard when he

OPPOSITE: FRONT DOOR

GRAND STAIRCASE

announced his engagement to Solveig "Sunny" Jarman (1910–1984), an American musical-comedy dancer, in 1929.[3] He was a noted amateur airplane pilot with a strong interest in the latest design and architecture; she was a petite platinum blonde of Norwegian ancestry who had met her husband in a whirlwind stage-door romance. Soon after their marriage, the Francises, who would have two sons, moved to Gland—a tiny village on the banks of Lake Geneva, between Geneva and Lausanne—where they built Château Solveig in 1934–35. A vast red-brick mansion with a steeply angled roofline modeled after traditional Norwegian

architecture, the Francises' house was designed by the prestigious Geneva architecture firm Peyrot & Bourrit.[4]

Although its exterior followed historical Scandinavian precedents, the interiors of Château Solveig were all representative of French modernity. The dramatic foyer had matching bronze panels reminiscent of the work of the artist Edgar Brandt, with stylized renderings of hunters, gazelles, boars, and stalks of grass, framing the opaque glass entrance doors. The main hall was theatrical, as well, with a tri-color marble floor of yellow, green, and white that led to a three-story central stair of white marble with

LIVING ROOM

FAR END OF THE MAIN FLOOR STAIR HALL

waterfall terminations and with hand railings and balusters of clear crystal. Near the staircase stood a mixed-metal globe on a six-column glass-and-chrome stand. At the far end of the hall was a white marble fireplace, crowned by an actual birdcage that extended above mirrored-glass doors at either side of the mantel breast.

The living room was painted beige—the color of Solveig Francis' wedding dress—with a complementary mantelpiece of polished Hauteville limestone. A modern point de Beauvais tapestry representing the Francis family crest was framed in stone above the mantel. Twin serpentine-back sofas, upholstered in heavy cream linen embroidered in cerise, were positioned before the fireplace, along with matching club chairs and a low crystal-and-glass variation of a Renaissance-style trestle table, a Jansen design in the manner of Serge Roche. Opposite the mantel wall were broad glazed doors that opened to a terrace and the gardens; these doors were framed by trisection windows with suede-upholstered banquettes paired with characteristic Jansen lacquered tables.

SMOKING ROOM, WITH FALL-FRONT DESK BUILT INTO FALSE DOOR

STUDY

DINING ROOM

VIEW OF SMOKING ROOM DISPLAYING A DIVIDED 20-PANEL COROMANDEL-STYLE SCREEN

Next to the living room was the music room, where cabinets veneered with mother-of-pearl were installed for the display of porcelains and ivories. Positioned in front of the music-room window was a metallic-leaf card table with ebony tub chairs upholstered in satin.

The dining room had walls of chartreuse lacquer with pilasters of mirrored glass etched and painted with stylized grapevines, a modern interpretation of late-18th-century Directoire painted paneling. As in several of the primary reception rooms, the floor treatment in

this space consisted of geometric planes of light walnut with insets of chrome-plated metal banding. The dining table was made of green-lacquered metal, crowned with polished plate glass that reflected the recessed lighting cove above. Chair upholstery was of peach-colored leather, trimmed in silver welt.

The smoking room reflected a somewhat more traditional Jansen design vocabulary. It was divided into two sections, the larger of which was framed in each corner by five panels of a 20-panel Coromandel-style

MUSIC ROOM

lacquer screen; the division of such screens to frame walls, doors, or cabinets became a Jansen standard in the 1920s and 1930s and remained popular with the firm's designers into the 1960s. In the room's smaller section, Schwartz devised a sécretaire à abbatant using a mock door and frame; when closed, the desk disappeared into the architecture of the room.

Francis Francis' study displayed photographs of airplanes, with one wall dedicated to a global map where he documented air routes and his own family's travels.

Subdued in its overall decoration, this room demonstrated some of the more pleasing interior architecture, with modernistic stepped wood-veneered panels framing the mantelpiece and a serpentine-shaped treatment for the recessed lighting. The mantelpiece was skinned in polished sheet metal attached with exposed rivets, a reminder of the owner's Sikorsky S-38 amphibious airplane, known as *Blue Falcon*.

Although each of Château Solveig's rooms was handsome, Schwartz seems to have taken particular

MASTER BEDROOM

pride in the design of the second-floor master bedroom, which was planned around the blond coloring of
Sunny Francis. Emphasizing a sense of lightness for
the room, Schwartz specified the gilding of column
footings, baseboards, and the feet of the centrally
placed dressing table, and as a result, the walls and furniture appeared to float above the walnut floor. The
monumental commode opposite the dais-supported
bed was veneered with mirrored glass and mountings
of gilded bronze and crystal; this was complemented
by mirrored-glass pilasters, which framed the com-

mode and dais and were decorated with gold and sepia-
colored engraved laurel branches and birds.
Upholstered in cream satin, the modern, geometric
armchairs were made of polished, rose-tinted plane
tree wood.

Although Sunny and Francis Francis divorced about
a decade after the house's completion, Château Solveig
retained its Jansen decorations into the early 21st century.[5] At that time, the house was sold by the Francis
family, and its furnishings were dispersed.[6]

MASTER BEDROOM WITH MIRRORED-GLASS COMMODE

Lady Honor and Henry Channon

LONDON, ENGLAND

A MONG THE COMMISSIONS THAT GAVE MAISON JANSEN ITS STATUS as the world's greatest decorating house, the dining room of 5 Belgrave Square has no rival. It was the first highly publicized example of the firm's post–Jean-Henri Jansen work. It also was one of the few commissions for which Stéphane Boudin was cited as decorator or creator. This fact alone should reveal something of the importance of Boudin's stature in the design field at the time, for his client, Henry Channon, an American expatriate universally known as Chips, required a background impressive enough to underscore his position as a member of London society—Conservative politician, friend of royalty, husband of a well-known heiress. With Boudin apparently about to be employed by England's Prince of Wales, the future Edward VIII, Channon was well aware that in hiring the Frenchman, he was securing the services of "the greatest decorator in the world."[1]

Henry Channon III (1897–1958) was born in Chicago and inherited a fleet of transport vessels that plied the Great Lakes. He briefly worked for the Red Cross during World War I and was later assigned an attaché position with the American Embassy in Paris. He attended Oxford and soon embraced the role of social climber, leading Cynthia Gladwyn, the wife of a British ambassador to Paris, to speak for many in English society when she described

OPPOSITE: DETAIL OF GREAT DINING ROOM

GREAT DINING ROOM

Channon as "that American pipsqueak (alas natural-ized British)." In 1933, Channon married Lady Honor Guinness, the eldest daughter of the second Earl of Iveagh and a scion of the sprawling Guinness brewing dynasty. Thus Channon's marriage connected him to some of the most glamorous figures of the day, including the infamous Mitford sisters.[2] Until their divorce in 1945, the Channons were one of London's best-known couples, noted for their close friendships with English and Continental royalty. After being elected to succeed his mother-in-law, Lady Iveagh, as a

member of Parliament, Channon became a well-known political figure.[3] But he is best remembered for his somewhat snobbish, posthumously published diaries that documented English high society in the mid-20th century. As he explained in that publication, "I have flair, intuition, great good taste but only second rate ambition; I am far too susceptible to flattery; I hate and am uninterested in all the things most men like such as sport, business, statistics, debates, speeches, war, and the weather; but I am rivetted by lust, furni-ture, glamour and society and jewels."[4]

DETAIL OF GREAT DINING ROOM WITH ORNAMENTAL CERAMIC STOVE

Stéphane Boudin seems to have recognized the easily bedazzled elements of Channon's personality from the moment the two men met to discuss the decoration of the Belgrave Square dining room on June 17, 1935.[5] "Monsieur Boudin from Jansen's in Paris has come over, and we hope he is to do our new dining-room built like the Amalienburg," Channon recorded in his diary. "It will be a symphony in blue and silver . . . cascades of aquamarine." The client finished the day's entry by posing the question, "Will it be London's loveliest room or is my flame dead?"[6] He needn't have worried. Boudin was well aware of his client's weakness for ceremony and showmanship, and he delivered a room, completed in 1936, that "intoxicated" all who saw it, including Queen Mary, who stopped by during a visit to Channon's next-door neighbor, her son the Duke of Kent.[7]

The Frenchman based his designs on the Hall of Mirrors in the Amalienburg, a hunting lodge in the park of Nymphenburg Palace, near Munich.[8] Completed between 1734 and 1739 by François Cuvilliés, a court dwarf turned architect, for Maria Amalia von Hapsburg, the wife of Elector Karl Albrecht of Bavaria, the hall was a fantasy of silver, crystal, and mirrored glass—an unlikely source of inspiration for a mid-19th-century London townhouse. Its exaggeratedly carved high-relief wood and plasterwork—painted pale blue and lavishly silvered—employed a naturalistic vocabulary of flora and fauna that was reflected into infinity by the room's 12 large mirrors.

It is possible that the architectural concept for the Belgrave Square dining room was born of Channon. He had written *The Ludwigs of Bavaria*, a history of the royal house that was published in 1933, and so was familiar with the ornamental extravagances of the Wittelsbach family. However, Boudin may have pro-posed the Amalienburg room as a model—he had recently installed 18th-century Rococo paneling from Vienna's Paar Palace in the London residence of Sir Philip Sassoon, a socialite whom Channon saw as an aesthetic rival. After an additional seven-hour meeting with Boudin on July 6, Channon predicted that the room "is going to be stupendous."[9] It would, he hoped, surpass in elegance any room in London.

After traveling to Munich to study the Amalienburg for inspiration, Boudin began to adapt the hall's 18th-century decorations to fit the Channons' 19th-century dining room, a rectangular space with an arched three-window bay. Boudin replaced an existing Regency cornice and frieze with a coved ceiling, framing it with masterful recreations of scallop shells, scrolls, and nymphs, all executed in plaster and subsequently burnished with silver leaf. Painted a crisp, cool shade of aquamarine, the two long walls were divided into three bays each, the end sections incorporating mirrored double doors with silver-plated hardware. Centered on one long wall, parallel with the dining table, stood an 18th-century silvered side table purportedly designed by Cuvilliés. Inside the central niche along the opposite wall stood a tall, Baroque-form ceramic stove with elaborate leaf and vine decoration.

The custom-made dining table was a melding of Rococo and modern elements, with silvered wood cabriole legs, intertwined ribbon-form stretcher, and ornamented skirt crowned by uniform squares of mirrored glass, a material that was frequently used in furniture made by the Jansen ateliers in the 1930s. On the table were placed some of the Channons' collection of Meissen porcelain, including pieces from the famous swan service, commissioned in 1737 by Count Heinrich von Brühl, prime minister to Augustus III, elector of Saxony. Boudin also provided silver-leafed

GREAT DINING ROOM

open-backed chairs; some stood around the table, others against the walls. All were copied from a surviving period example by Jansen's talented woodworkers and upholstered with the same aquamarine silk damask Boudin placed at the room's arched windows, which overlooked the four-and-a-half-acre private park at the center of Belgrave Square.

Boudin also devised two smaller adjacent spaces that gradually prepared guests for the dining room's splendor, a decision that revealed the Frenchman's understanding of ceremony and procession, as well as his recognition that a room as ornate as the one designed for the Channons could not be entered abruptly. The first transitional space was a small dining room for intimate, less grand dinners, its black-painted walls inspired by the background of the chosen Bessarabian carpet. Faced with an enclosed area with no source of natural light, Boudin created display cases shaped like false windows. Illuminated with hidden bulbs and lined with white silk, these cases were filled with 18th-century porcelains arranged on shelves of black glass and framed with tightly drawn draperies of white silk. At the far end of this room were double doors, also framed with white silk and flanked by a pair of theatrical candlestands—one in the form of a Chinese servant, the other representing a Nubian counterpart—that led to a narrow passage painted a dark shade of apricot and adorned with silvered relief ornament. Based on a bedroom at the Amalienburg, this second space led to the grand dining room. When the Channons entertained, this narrow hall was lighted by candles, placed in matching sconces and in a small

porcelain and ormolu chandelier suspended from the arched ceiling; electric lights fitted behind the intricately molded cornice cast an additional glow.

These smaller rooms, although rarely referred to by Channon in his writings or by any other visitors to 5 Belgrave Square, were astonishing successes. They established momentum and suspense as guests passed from the darkness of the black dining room through the candlelit warmth of the orange hall and into the cool brilliance of the aquamarine and silver dining room beyond. Given that this dramatic suite of rooms was completed during Edward VIII's short reign and visited on a number of occasions by the king in the company of Wallis Simpson, for whom he abdicated his crown, it should not be surprising that its creator later became a contributor to the iconic Windsor style. Both the king and his future wife were impressed by the theatrical decor that Boudin created for the Channons and surely remembered it when, as Duke and Duchess of Windsor, they commissioned him to create similarly dramatic confections for their Paris residence in the early 1950s.

The Belgrave Square house was damaged by German bombs in 1944 and later restored by Channon. It is presently divided into luxury apartments. The dining room was disassembled when Channon's family sold the property after his 1958 death, a year after he received a knighthood. Its architectural elements and furnishings are reportedly stored at Kelvedon Hall in Kelvedon Hatch, Essex, the country house of his only child, Paul Channon, Baron Kelvedon of Ongar.

VIEW FROM SMALL DINING ROOM THROUGH PASSAGE TO GREAT DINING ROOM

1935–c. 1967

The Hon. Lady Baillie

LEEDS CASTLE

MAIDSTONE, KENT, ENGLAND

D AUGHTER OF A BRITISH BARON AND GRANDDAUGHTER OF AN American multimillionaire, Olive Baillie met Stéphane Boudin in 1933. Their intense client–decorator relationship involved several houses and spanned more than three decades. Initially, she commissioned the Frenchman to assist with the decoration of her London residence at 45 Upper Grosvenor Street. In this sizable townhouse, Boudin introduced a melding of French and English 18th-century styles, as well as the then somewhat lost art of trompe l'oeil painting. For his client's bedroom, he designed a pair of decoratively painted chests of drawers, ornamented with faux sheet music and instruments, lace handkerchiefs, a masquerade mask, and an opened date book that recorded the name Boudin. Greatly celebrated and subsequently imitated, these magnificent and very personal pieces further ingratiated the decorator into the life of his client (although they paled in comparison with what Boudin created for Lady Baillie in later years). As a result of her association with Jansen, she became the iconic tastemaker of pre–World War II England.

The Hon. Olive Paget (1899–1974) was the elder daughter of the first and only Baron Queenborough (1861–1949), a member of Parliament who made a fortune in the Canadian

OPPOSITE: LEEDS CASTLE

VIEW OF RESTORED LEEDS CASTLE

steel industry.[1] Her mother was Pauline Payne Whitney, the eldest daughter of William Collins Whitney (1841–1904), a powerful financier who served as secretary of the navy under Grover Cleveland.[2] She was first married to the Hon. Charles Frederick Winn, a British army officer, in 1919, but divorced him in 1925. Before the announcement of her divorce had even reached family and friends in the United States, she married Arthur Wilson Filmer, but this marriage also lasted only six years. Her last husband was Sir Adrian Baillie, sixth Baronet of Polkemmet and a Conservative member of Parliament, whom she wed in 1931; this marriage was dissolved in 1944.

In 1935, with the decoration of her house in Upper Grosvenor Street complete, Lady Baillie turned to Stéphane Boudin with a new challenge. Nine years earlier, at the height of the American fashion for acquiring English houses, she and her second husband had pur-

chased Leeds Castle, near Maidstone, Kent, about 30 miles southwest of London. Once home to Anne Boleyn, among other English queens, the castle, built across two small islands and equipped with turrets and drawbridges, was considered so "beautiful and so perfectly medieval" that one observer noted, "some Americans suspect its being a piece of scenery erected overnight by a motion-picture company."[3] The newspaper publisher William Randolph Hearst had rejected the opportunity to buy the romantic fortress, however, because of the building's primitive condition, including the fact that there was "not a bath in [the] place."[4] But Lady Baillie saw beyond the realities of the property, which dated back to the ninth century and was largely built in the 12th, and acquired it for a reported $873,000.

After installing electricity and other modern conveniences—included 15 bathrooms—she employed fashionable French designer Armand-Albert

MAIN STAIRCASE

Rateau to assist with the transformation of the castle's vast interior. Rateau's rooms represented 1920s fantasy and luxury: fairy-tale winding staircases and Art Moderne alabaster bathrooms befitting a Gloria Swanson movie. By the mid-1930s, Lady Baillie wanted a more serious approach to the decoration of her country house. Boudin's historically based work for her London residence had proven him an ideal collaborator; his ability to tolerate and satisfy Lady Baillie's endless lists of projects no doubt enhanced his qualifications.[5]

Among the decorator's first projects at Leeds Castle was the design of the master bedroom in 1936. It remains one of his most justly celebrated interiors. Here the Frenchman installed Louis XV–style paneling that had been painted a rich medium blue with ivory detailing and distressed to such a degree of apparent antiquity that it fooled even the greatest connoisseurs of period architectural detail. David A. H. Cleggett, a historian of the castle, described the process of forced aging as follows: "The bedroom panels were first brushed with a steel brush to bring up the grain, and then painted with about three thin coats of glaze, followed by the rubbing in of the final dry blue colour. The panels were then waxed."[6] Against this artfully

DINING ROOM AS DECORATED BY BOUDIN

conceived backdrop was placed a large half-tester bed of luxurious ivory silk, modeled on the royal bedsteads at Versailles; the headboard was outfitted with shell-shaped reading lights. Facing the bed, Boudin arranged a handsome grouping that consisted of a Louis XV commode, Meissen porcelain birds on brackets, and a pair of Louis XVI painted fauteuils, upholstered in vibrant orange velvet.

In place of the former breakfast room, Boudin and Lady Baillie created a large drawing room, with antique yellow damask upholstered walls, capped by a contin-

uous quilted valance of similar coloring and somewhat Baroque design, which was elaborately detailed with ornamental tapes and tassels. The existing windows were lowered to the floor, an architectural alteration that allowed the room to visually extend out to the landscape—a rather modern concept for a medieval castle. A large yellow, green, and white marble mantelpiece, based on a design by the 17th-century English architect Inigo Jones, was installed here, in front of which was arranged a long sofa upholstered in deep-green cut velvet, a Boudin hallmark velvet-draped

DINING ROOM

table, and a yellow satin-covered Louis XV ottoman. Pieces from Lady Baillie's collection of 17th- and 18th-century Chinese porcelain were displayed on the mantelshelf, the tops of Jansen-designed ormolu-mounted bookcases, and small lacquer-and-brass tables selected by Boudin. For the floor, the Frenchman chose a handsome 18th-century Russian carpet with bold vine patterning in shades of green, indigo, turquoise, red, and gold against a deep brown background. Though later ridiculed by purists such as the historian John Cornforth, who saw Boudin's approach as inappro-

priate for British houses, this room, with its luxurious Continental elegance, was an impressive creation. It was an excellent example of the collector-oriented compositions that had become standards of Maison Jansen in the prewar years.

Elsewhere in the castle, Boudin altered stairwells, removed existing walls, and defined dramatic new spaces. The somewhat histrionic broad main stone staircase designed by Rateau was replaced by a fluid flight with a central window-lighted landing that offered a formal descent for guests staying in one of

DRAWING ROOM

the second-story suites. A schoolroom used by Lady Baillie's children was reconfigured into a magnificent library, lined with ivory-painted paneling and casework, all highlighted with red-gilt coloring reminiscent of leather book bindings. The architecture of the room was based on late-17th-century designs of French Huguenot architect Daniel Marot, but the recess of the central bay of each section of cabinetwork is a subtle and unexpected Boudin gesture that enhances the openness of the overall room. Etienne Drian's group

portrait of Lady Baillie and her daughters eventually took center stage above the room's mantelpiece.[7] Velvet-upholstered banquettes, with low backs and numerous tapestry-adorned bolsters, were made for the room and placed in front of the bookcases, along with the firm's popular low lacquer tables, here used as end tables for small brass lamps.

For the new dining room, Boudin combined several small rooms at the east end of the castle to create one large space. He and Lady Baillie selected from Jansen's

LADY BAILLIE'S BEDROOM, DESIGNED IN 1936

stock of antiques five late-18th-century tapestries as the centerpiece of this new room's decor. Each panel had a picturesque scene of bathing swans, strutting roosters, or like subjects—framed by trompe l'oeil horticultural, musical, or sporting trophies and flower-adorned columns—and was incorporated into new paneling that melded late-18th-century French and English designs. Perhaps bowing to a sense of nationalism on the part of Lady Baillie, the paneling was made in England by the firm of Henry & Farthing, not in Jansen's Paris ateliers.

The woodwork was glazed in soft water green and ivory. Gilt brackets displayed rare Celestial Empire Chinese porcelains, as well as some Export wares, including examples of famille verte and famille rose patterns. Complementing these colorful enameled porcelains was a large Bessarabian carpet, with pink floral rosettes framed in ivory tracery against a deep chocolate brown ground. The English pedestal-base banqueting table was surrounded by Louis XIV–style painted chairs, upholstered in white leather that had

GUEST BEDROOM WITH A TROMPE L'OEIL-PAINTED CABINET MADE IN THE JANSEN ATELIERS

been tooled to look like damask. White was also the color of the straight-falling damask draperies, which were capped by flat scalloped valances and trimmed with spiraling white decorative tapes. The room was a stylish backdrop for Lady Baillie's lavish weekend entertaining for guests, who included Queen Marie of Romania, the actor Errol Flynn (Sir Adrian Baillie was involved in the film industry), and a heady array of politicians, statesmen, authors, and art connoisseurs.

The firm worked at Leeds Castle from the mid-1930s through the mid-1960s, providing design services, furniture, and antiques, and Boudin and Jansen decorated almost every room. Corridors were given the minimalist formality associated with royal pageantry, whereas drawing rooms were assigned intimate arrangements of furniture suitable for small gatherings

and private conversation. Bedrooms received especially high attention to detail, emphasizing the importance of guests to Lady Baillie's vision for the castle; beds were given elaborately detailed hangings unrivaled by any in other Jansen commissions, each enriched with braids, tapes, and fringes. Some rooms were decorated two and three times, their alterations dictated by the requirements of Lady Baillie. Jansen also later oversaw the cleaning and reinstallation of bedhangings, draperies, and carpets, an aspect of the client–decorator relationship that is rarely written about.

The firm's Leeds Castle interiors played an important role in the formulation of designs for later clients. The distressed blue paneling of Lady Baillie's bedroom served as the model for the Duke and Duchess of Windsor's Bois de Boulogne dining room, and the

GREEN BEDROOM

palette of the library, as well as the pattern of the dining room carpet, were copied for the Kennedy White House.

Lady Baillie remained close to Stéphane Boudin, insisting that he continue his involvement with the decoration of Leeds Castle after his 1961 retirement as president of Jansen. She was one of the few clients who visited him during his final illness. A further indication of her devotion was her decision, after his 1967 death, to discontinue his in-progress plans for her private office. Instead, she closed the room and left it uncompleted in an unspoken tribute, though she did retain the services of Boudin's nephew, Claude Mandron, to oversee other aspects of the castle's transformation. Work stopped only upon Lady Baillie's death in 1974, after which the castle and its property were transferred to the Leeds Castle Foundation. Since 1976, it has been open to the public as a museum and conference center.

1938

The Duke and Duchess of Windsor

24 Boulevard Suchet

Paris, France

Along with leasing Château de La Cröe, on the French Riviera, the Duke and Duchess of Windsor rented a large mansion at 24 boulevard Suchet in Paris. Within its existing paneled rooms, Boudin and Maison Jansen created regal drawing rooms and galleries reminiscent of those in royal palaces. The house also included further expressions of the evolving Windsor style.

Entering the house at street level, guests were greeted by liveried servants in a minimally furnished hall. As at La Cröe, Boudin established a sense of ceremony through the restraint of the decor. Exceptions were a Louis XVI lyre-form pendulum clock in case, a painted Venetian screen, and a pair of alabaster urns on black marble columns, which were wired as light fixtures.

After ascending to the first, or main, floor of the house, one found a suite of four rooms. The largest was the salon, which had ivory-colored paneling modeled on the Corinthian order. Most of the furniture adhered to the Louis XV style, with examples of the earlier, less fluid Louis XIV period interspersed. Elaborate draperies of ivory silk, trimmed in red, were tied back within arched openings. Antique red velvet, found on one of the duchess' antiques excursions with Boudin and reputedly from a cardinal's vestments, was used to upholster a

Opposite: Banquette room

FRONT FACADE, C. 1946

gilt-framed sofa and some chairs. Opposite the white marble Louis XVI–style mantelpiece stood the main seating group, dominated by a button-tufted ivory sofa with red detailing. An elaborate Louis XV–style bureau plat, adorned with ormolu tracery against mirrored glass panels (and likely a Maison Jansen creation), also stood in the room.

Through the double doors to the left of the mantelpiece, one entered the gold drawing room, a more delicate and intimate interior. With a slightly lower ceiling and Louis XVI–style paneling, the room was decorated in shades of yellow and blue, accented by gilt. The single window was framed in light yellow silk, with both drapery panels and scalloped valance trimmed in fine white fringe. Two seating areas were devised, with an array of silk-upholstered Louis XV and Louis XVI chairs, as well as a painted sofa, all neatly arranged

before the fireplace and its opposing wall. Jansen faux-bamboo gilt-metal tables, of varying heights and forms, were mixed among the period pieces, providing elegant surfaces for the display of small collections of boxes and porcelains. Used by the duchess to greet female visitors, this elegant room also served as a passage to dinner in the formal dining room beyond.

The formal dining room was decorated in the Louis XV taste, with handsome gold and ivory boiserie. Jansen added a large panel of mirrored glass to one of the interior walls, which reflected the opposing two windows and helped define the whole as an architecturally independent space, standing separate of the rest of the building. This illusion was further encouraged by arched, mirrored doorways designed in imitation of additional windows on the remaining inside wall. More mirrors were applied to the shutters of the room's four

SALON

actual windows, which were cloaked in elaborate double-tied draperies of red velvet. The regal color was repeated in the plain field of the room's large Persian Khorossan carpet, in the painting of the Louis XV–style chair frames, and in the trimming of the chairs' ivory silk damask upholstery. The Boudin-designed dining table, with elaborate giltwood base and glamorous surface of dark mirror, harkened back to the Rococo designs for the Channons in London four years before.

The final room on the floor, referred to as the banquette room because of the low Turkish-style seating, was less formal. The seemingly continuous sofa was actually made up of five similarly sized upholstered units, covered in buttoned green velvet, with matching bolsters and pillows. Modern in overall look, this type of seating had become part of the Jansen vocabulary by the mid-1930s and closely resembled similar sofas made for Lady Mendl's house in Los Angeles a decade later. Adding to the exoticism of the room were three-dimensional plaques and stands representing black-amoors, Chinese lacquer tables and bamboo chairs, and a Venetian-style rocaille garden seat. The windows were given straight-falling panels of diamond-quilted green silk, similar in color and motif to the room's latticework-patterned green carpet, which was designed by Boudin.

The former king's bedroom was decorated in ivories and red, with the existing paneling painted a uniform off-white. Wall-to-wall regal red carpeting provided a dramatic field for the mostly French furniture, which included a Louix XVI sécretaire à abattant placed between the silk-hung windows. Boudin assembled a suite of painted furniture, consisting of actual early-19th-century period antiques as well as new pieces. In the Empire taste, the chairs, chest of drawers, and sleigh-form bed were painted red and black, with gilt

highlights that included cast-metal, plume-adorned helmets. The chairs were upholstered in cream-colored velvet and trimmed with red and gold-on-gold passementerie. Next to the bed, on a bearskin rug, stood one of Jansen's minimalist, multitiered occasional tables in mahogany and gilt brass. A comfortable club chair was slipcovered in ivory silk with red welting.

The duchess' bedroom was much more dramatic, with pleated walls of royal blue silk. The windows were finished with the same fabric, with white voile under-curtains. The wall-to-wall carpet was dyed to match the walls. Against this jewel-box setting, Boudin added sharply contrasting objects in white, including a Rococo-style mirror and nightstands, a Venetian-style chest of drawers whose blue and white painted decoration was inspired by antique porcelian, and a stylish fur rug in the form of a large chrysanthemum or dahlia. The Baroque-inspired, thronelike bed consisted of upholstered blue head- and footboard, trimmed with broad white woven tape. The bedcover was also trimmed in white tape, and its theatrical scalloped skirt included four-inch-long white fringe.

The Windsors enjoyed the boulevard Suchet house for a short time before being evacuated from Paris on the threshold of war. Surprisingly, the interiors were largely intact when the couple returned in 1945. Boudin and his staff assisted in the cleaning and reinstallation of draperies, carpets, and furniture, some of which had been stored in the interim, possibly in the Jansen ateliers. However, the Windsors remained in the rented house for just another year; it was sold in the spring of 1946. Before repacking the furnishings, the duchess commissioned Russian-born artist Alexandre Serebriakoff to record the formal reception rooms in a series of watercolors. A photographer was also brought in to document both the public and private rooms prior to their disassembly.

DINING ROOM

THE *PASTEUR*

BORDEAUX, FRANCE

THE *PASTEUR* IS REMEMBERED AS A SHIP WITH A HEROIC ROLE IN World War II, but it was originally intended as a promoter of French modernism and creativity. Designed as a luxury passenger liner for the French–Argentine route of Cie sud Atlantique, the *Pasteur* was delayed in serving its intended function for 20 years. The ship's September 1939 maiden voyage was canceled as a result of the outbreak of war in Europe, and the inaugural run, rescheduled for the following June, turned into a successful mission to save the French gold reserves on the threshold of German occupation. By making a high-speed run across the Atlantic, the *Pasteur* delivered just over 213 tons of bullion from the Bank of France to New York, and then to Canada for safekeeping.

Built by the Penhoet shipyards at Saint-Nazaire, France, the *Pasteur* was 697 feet long, with quadruple propellers that could provide a maximum 25.5 knots. As planned, it was to be a more luxurious replacement for the *Atlantique,* which had recently burned at sea. At nearly 30,000 tons, the *Pasteur* was the third-largest of France's prestige liners, exceeded in size only by the *Ile de France* and the iconic symbol of modernism, the *Normandie.*[1] In fact, the ship was promoted as a smaller version of the *Normandie,* and its interiors intentionally emulated the larger vessel's elegant contemporary appointments. Stéphane Boudin's daughter later recalled

OPPOSITE: DECORATOR'S RENDERING OF FIRST-CLASS CABIN, C. 1938

THE *PASTEUR* AT SEA, JULY 1939

her father "designing the entire interior of the ship," but records indicate this was not the case.[2] *Pasteur* historian Jean-Yves Brouard lists Boudin as one of four chief designers, including architects Raguenet & Maillard, who designed the Parfumerie Française at the 1925 Exposition Internationale des Arts Décoratifs et Industriels Modernes, and architect Roger Lardat, the designer of the gardens of the 1937 Exposition Universelle de Paris. Partnered with men who were more directly invested in the espousal of French modernism, Boudin's role may have been twofold. Certainly his experience as a decorator came into play with the creation of both public and private spaces, albeit all of them representative of modernism. However, his capacity to organize and manage the global Jansen enterprise could have been viewed as ideal experience for overseeing the multifaceted *Pasteur* project. A series of photographs, taken in 1938 and now lost, suggest

such a role; they depicted Boudin walking through the ship, examining various aspects of its fitting-out.[3]

The *Pasteur's* most imposing interiors were the mahogany-paneled salons, which included suites of tapestry-upholstered furniture with Brazilian rosewood and ebony veneers, reminiscent in luxury and overall form of furniture designed by Emile-Jacques Ruhlmann for his Pavilion d'un Collectionneur at the 1925 Paris exposition. The dining rooms were not as grand as those of the larger *Normandie,* but they all the same conveyed a sleek, youthful energy with streamlined tables and chairs. The indoor swimming pool included a large modernistic glass mosaic representing tropical fish and dolphins, illuminated from above by skylights. First-class staterooms featured restrained interpretations of Napoleonic sleigh beds next to futuristic built-in dressing tables and nightstands, all set against highly polished floor-to-ceiling burl paneling.

SWIMMING POOL, 1939

Other cabins had upholstered walls, incorporating both solid, linenlike textures, framed by exotic wood banding, and vibrant geometric printed patterns. Unfortunately, given the outbreak of war and the consequent difficulties posed by transatlantic travel, the luxurious interiors of the *Pasteur* were never used. They were scrapped when the ship was converted to troop transport service in the summer of 1940.

The *Pasteur* carried thousands of Allied troops to Europe and Africa during World War II. On its return trips, it transported German and Italian prisoners to internment camps in Africa, the United States, and Canada. After the war, the ship continued to be utilized as a troop carrier. Awarded the Croix de Guerre for service in October 1947, the *Pasteur* went on to transport thousands of French soldiers during the Indo-China War. Sold to West Germany in 1956, the *Pasteur* was renamed the *Bremen* and placed into Atlantic passenger service. Later, after serving under the flags of Greece, Saudi Arabia, and the Philippines, it sank in 1980, while being towed in the Arabian Sea.

FIRST-CLASS SALON, 1939

OFFICERS' DINING ROOM, 1939

Audrey and Hon. Peter Pleydell-Bouverie

THE HOLME

LONDON, ENGLAND

BUILT IN 1819, THE HOLME WAS THE FIRST VILLA TO BE BUILT IN Regent's Park, an aristocratic pleasure ground that was partly developed for residential use in the early 1800s by John Nash, the favored architect of George IV. Originally the villa was the home of James Burton, a speculative builder, and designed by his teenage son, Decimus, who later became a prominent architect. Greatly enlarged in 1911 by the Marquess of Crewe, The Holme was further altered by the architect Paul Phipps after its acquisition by the Hon. Peter Pleydell-Bouverie and his wife, Audrey, who had recently married.[1] For the interior, Stéphane Boudin of Maison Jansen was employed to oversee the decoration of the main reception rooms; the gardens were designed by Geoffrey Jellicoe and his young associate, Russell Page, who worked on numerous Boudin-decorated properties over the years.

The last of 10 children, Peter Pleydell-Bouverie (1909–1981) was a son of the sixth Earl of Radnor. Little is known of him beyond his noble connections, but his wife, whom he married in 1938, was a prominent member of transatlantic society and referred to as "a longtime glamour girl."[2] A girlfriend of the future Duke of Windsor and a goddaughter of Edward VII of Great Britain—rumor had it that the king was actually her maternal grandfather—Audrey James (1902–1968) was the daughter of William Dodge James, an American

OPPOSITE: DINING ROOM

FRONT FACADE

lumber and steel millionaire, and his wife, the former Evelyn Forbes, a popular London hostess known to posterity as Mrs. Willie James. Following the death of her first husband, Captain Dudley Coats, heir to an English cotton-thread fortune, Audrey went on to marry and divorce Marshall Field III, the Chicago mercantile millionaire, and four years later she became the wife of Pleydell-Bouverie.[3] A sportswoman, breeder of Labrador retrievers, and avid collector of French Impressionist paintings, she was not a force in the world of art and design like her eccentric younger brother, Edward (a patron of surrealist artists, who commissioned Salvador Dalí to reinterpret the interiors of the family house in Sussex), but she did make a creative mark through establishing elegant residences and gardens.

The Pleydell-Bouveries may have selécted Jansen after seeing the firm's famous dining room for the Channons at Belgrave Square or its less touted interiors for Lady Baillie's Grosvenor Square residence and Lady Ribblesdale's Regent's Lodge, which adjoined Regent's Park. They also may have become aware of Boudin

through their architect; Phipps was an uncle of Jansen client Nancy Tree.[4] The decorator's reputation in London in the 1930s, in any case, had acquired a certain cachet; he was noted for creating stylish backdrops for equally stylish people. The Holme likely was the Pleydell-Bouverie project listed among the firm's works in progress when German soldiers marched into Paris in 1940.[5]

For the dining room of The Holme, Boudin skillfully melded an unusual but stylistically related combination of English Regency, French Directoire, and German Neoclassicism. The tightly pleated upholstered walls were borrowed from those seen in a German palace, possibly a room within the Residenz, an 18th-century Baroque palace in Würzburg. Boudin was a great enthusiast for German historical models, as shown by his work for the Channons and his much later redesign of the Blue Room of the Kennedy White House. The overmantel looking glass and medallion-patterned fitted carpet were true to the Regency vocabulary; the chairs and pier table—with Egyptian figural supports—adhered to the designs of Englishmen Thomas Sheraton and Thomas Hope, but through their decoration and ornamentation they came much closer to representing the French Directoire. Boudin's sensitivity to proportion and balance is well represented in a surviving photograph of the finished room, where the verticality of the chairs, the walls with their vertical silk pleats, and the minute crystals of the Russian-style Neoclassical chandelier work together to counter the otherwise squat proportions of the architecture.

The ballroom was perhaps less successful as an interior scheme; the architectural historian John Cornforth later described it as an example of how "Boudin found English proportions difficult."[6] For this grand party

BALLROOM

space, as in the dining room, the decorator attempted to counter the strong horizontality of the architecture with linear parcel-gilt chairs, eagle-supported pier tables, a Grecian-form sofa, and stools in the form of crouching blackamoors. His very delicate valance treatments for the windows—the straight-falling panels were installed within the architectural moldings—support this theory. A more substantial design for the windows, perhaps of a contrasting color to the walls, would have only reinforced the lack of balance between the room's great breadth and limited height. Unfortunately, an existing Regency chandelier, too long for the room, undermined Boudin's ambitions for the decoration, which also was dominated by a series of theatrical gilt trophies of musical instruments hung on the walls.

Audrey and Peter Pleydell-Bouverie were divorced in 1946. Soon the interior furnishings of The Holme were transferred to her country house, Julians, near Rushden, Oxfordshire, where they were reinstalled by Boudin.[7] Never remarrying, she later served as a trustee of the Tate Gallery in London, where her collection of French Impressionist paintings was exhibited in 1954.

c. 1940

Hattie Carnegie and John Zanft

1133 FIFTH AVENUE

NEW YORK CITY

L OCATED AT 1133 FIFTH AVENUE, THE DUPLEX APARTMENT OF fashion entrepreneur Hattie Carnegie and her third husband, movie industry executive John Zanft, was completed by Jansen's New York office, independent of the Paris headquarters and ateliers because of France's occupation by Germany during World War II.[1] Presumably the work of Francis Chaillou, the director of Jansen, Inc., the apartment was described by a later Jansen employee, Arthur Bennett Kouwenhoven, as "spectacular . . . very comfortable and elegant at the same time."[2] It was an astute observation of a decor that neatly mirrored Carnegie's pioneering vision for women's fashion.

Adopting the surname of one of America's best-known millionaires, Andrew Carnegie, the Austrian-born hat designer Henrietta Kanengeiser (1886–1956) started a clothing business in New York City with seamstress Rose Roth in 1909. After buying out her partner and changing Roth & Carnegie to Hattie Carnegie, Inc., she began a successful career as a trend-setting promoter of women's clothing, accessories, and perfumes. Nothing the company produced, not even the famous Carnegie suit, actually was designed by its diminutive founder, who acknowledged that she couldn't sew, cut a pattern, or construct a dress. Instead, she managed a team of exclusive in-house designers—among them Jean Louis, Norman Norell, and

OPPOSITE: PLAYROOM WITH AN ADJOINING LIBRARY-OFFICE

129

ENTERTAINING SPACE DETAIL

ernism of Gaston Schwartz. The 12-room duplex—probably not coincidentally, it was in the Carnegie Hill section of Manhattan, just three blocks south of Andrew Carnegie's mansion—easily blended these two extremes of Jansen taste, with a gracious end result. The off-white entertaining space known as the playroom was particularly illustrative of this successful melding of styles, where Louis XV–style fauteuils and bergères, as well as 18th-century blackamoor candlestands, were masterfully partnered with modern sofas covered with pale raw silk, low tables with figured Chinese lacquer tops, and trellis-patterned panels of etched mirrored glass that stretched floor to ceiling and gave the space a Hollywood sense of glamour. Chaillou divided the rectangular room into four sections, including two opposing conversation areas, a writing corner, and a games area with a bridge table positioned in front of the bank of windows. These spaces were further defined by divisions in the ceiling—partially structural—and applied pilasters along the walls.

The decoration of Hattie Carnegie and John Zanft's dining room was much more atmospheric, being a reduced and simplified variation of Boudin's celebrated Amalienburg reincarnation for Chips Channon of a decade before. Lightly gilded off-white paneling was set with Chinese lacquer landscapes and space-enhancing lengths of mirrored glass; there was no chandelier, a decision that caused the intimate room to seem larger than it was.[5] The deeply veined marble mantelpiece was set within a subtle recess, an architectural detail that complemented the chamfered corners of the boiserie; these simple features belied the repetition and uniformity of the modern New York apartment building that housed it. Following Jansen's practice in dining rooms the firm executed for the Channons and the Duke and Duchess of Windsor, the

Pauline Fairfax Potter—and edited their luxurious creations, many of them adapted from Paris haute couture examples, for a largely American clientele that included socialites such as the Duchess of Windsor, Millicent Hearst, and Mona Williams, and the actresses Ina Claire and Tallulah Bankhead.[3] After two brief marriages, in 1928 Carnegie wed John Zanft (1883–1960), a newspaper columnist who became the vice president and manager of the Fox chain of movie theaters.

The likely decorator of Carnegie and Zanft's apartment, Francis Chaillou, started his Jansen career in the firm's Havana office.[4] He was especially gifted at combining Stéphane Boudin's historicism with the mod-

DINING ROOM

white painted table was topped with mirrored glass that reflected the room's main source of illumination: eye-level candlelight.[6] Additional lighting was provided by ormolu sconces mounted on either side of the mantel-piece and the room's main door. The final touch consisted of pinch-pleated, unadorned white silk panels at the windows. It was a treatment not unlike the draperies used to unveil a new Carnegie line of clothing at the company's headquarters at 42 East 49th Street, a remodeled townhouse that also was decorated with Jansen-style rooms equipped with similar off-white paneling and furniture ranging from 18th-century antiques to modern reproductions.

The businesswoman's paneled bedroom also was classically French in appearance. The focus of the space was a Louis XVI–style twin bed of carved wood that appears to have been given a limed or whitewashed finish. The bed was set into a shallow alcove lined with gathered panels of silk and framed with matching ruf-fled silken draperies.

After Carnegie's death, the duplex was sold to New York City socialite Ann Woodward.[7]

Ava Ribblesdale

MAISON JANSEN HAD A LONG HISTORY WITH AVA RIBBLESDALE, a Philadelphia debutante who went on to be a leading figure in New York City and London society, first as the wife of America's most famous millionaire and then after her marriage to an equally prominent British nobleman. The firm had been involved with the decoration of Regent's Lodge, her 20-bedroom house in Regent's Park, London, and it likely had some input on the extensive redecoration and remodeling of another magnificent London mansion that she earlier rented, 18 Grosvenor Square.[1] The relationship between client and firm must have been strong, because in November 1941—a year after she and more than 700 American refugees fled the growing European war aboard the *USS President Roosevelt*—Ribblesdale called on Francis Chaillou of Jansen's Manhattan office to decorate the 17-room apartment she had leased at 420 Park Avenue, near East 55th Street.

Noted for her beauty, hauteur, and abilities as a sportswoman, Ava Lowle Willing (1868–1958) was married, from 1891 until 1910, to Colonel John Jacob Astor IV (1864–1912). He later perished on the *Titanic,* though not before they had produced at least one child and weathered a much-publicized 1909 divorce that won her a reported settlement of $50,000 a year.[2] Following the divorce, she devoted more time to life in England, a world

OPPOSITE: ENTRANCE HALL

DRAWING ROOM

she much preferred, renting several houses before settling on Grosvenor Square. Eight years later, Ava Astor surprised society on both sides of the Atlantic by announcing that she had wed Thomas Lister, the fourth and last Baron Ribblesdale (1854–1925), a former lord-in-waiting to Queen Victoria, a man whose appearance was so distinguished and wardrobe so old-fashioned that King Edward VII reportedly called him "The Ancestor."[3] She returned to the United States at the outbreak of World War II, at which time she renounced her title, reclaimed her American citizenship, and began calling herself Mrs. Ribblesdale.[4]

The Chaillou-decorated entrance hall of Ribblesdale's single-floor apartment—the building was constructed in 1916 to the designs of Warren & Wetmore, the architects of Grand Central Terminal—melded modernism and historicism. The room encompassed three walls of traditional glazed paneling with ivory detailing, but the fourth wall was hidden beneath sheets of stark mirrored glass. The contemporary reflective surface hid two flush doors, one of which led to the dining room, the other to the service area of the apartment. Against one wall stood a marble-topped Rococo console table, above which was placed an elaborately carved remnant of

DRAWING ROOM

18th-century paneling that had been made into a mirror frame. To either side of the table stood a George III gilt armchair brought from Ribblesdale's house in Grosvenor Square.

From the entrance hall, double doors opened to a large paneled drawing room overlooking Park Avenue. Chaillou divided the space into two opposing seating areas, each arranged beneath matching Louis XV rock crystal and ormolu chandeliers. At the left end of the room, framing the fireplace wall, were arranged Louis XV fauteuils and bergères, covered in cut velvets and silk damasks, and

a contemporary upholstered sofa. A focus of this part of the room was a handsome Louis XV cylinder desk with intricate flora-patterned marquetry. The room's opposite end was more formal in execution and contents, with an exceptional ormolu and lacquer bureau plat facing a settee and fauteuils neatly disposed between the divided panels of a Coromandel lacquer screen, by this time a Jansen trademark.

The dining room was given a similar treatment to that of the drawing room, with a marble mantelpiece flanked by the separated sections of a landscape-patterned Chinese screen. The walls were painted light gray, and

DINING ROOM

the only addition to the existing architecture was a formidable marble-topped serving table designed by Chaillou. The round, pedestal-base English dining table at the center of the room was surrounded by reproductions of Louis XV painted armchairs with caned seats and backs. The spare composition was somewhat unusual compared to other Jansen dining rooms of the period—the chandelier, for example, was a fanciful creation resembling a Chinese pagoda or parasol—but like Jansen client Hattie Carnegie, who had a similarly color-

less dining room, Ribblesdale would have known that the restraint of the room's decor and neutral gray walls made a highly effective background for men in dinner jackets and women in jewels and colorful gowns.

The last room of this apartment to be documented in photographs was a small sitting room, which guests must have found antiquated in its formality and composition, especially when compared with Chaillou's more contemporary entrance hall. Simple painted paneling served as backdrop for a predictable gathering of

SMALL SITTING ROOM

Louis XV chairs, an Aubusson carpet, and small tables adorned with marquetry. There was little to identify it as a room of the 1940s, as opposed to one decorated 50 years before. Indeed, it represented the era in which Ava Ribblesdale had been born and raised and in which Maison Jansen first entered service to society's elite.

Ribblesdale continued to stay in the United States after the end of the war, dividing her time between the Park Avenue apartment and a house in Southampton. A year after her death, her collection of French furniture and art objects was sold through Parke-Bernet Galleries.[5]

Lydia and George H. Gregory

903 PARK AVENUE

NEW YORK CITY

FTER THEY FLED THE NAZI INVASION OF FRANCE, GEORGE Gregory and his wife, Lydia, leased a 17-room apartment at 903 Park Avenue in April 1941 and commissioned Francis Chaillou of Jansen's Manhattan office to be its decorator.[1] Decorated in an elegant beige, tan, cream, and white color scheme and accented with mirrors and gilt, the Gregory apartment was consistent with the New York branch's work during the war, combining a sophisticated degree of historicism with more modern features.

Though not as well known as two of his three sons—the Renaissance-bronze collector and art-book publisher Alexis Gregory and the actor-director André Gregory—the Lithuanian-born Gregory (1895-1983) achieved prominence and wealth in Europe as the representative of the German chemical company I. G. Farben in the Soviet Union. After Joseph Stalin came to power, he immigrated to Berlin and then Paris, where he married a beautiful young woman he had met in Russia, Lydia Sliosberg (1905–1978). Joined by his wife and family, he fled once again as the Nazis overran Europe, finding sanctuary in New York City and a new career as a real-estate developer and financier.[2]

Located on the 10th floor of a 17-story building that had been constructed in 1913 by Bing & Bing, the most dramatic room in the Gregorys' full-floor apartment was the circular

OPPOSITE: CIRCULAR ENTRANCE HALL

SALON LOOKING INTO THE PETIT SALON

entrance hall with a coved dome ceiling.[3] Beautiful in its proportions, the room was representative of Chaillou's masterful use of mirrored glass and dramatic woodwork. The hall had four shallow, rectangular alcoves framed by high-relief moldings, three of which were lined with multiple small sheets of mirrored glass; in the fourth was set the carved door to the elevator. Of the three mirrored alcoves, two incorporated flush double doors that led to various areas of the apartment, and the third acted as a backdrop for a pedestal holding a stone statue of a young boy in rural 18th-

century costume. Furnishings were limited to a marble-topped bronze gueridon in the center of the room and Louis XV cane-back armchairs placed against the walls. Lighting was provided by four double-branch sconces, possibly giltwood, with mirrored reflectors, as well as recessed lighting above the cornice.

The large salon was furnished with Louis XV canapés, bergères, and fauteuils, which the Gregorys brought with them from Europe. There was none of the typical Jansen woodwork. Instead, the room was anchored by a Savonnerie carpet and focused on an

VIEW OF THE SALON

important Savonnerie tapestry of a pastoral scene that covered the largest span of wall, between the windows overlooking Park Avenue. Chaillou installed two mirrored doors and door surrounds with raised gilt moldings in a modernized Louis XV–style. An almost cliché arrangement of art objects—Meissen porcelain birds mounted on giltwood brackets, a French 19th-century landscape, a terra-cotta bust of a child, and an elaborate marquetry commode—was grouped between two of the mirrored doors, affording a textural counterpoint to the previously noted tapestry.[4]

At one end of the large salon, framed by a divided Coromandel screen, was the entrance to the petit salon, which served as an intimate sitting room. Here, Chaillou encased the chimneybreast in mirrored glass, against which was installed a red marble mantelpiece and partial 18th-century painted overmantel frame. Against the window stood a modern silk-upholstered love seat that seemed to have taken its sculpted form from Venetian Baroque models; it was accompanied by a Jansen mirrored coffee table with cabriole legs.

DINING ROOM

The dining room combined English and French design themes, with walls partially covered by sections of unpainted, delicately carved Louis XV–style woodwork inset with large sheets of mirrored glass, one facing the large window looking onto the avenue, the other surmounting a mantelpiece in the Louis XV style and made of dramatically figured marble. Louis XV gilt-bronze sconces and a handsome ormolu cartel were the only additional decorative features. The mahogany double pedestal table was surrounded by Queen Anne–style side chairs upholstered in leather,

and around the room stood marble-topped serving cabinets bearing porcelain tureens and other decorative objects. Beyond a Louis XV fire screen with needlework insert and two bombé pedestals bearing large urns containing uplights, the furnishings seemed more in keeping with those of a gentlemen's club.

The decoration of the master bedroom, however, borrowed less from historical models and more from Hollywood. Numerous thin pilasters of mirrored glass framed with white-enamel moldings trimmed the pastel walls. The headboard and footboard of the bed

MASTER BEDROOM

were covered in button-tufted white silk damask; above the bed hung a portrait of the Gregory's two elder sons. Wall-mounted nightstands of enameled wood and mirrored glass continued the streamlined theme, whereas delicately painted fauteuils, a marquetry work table, and fur rugs laid across the pale wall-to-wall carpeting introduced hints of 18th-century royal refine-

ment. Opposite the bed was a sitting area composed of a French Provençal settee, two more small marquetry tables, and a Louis XV–style armchair.

In 1958, when the rent on the apartment was raised to a point that the Gregorys found excessive, they moved to 820 Park Avenue. All of their Jansen decorations were reinstalled in the new apartment.

1947–48

Roberta and Robert Goelet

CHAMP SOLEIL

NEWPORT, RHODE ISLAND

THE ROBERT GOELET COMMISSION REPRESENTED A REUNITING OF
the Paris headquarters with the New York office of Jansen, following their forced
separation during World War II. Jansen was hired to install 18th-century paneling
in one room, reconfigure the upstairs bedrooms, and design a new wing for dining
and entertaining. The firm also supplied new paneling for a small dining room and
some of the second-floor rooms. The amount of work proved less extensive than most prewar
Jansen undertakings—in part, this reflected an American conservatism, born partly of the lin-
gering affects of war rationing—but it provided for a socially prominent reintroduction of
Jansen into American society, something Stéphane Boudin made a personal priority.

Robert Goelet (1880–1966) was a descendant of the French Huguenot Philip Jansen
Goelet, whose family fled France for Holland, and then for the New World in the last quarter
of the 17th century. The possibility of a blood relationship between Goelet and the family of
Jansen's founder, however fanciful, was no doubt attractive to the Harvard-educated
Francophile. Real estate and investment businessman, sportsman, author, motion picture producer, opera enthusiast (he was a director of the Metropolitan Opera for 30 years), and art
collector, Goelet was a passionate connoisseur of 18th-century French furniture and decorative arts, a trait that was shared by several members of his family, including his aunt Grace

OPPOSITE: VIEW FROM NEW DINING ROOM TO ADJACENT HALL

GARDEN FACADE WITH NEW DINING ROOM WING AT LEFT

Vanderbilt and his sister May, the Duchess of Roxburghe.[1] As an educated admirer of the art and architecture of the ancien régime, he must have become an admirer of Jansen, as well.

Following the 1947 donation of his family's Newport residence, the Richard Morris Hunt–designed Ochre Court, to the Archdiocese of Providence for the establishment of Salve Regina College, Goelet and his third wife, Roberta Willard, acquired the much smaller residence called Champ Soleil, or Sunny Field.[2]

For this Louis XIII–style house, Jansen worked in collaboration with its original architects, Polhemus & Coffin of New York, who designed the house for Philadelphia banking heiress Lucy Drexel Dahlgren and modeled it after La Lanterne, a hunting lodge near Versailles.[3] The landscape design was by Umberto Innocenti and Richard K. Webel. The leading design

voice in the project was no doubt Jansen, as is suggested by the numerous surviving plans bearing the firm's name.

The most notable room of the commission was the library, which included magnificent Louis XV–period paneling brought directly from Paris. Jansen devised a symmetrical theme, with mirrored alcoves opposite the room's existing windows and a bookcase-framed mantelpiece centered opposite the room's only door. The paneling was generously rubbed with gold- and brown-pigmented waxes, further encouraging the kind of warmth expected of such a secluded room. As a later owner, Irene Aitken, said, the "room was magnificent—easily everyone's favorite."[4]

Because Newport houses are designed for frequent entertaining, Jansen devised a separate dining room wing for the garden side of the house, an addition that brought the house's square footage to more than

146

DETAIL OF NEW HALL JOINING MAIN HOUSE WITH DINING ROOM WING

13,000. It is possible that the dining wing's construction was planned with the wedding festivities of the Goelets' only child, Mary, in mind; in 1948, soon after the wing's completion, she announced her engagement to Eliot Cross, a member of the Office of Strategic Services (OSS) and a recipient of the Medal of Freedom. The room was basically square, with new classically inspired ivory-painted paneling measuring 12.5 feet in height, and as it would be used mainly in the summer months, Jansen's design included no fireplace. Centrally placed in the fireplace's stead was an ivory and gilt coffered niche, which housed an 18th-century Austrian white faience stove with a chimney in the form of a palm tree adorned with putti; mainly decorative, this stove could all the same produce enough warmth for the occasional cool summer

147

Living room, c. 1950

Library, c. 1950

DINING ROOM, C. 1950

evening. Along each of the sidewalls was centered one of a pair of Louis XVI–style gilt console tables with fleur-de-lis bases, presumably made by Jansen in Paris. Above each table hung one of a pair of gilt-framed looking glasses that reflected the light of the rock crystal chandelier. Lighting was also supplied by a set of four bronze doré sconces with reliefs of young boys and intricate representations of the French royal crown, as well as by varying examples from Goelet's collection of 18th-century candelabra. It was here that Goelet (his wife had died in 1949, shortly after their daughter's wedding) gave one last grand entertainment, in 1964, a dinner-dance in honor of the finish of the America's Cup Race.

After Goelet's death, the 18-room Champ Soleil was purchased by Mary and James Gordon Douglas Jr.[5] It

DINING ROOM, C. 1950

later became the summer residence of Annie-Laurie Aitken, the widow of a Pittsburgh utilities magnate, and her second husband, Russell Barnett Aitken, an artist, adventure writer, and former associate editor of *Field and Stream*.[6] The house, and the backdrops of carved paneling that Jansen provided, served as a perfect repository for the couple's collection of fine European furniture and art objects. Champ Soleil was sold by Aitken's widow, Irene, in 2003.

c. 1950

Margaret Thompson Biddle

LES EMBRUNS

SAINT-JEAN-CAP-FERRAT, FRANCE

L
ES EMBRUNS WAS ONE OF SEVERAL HOUSES THAT STÉPHANE BOUDIN and Maison Jansen decorated for Margaret Thompson Biddle, an American mining heiress who wrote about the Paris social and political scene for French and American publications and who successfully carried the 19th-century fashion of salon entertaining into the post–World War II era. Noted for her intelligence, political connections, and experience as a diplomat's wife, Biddle was a well-known hostess and art collector, her life spent shuttling between an apartment in the former Joseph Pulitzer mansion in New York City, a house on rue Las Cases in Paris, and the Riviera villa.[1] As described in the *The New York Times*, all these residences witnessed "notable gatherings of headline figures."[2]

Biddle (1896–1956) was born in Helena, Montana, the only child of William Boyce Thompson, a philanthropist whose fortune was built on diamond mines in South Africa and copper and sulfur mines in the American West; he also served as a director of the Federal Reserve Bank of New York. Upon his death in 1930, Margaret, then the former wife of Theodore Schulze, and her mother, Gertrude, shared an inheritance of more than $16 million.[3] A year later, in London, she married Anthony J. Drexel Biddle Jr., a banking heir who went on to serve as America's minister to Norway and Poland, ambassador and minister to

OPPOSITE: CORNER OF A GUEST BEDROOM

SALON

SALON

DINING ROOM

governments in exile during World War II, and ambassador to Spain.[4] The couple divorced in 1945, but Margaret Biddle, who had long maintained a foothold in Paris, remained in Europe, where she worked as the Paris editor of *Woman's Home Companion* and a correspondent for the French magazine *Réalités*. With an avid interest in politics and world affairs, she boasted of having hosted the initial meeting between General of the Army Dwight D. Eisenhower and Republican Party leaders. This connection led her to bequeath a $100,000 collection of antique English and French vermeil, or gilded silver, to the White House in 1956. Accepted by the U.S. government a year later, the col-

lection, which was intended to be used at state dinners, was eventually stored in the Vermeil Room, which, appropriately enough, was decorated during the Kennedy administration by Stéphane Boudin.[5]

Boudin probably met Biddle in Paris before the war, but Maison Jansen may not have counted her as a client until the liberation of France in 1944.[6] For Les Embruns, the Frenchman created a comfortable vocabulary befitting the villa's lush Riviera setting and its owner's reputation as a hostess. Whitewashed walls, slipcovered chairs, and a mélange of Italian 18th- and 19th-century painted furniture established a somewhat informal feeling in the stone and stucco mansion. To

SUN, OR MORNING ROOM

this, Boudin added a degree of whimsy with the introduction of painted trompe l'oeil decorations, asymmetrical floral vines for bedroom ceilings, and flowering trees inside the pool house.

The most formal and recognized room of this residence was the dining room, which was lined with an early-19th-century French scenic wallpaper. Aware that such a wall covering could be overpowering, Boudin made it inviting and playful through the inclusion of polychromed blackamoor candlesticks, gilt torchères in the form of swaying palm trees, and a pair of painted-metal faux potted palms that had been converted into lamps. Complementing these fixtures and further

playing on the naturalistic theme was a set of four Italian gilt-wood sconces representing asymmetrical, intertwining branches. A fantasy landscape, Les Embruns's dining room was the centerpiece of Biddle's Riviera entertaining. With her table acting as a bastion of civilized life in an otherwise untamed world, she led her guests in lively, spontaneous conversation, solving society's challenges with each course.

After dinner, guests would retire to the salon, another whitewashed room, whose numerous doors led to paved terraces and flowering gardens. In front of the fireplace, Boudin positioned matching sofas covered in blue raw silk alongside two highly sculptural

GUEST BEDROOM

late-18th-century parcel-gilt Venetian chairs; these were arranged around a gilt faux-bamboo low table from the Jansen ateliers, near a leopard-skin rug. For the windows and the glazed doors, which were usually kept open, Boudin designed straight-falling panels of blue and ivory striped silk, capped by jagged-edged valances of the same material. At one end of the room, between two windows, stood a white silk loveseat that imitated in line and detailing the curvaceousness of the thronelike Venetian chairs.

Off the main salon was a smaller, more intimate room with white-on-white silk damask draperies of simple design and matching carpeting and painted walls. Against this blank canvas, Boudin installed chairs and sofas covered in glazed green, yellow, and white chintz with a pattern depicting branches of coral. This fresh, sunny space was used for morning gatherings, and as its more feminine decor might suggest, it also served as a private hideaway for the owner of the house.

The informality of Boudin's reception rooms for Margaret Thompson Biddle was carried over into the numerous bedrooms. Almost every one was furnished with painted chests, tables, mirror frames, and headboards displaying delicate flowers, scrollwork, and an

BEDROOM

array of miniature landscapes. Walls were painted in shades that complemented the printed cottons and striped silks selected for the windows and beds. Far from ostentatious, these rooms were inviting and comfortable and reminiscent of the decorator's playful designs for Biddle's friends the Duke and Duchess of Windsor, at their country house, the Moulin de la Tuilerie.

Margaret Thompson Biddle died on June 9, 1956, soon after attending a gala in Paris, in honor of King Paul and Queen Frederika of Greece.[7] Her funeral was attended by three former prime ministers of France and the supreme allied commander in Europe. Les Embruns was left to Biddle's two children from her first marriage, and many of its contents were eventually sold through Christie's of Monaco in June 1994.[8]

The Hon. Lady Baillie

Harbourside

Hog Island, Nassau, the Bahamas

T HE ROMANTIC ENGLISH COUNTRY HOUSE LIFESTYLE OF THE 1930s, which had become intertwined with the success of Jansen and the celebrity of Stéphane Boudin, greatly faded in the years immediately following World War II. Increased property taxation and rising costs for upkeep played roles in this antiquation, as did a redefinition of the workforce through war and further industrialization; for the most part, the formerly plentiful servant class that made the country house possible no longer existed, having moved on to urban centers and factory employment. A downsized, less ostentatious manner of living resulted, dictated by the horrors of war and the rationings of its aftermath.

Lady Baillie's Leeds Castle was one of the few English country houses to survive this transformation. Great weekend gatherings continued to be planned and staged, but Olive Baillie soon envisioned a smaller, less formal retreat as an escape for herself and her closest friends and family. In or around 1950, while continuing to renovate and expand her famous English castle with Boudin, she purchased an enclave of buildings on Hog Island, near Nassau, the Bahamas.[1] She employed a local architect, John Wolfe, to refine and aggrandize the main house and guest quarters, and commissioned Jansen to oversee the decoration of the interiors of the house, which she called Harbourside.

OPPOSITE: DETAIL OF A GUEST ROOM MANTLEPIECE

<small>ENTRANCE HALL</small>

Not much more is known about the architectural changes or the construction history of this very private domain. What does survive is a series of archival photographs that document the primary rooms. Clearly the decor was less formal than previous work accomplished by Jansen for Lady Baillie. The rooms display a whimsical quality more commonly associated with Lady Mendl's Circus Ball of 1938 than the serious formality of Leeds Castle. Indeed, at Harbourside, Boudin created rooms in keeping with the follies or spaces of a secret garden, not with the traditional decoration for which he was known.

The most welcoming space in the main house was the drawing room, which served as the primary sitting room. It was a long, rectangular space with fireplaces at either

end—a downsized variation of the English manor house great hall—and its plaster walls were scored in imitation of more formal, trellis-like wood paneling. The walls were painted in white and pale green, with winding vines defining each of the wall panels, mantels, looking glasses, and door surrounds; crossed green and white parasols, positioned in the manner of ornamental swords, framed the central door of the room's long wall. The room was also treated like a garden folly with a forced perspective surround. Another illusionary technique was used for the ceiling, where a multitude of thin white beams gave the impression of a pergola. Continuing the botanical theme was a pair of white-painted iron chandeliers, ornamented with naturalistic green leaves, and walls hung with framed butterfly specimens.

TOP AND ABOVE: ENTRANCE HALL DETAILS

The furnishing of this glamorous space was in keeping with traditional interior design vocabularies. In the center of the room, on a white carpet, stood a large inlaid table, capped with a pair of gilt greyhound statuettes and flanked by mahogany curule-base stools. To one side of the room, gathered around a palm-ornamented mantelpiece hosting an early-19th-century Anglo-Indian rosewood and brass architectural clock, were tailored sofas and club chairs, all upholstered in light gray-green velvet. On the opposing side of the room, before a duplicate mantel surround, were arranged five large Louis XV–inspired chairs; these were upholstered in an ivory-on-ivory striped silk and trimmed with green and ivory gimp. A pair of George III marble-topped console tables framed the central door; their carved gilt clamshells subtly introduced a decorative leitmotif that dominated the decoration of the house's private quarters.

The nearby dining room continued the green and white color scheme. The walls were painted a highly reflective, extremely dark green and overlaid with Chippendale-inspired chinoiserie trelliswork, painted the same cool white as the doors and window surrounds; the central ornament of each wall was a recessed circular plate of mirrored glass. Spread across the floor was natural grass matting in a basketweave pattern, against which was arranged traditional 18th- and 19th-century English mahogany dining furniture. The simple open-back chairs were upholstered with green-and-white horsehair woven in a diaper pattern. Instead of a chandelier, lighting came exclusively from sconces and crystal and gilt-bronze mounted oil lamps.

The main house's less formal sitting room was treated to three-quarter cast-plaster walls in imitation of gathered and tied bamboo stalks; the illusion was of a fence or privacy screen. The stalks were painted white, the faux ties and bands picked out in red. Sky blue paint covered the unadorned upper portion of the walls, further emphasizing the open-air effect. Straight-falling panels of bold crimson and blue striped cotton hung at the five windows. The floor was covered in woven matting, whereas the furniture consisted of a mélange of early-19th-century English Regency consoles, a Louis XVI writing table, and various faux-bamboo chairs and small tables. Facing the ocean view was a comfortable sofa upholstered in quilted white cotton. Continuing the naturalistic motifs of the entrance hall was a vine-embroidered white cotton used to upholster a group of comfortable, caster-based chairs. Off in a corner was a card table, where Lady Baillie spent hours with friends playing bridge.

The last room documented in this series of photographs is a guest bedroom whose fanciful decoration surely reveals aspects of Lady Baillie's own private suite. Inspired by Harbourside's views, Jansen used white, ivory, and brown seashells to define architectural panels against painted blue plaster. The simple mantelpiece was an example of shellwork Neoclassicism, with clusters of clamshells ornamenting the corners like Grecian urns, mussel shells forming symmetrical garlands and beadwork, and a large conch shell serving as the traditional central tablet or plaque. The bed had a clam-form headboard made of gilt bronze. Three-tier bronze and mahogany tables from Jansen's workshops served as nightstands. For the window and bedcover, Boudin selected a bold coral, blue, and ivory striped silk. Solid-blue satin was used on club chairs and stools, and the floor was covered with simple pink, blue, and white cotton rugs.

Lady Baillie continued to use Harbourside until her death in 1974. The property was then sold by her heirs.

DINING ROOM

ABOVE AND TOP: VIEWS OF SITTING ROOM

GUEST BEDROOM

1950–65

Jayne and Charles B. Wrightsman

PALM BEACH, FLORIDA

DESIGNED IN 1917 BY H. HASTINGS MUNDY, THE WHITE STUCCO house at 513 North County Road was purchased in 1947 by millionaire Charles B. Wrightsman and his second wife, Jayne. Originally known as Blythedunes, it had been built for Robert Dun Douglass, a New Jersey financier whose family founded Dun & Bradstreet, but in 1930 it was sold to one of the era's most publicized couples, the utilities magnate Harrison Williams and his wife, Mona, a noted fashion plate. They gave the house a dramatic exterior refitting by the architect Maurice Fatio and interiors by the English decorator Syrie Maugham.

Charles Bierer Wrightsman (1895–1986) was born in Pawnee, Oklahoma, the son of Charles John Wrightsman, an English-born lawyer turned oilfield wildcatter who also was celebrated for devising the still-vital tax write-off known as the oil-depletion allowance. After being educated at Phillips Exeter Academy and Stanford and Columbia universities, the younger Wrightsman began his own career in the oil industry, eventually serving as the president of Standard Oil of Kansas. He met his second wife, a stunning beauty named Jayne Larkin (born c. 1920), when he was trying out new fragrances in the West Coast department store where she worked.[1] Married in 1944, the Wrightsmans gradually infiltrated the elitist art world, befriending such important figures as National Gallery director John Walker and

OPPOSITE: JAYNE WRIGHTSMAN IN THE LIBRARY, 1959

elderly art scholar Bernard Berenson. For Berenson, who could no longer travel, Jayne Wrightsman personally photographed the entire collection of the National Gallery so that he could see it and provide his thoughts and opinions. This was one of many stages of the couple's unusual education in art history and connoisseurship. Friendships with Baroness Renée de Becker and Baron Eric von Goldschmidt-Rothschild—Jansen clients who were New York–based purveyors of 18th-century pedigreed French taste—as well as with the influential Stéphane Boudin of Jansen, provided similar tutorials in the then-undervalued taste of the Bourbon kings.

With the purchase of the Williams house in Palm Beach, the Wrightsmans at first basked in their inheritance of the often-touted taste of the previous owners. The rooms remained furnished with mostly 18th-century English pieces, and the main drawing room's 18th-century Chinese hand-painted wallpaper continued to dazzle visitors. But as Jayne Wrightsman took a greater interest in the history of decorative arts, the decoration that Maugham devised for the Williams gradually gave way to the influences of 18th-century France. "When the Wrightsmans acquired a French commode and . . . tried it out in the living room," recalled John Walker, "friends were shocked and disapproving. Mona's décor was in perfect taste . . . What right had anyone to alter it?"[2]

Eventually Boudin and Maison Jansen were invited to see the house, and soon alterations to the interiors went well beyond the placement of a single case piece. Three rooms eventually were paneled in 18th-century French woodwork, and four rooms received parquet floors with royal provenance. The English antiques, many of which proved not as old as originally believed, were replaced with exceptional examples of 18th-century French court taste.

The best-known room in the Palm Beach house was the drawing room, for which Boudin and Jayne Wrightsman maintained the Chinese paper that Maugham had purchased for the Williams; the exotic, asymmetrically patterned wall treatment proved an ideal backdrop for an ever-growing collection of French Rococo chairs, tables, and art objects. The one architectural change was the substitution of a Louis XV rouge marble mantelpiece and mirrored-glass surround for the sizable stone-and-wood English baronial mantel. Boudin arranged the room around a large, late-17th-century Savonnerie carpet originally designed for the Louvre, which was eventually given to the Metropolitan Museum of Art for inclusion in the Wrightsman Galleries. Standing in the central medallion of the carpet was a circa-1740 ormolu-adorned writing desk, designed by Bernard II Van Risamburgh, which the Wrightsmans had acquired from descendants of the Duc de Richelieu.[3] Around the writing table were placed a pair and a single example of mid-18th-century gilded upholstered stools, positioned as though they awaited a tutorial on some aspect of Louis XV design.

Additional groupings of bergères, fauteuils, and other seating forms lined the walls; a set of four Louis XV gilded armchairs, signed E. Meunier and featuring colorful embroidered silk upholstery, stood before the fireplace.[4] Elsewhere in the room were such rare pieces as a Louis XV ormolu-mounted cartonnier, or shaped cabinet, the highly reflective lacquer surface of which displayed chinoiserie-style red and gold flora and fauna against a rich black field. For the windows, Boudin selected multicolored, floral-patterned, striated silk that reached the floor in elegant straight-falling panels, above which were mounted chinoiserie openwork cornices.

In the dining room, Jansen installed two Louis XIV–style purplewood, oak, and parcel-gilt tables. The

DINING ROOM

bases of these tables consisted of four acanthus-adorned cabriole legs, joined by C-curve stretchers; the bases were nearly identical to Boudin's prewar design for the Duke and Duchess of Windsor's dining

table at 24 boulevard Suchet, which was later removed to the couple's residence in the Bois de Boulogne. One table, slightly smaller in length, could be used as an extension for the larger example with the removal

JAYNE WRIGHTSMAN IN THE ENTRANCE HALL, MID-1960S

of its gilt edging. Louis XV chaises en cabriolet served as dining chairs.

One of the rooms chosen to receive period woodwork was the library, painted in variations of primrose yellow and white. Here Jayne Wrightsman wrote some of her famous long letters to Bernard Berenson and other art historians, sharing insights while seeking additional perspectives on any of a number of considered acquisitions.

She sat at another handsome writing desk, this one standing beneath a trademark Boudin arrangement of Meissen porcelain birds on giltwood brackets. Drawn to the desk was a painted circa-1720 Régence fauteuil de cabinet. Nearby stood a pair of Louis XV beechwood fauteuils à la reine, signed L. Cresson. Presumably it was in this scholarly domain that Sir Francis Watson sat "beside her . . . showing her . . . two hundred and forty illustrations of a book he was

writing on furniture of the period of Louis XVI. They were not captioned. To his amazement Jayne knew the name of the ébéniste responsible for making the piece and in most cases the present owner, the sale at which it was purchased, and the price paid."[5]

Jansen style extended out to the pool area, where Boudin created arrangements of contemporary sofas, chairs, and tables in imitation of the vastly more formal seating areas inside. Much of the rattan, tailored-upholstered furniture duplicated pieces Boudin had devised for Gianni Agnelli and Pamela Churchill at La Leopolda and Margaret Thompson Biddle at Les Embruns. But for this Florida commission, Boudin added vivid pink to his standard white sailcloth cushions, thus drawing the flowers of nearby plantings into the overall decorative composition; this addition was complemented by the blue of the swimming pool's water and the green of the lush lawn, intentionally or

JAYNE WRIGHTSMAN IN THE THE DRAWING ROOM, MID-1960S

otherwise emulating the palettes of some of the Wrightsmans' Impressionist paintings. Though comfortable, the composition was made formal through its meticulous maintenance. "Every palm tree is perfectly placed," wrote one observer.[6]

The elegance of the decor was enhanced by the Wrightsmans' regal style of entertaining. Borrowing from standards set by the Duchess of Windsor and Lady Baillie, Jayne Wrightsman made it a point to have the favorite flowers of overnight guests in their rooms, while also providing a stack of books and magazines tailored to their particular interests. The presentation was flawless. "To stay at North County Road," later wrote a guest, "was an unforgettable experience, a tangible reminder of the douceur de vivre the passing of which was lamented by Talleyrand. The company, the life, the service . . . the gardens, the swimming, the conversation and not the least the cuisine were all incomparable."[7]

When Boudin died in 1967, Jayne Wrightsman wrote to his daughter: "I loved Boudin deeply—I considered him one of my dearest friends. It is a great loss for me but I am so happy that I can live surrounded by all the lovely rooms he made for us—all happy reminders of [him]."[8] By this time, the Wrightsmans had moved beyond the influence of Maison Jansen. They subsequently used the talents of other designers in Palm Beach, notably Vincent Fourcade in the early 1980s. However, the core of the Boudin–Jansen work remained in place until the house was sold in May 1984 to the women's apparel millionaire Leslie Wexner, who demolished it. The Wrightsmans' collections of furniture and art were removed, some being transferred to the Metropolitan Museum of Art, and lesser pieces were sold through Sotheby's New York.

c. 1953

Marguerite and George Tyson

LES ORMES

WASHINGTON, D.C.

L ES ORMES, OR THE ELMS, IN THE SPRING VALLEY SECTION OF Washington, is a Jansen commission with a multifaceted history. It was built in 1930 for career diplomat Robert Dudley Longyear, on a site that originally encompassed 18 acres.[1] Purchased in 1953 by Marguerite and George Tyson, a retired stockbroker, the picturesquely gabled French Normandy–style house was also the residence of Marguerite Tyson's sister, Perle Mesta, a politically savvy socialite who was best known as America's "hostess with the mostes.[2]" All three lived here together until 1961, when the Tysons sold the house to one of Mesta's favorite politicians, Lyndon Johnson, and his wife, Lady Bird, as a vice presidential residence more fitting than their suite at the Wardman Park Hotel.[3] Stéphane Boudin decorated Les Ormes for the Tysons over a year-long period, completing his work in 1954. When the Johnsons moved to the White House in December 1963, following President Kennedy's assassination, an exuberant Boudin claimed Lady Bird Johnson as a kindred spirit if not client, noting, "I will love Madame Johnson . . . she has lived in my house . . . Les Ormes."[4]

One didn't have to enter Les Ormes to see the presence of Jansen. Boudin created a stationary canopy above the front door of the house, perhaps influenced by his late-1930s work for Lady Mendl at Villa Trianon. Painted with broad stripes, the sheet-steel cover had the

OPPOSITE: DINING ROOM

175

definite and intentional appearance of a tented awning. Surely more appropriate for the theatrical Mesta or her sister, a former actress, than a vice president of the United States, the canopy was a conspicuous addition to an otherwise sedate residential neighborhood. Indeed, it appeared as if it could have been a stage prop from the Broadway musical *Call Me Madam,* which was based on Mesta's four years as America's first minister to Luxembourg.[5]

Raised in Oklahoma, Pearl (1889–1975)—who changed the spelling of her name in 1944—and Marguerite (1896–1963) were the colorful daughters of William Balser Skirvin, an oilman who built the Skirvin Hotel, considered the Ritz of Oklahoma City. After a brief career acting in silent films and on Broadway (she later claimed that her greatest career achievement was serving as her older sister's household manager in the American Legation in Luxembourg), Marguerite married Robert John Adams, heir to a Connecticut textile-mill fortune, and after their divorce she married the Boston-born Tyson.[6] As for Pearl, she studied music before marrying the much older George Mesta, founder of a major Pennsylvania manufacturer of steel machinery. He died in 1925, eight years into the marriage, leaving her in control of the $78 million company. Eventually Perle Mesta became congressional chairman of the National Women's Party and served as a fundraiser for both Republican and Democratic national campaigns.[7]

Boudin initially came into contact with the sisters when Marguerite Tyson hired him to redecorate the American Legation residence in Luxembourg.[8] His services were required again when the Tysons purchased the 12-room whitewashed brick house in Spring Valley, and he proceeded to decorate it with a collection of 18th-century furniture and art objects, many of which Marguerite had acquired during the stay in Luxembourg. In fact, Mesta stated in her memoirs that the house was specifically chosen because it had a room large enough to hold the rose-colored Aubusson carpet that the Tysons purchased in France.[9] The carpet, noted for its monumental size, was the central feature of the main reception or living room.

Equally large in scale, with a step-down entry opposite a Louis XV–style chimneypiece with mirrored overmantel, the sunny room had four windows, two overlooking a hillside and two the house's entrance. The cream-colored window treatment was a Jansen standard, with stationary valances of fringe-adorned tabs or tongues over tied-back drapery panels; the unlined panels were one shade lighter than the silk of the valances. The difference between the coloring of these two otherwise identical fabrics was not clearly apparent, for one was seen flat, and the other was always viewed with varying shadows through pleating and folding. However, such differences gave an almost undetectable weight or importance to the upper portion of the window treatment.

This subtlety was a longstanding leitmotif of Jansen and, specifically, Boudin. Linking the four windows were six similarly scaled floor-to-ceiling upholstered wall panels of rose-colored silk damask, vaguely described by Perle Mesta as having come from "another chateau."[10] So dominant was the pattern that no paintings, brackets, or other decorative features were displayed on the walls of this room. In contrast to the Jansen-manufactured mantel and the woodwork in the entrance hall, the living room's parquet floor was antique and purportedly had the pedigree of a château near Versailles.

As photographed during the Johnsons' short occupancy—at which time the furniture arrangements

ENTRANCE HALL

remained similar to those chosen by Marguerite Tyson—this room seems somewhat informal and in keeping with other Jansen commissions of the time, including the residence of the French ambassador in Washington.[11] Presumably this informality worked well with Mesta and the Tysons' entertaining style; one evening, groups of bargaining politicians would be found sequestered throughout the room, and the next night, Judy Garland would be giving a spontaneous concert to two hundred friends and fans. The adjacent

177

MRS. LYNDON B. JOHNSON HOSTS INDIRA GHANDI, 1962

entrance hall had a black and white marble floor, which made "a wonderful place for eight or ten couples to dance."[12] Opposite the front door, Boudin installed a mirrored wall, defined by a white Rococo-style frame carved with elaborate bow-knots and roses. A parcel-gilt, marble-topped console table stood here, typically bearing a large-scale floral arrangement.

On the other side of the entrance hall was the very theatrical dining room. A large rectangular space with windows facing the garden, it was decorated with nearly wall-sized 18th-century cartoons or studies for tapestries. Found in Venice, the large tempera-painted canvas scenes represented various social gatherings, including chess and cards being played among friends, music

being performed in a village street, and chocolate being served in a palace drawing room. Mesta noted in her autobiography that her sister selected the canvas renderings "because they give a lighter, less stuffy feeling than tapestries."[13] This noted, Boudin doubtless would have deemed tapestries inappropriate for the room's low ceilings.[14] Indeed, for another client in Washington—the young Jacqueline Kennedy, bride of the junior senator from Massachusetts—the decorator had suggested simplicity over formality for her 19th century Georgetown townhouse. Boudin "councelled [sic] me against so many large expenditures I thought I should make," Kennedy noted, "saying that they would all be too pompous in their surroundings."[15] He

MAIN SALON, OR LIVING ROOM

probably did the same for Marguerite Tyson. Dominating the room was a Sheraton-style four-pedestal mahogany extension table, surrounded by green leather-upholstered Louis XV–style side chairs; these reproductions, along with other French reproductions and some existing antiques, had been acquired by the Johnsons when they purchased Les Ormes. Totaling 20, the dining chairs could be supplemented by 14 cane-backed Louis XVI–style side chairs from the adjoining breakfast room. Opposite the windows of the dining room, and below the central cartoon panel, stood a long Adamesque console table with key patterning in the apron.

Les Ormes was sold by the Johnsons in 1964 to Luther B. Smith, who sold it weeks later to the government of Algeria.[16] Since then it has been the home of the Algerian ambassador to the United States.[17]

179

1957–74

Suzy and Pierre Delbée

PARIS, FRANCE

THE APARTMENT OF PIERRE DELBÉE, THE PRESIDENT OF JANSEN, and his wife, Suzy, a member of the Lazard banking dynasty, was both a backdrop for lavish entertaining and a testing ground for decorative schemes and ideas. As with so many residences of architects and designers, it was never really completed; it continued to evolve until Pierre Delbée's death in 1974. With this understood, there was no better example of the quality of workmanship and high level of creativity produced by Jansen than this chic, eclectic residence, the home of a man noted for his personal flamboyance.

The entrance hall, which served as a part-time dining room, took the firm's characteristic historicism and melded it with Dalí-esque surrealism. In just a few steps, a visitor was introduced to the extremes of Jansen's offerings, as well as to the highest levels of materials and craftsmanship available. The entire room, including the ceiling, was encased in Louis XV-style paneling, which had been painted varying shades of blue. Against this formulaic Jansen backdrop, the Delbées exhibited cabinetmaking treasures such as a circa-1760 pair of ormolu-mounted black lacquer corner cabinets. Above these cabinets, which flanked the apartment's front door, were displayed two imposing 16th-century Italian reliefs of ancient Roman senators, representative of Suzy and Pierre Delbée's interest in classical art objects. The room was

OPPOSITE: ENTRANCE HALL

ENTRANCE HALL–DINING ROOM

View of entrance hall—dining room

LIBRARY DETAIL

dramatically lighted by a pair of Renaissance-inspired silver chandeliers, as well as strategically placed Louis XIV-style gilt-bronze wall sconces with mirrored glass reflectors, and ormolu-mounted porphyry table lamps bearing black shades. The most striking features were the room's five doors. Made of ebony and ivory veneer, each of the three-panel doors was given a unique architectural theme, including variations of temples and follies with surrealist juxtapositions of an hourglass, spires, and geometric trophies. The double doors that led to the main salon were equally inventive in their design,

bearing a trompe-l'oeil representation of a grid-pattern floor that directed one's attention into the next room, even when the doors were closed. Designed by Pierre Delbée in 1957 and made within the firm's ateliers over twenty months by three artisans, the doors were sterling examples of the craftsmanship that was produced in Jansen's ateliers in the post–World War II era.

The main salon was devised as a combination library and Renaissance cabinet of curiosities. The walls were lined with floor-to-ceiling bookcases made of Myroxylon balsamum, or Brazilian red-oil wood, while

BEDROOM

the doors were upholstered in green suede framed with strips of gilt bronze. Here Suzy Delbée's passion for antique books was acknowledged, and interspersed among her library of fine bindings and rare volumes were dozens of globes of varying sizes, busts of male and female historical figures, and architectural models of every size and description. Excepting the red velvet sofa and some of the larger-scaled tables, the room's furniture was intended to be moved around and constantly rearranged, underscoring its ability to transform from after-dinner sitting room to scholar's study. There was no suite of matched pieces: each chair, table, and lamp had been acquired as an example of a work of art. An Empire fauteuil whose arms terminated in gilt lion heads faced off against a later-date ormolu table whose base was adorned with naturalistic serpents, which in turn countered a theatrical throne encompassing full-scale harps for arms. Elaborately carved ostrich eggs opposed chess boards made of ivory, ebony, and gold. Twenty-two antique baby rattles made of coral and silver were displayed on one table, while on another could be found a dozen leather boxes of various forms and sizes.

As might be expected, Pierre Delbée's bedroom was more intimate, but it, too, contained small collections of objects and works of art. The walls were upholstered like a jewel box in dark green silk velvet, which was divided into panels with vertical and horizontal strips of specially woven decorative tape. The bed was backed by a serpentine headboard, covered in fragments of an antique allegorical tapestry, and sur-mounted by an array of crucifixes. Framing the bed were Napoleon III Chinese lacquer trays, mounted on ebony stands made within the Jansen ateliers. Against the walls were arranged Italian bas-reliefs and portrait miniatures whose provenance ranged from the Renaissance to the 19th century.

The presence in this room of a highly fragile secrétaire à abattant of red lacquer, signed by the great ebéniste François Rubestück and dated circa 1766, reveals a great deal about how Delbée lived, and, more importantly, how he designed.[1] Adorning the narrow room more like an altar than a desk, the far-from-utilitarian work of art was surely selected by the decorator for the intense visual contrast between the gleaming red of the lacquer and the matte green of the velvet walls. Functionalism and practicality rarely entered into the decorator's vision for a room or project, as demonstrated by this personal selection; indeed, it would be impossible to sit at the desk because of its placement in relation to the bed. Unlike his predecessor to the presidency of Jansen, Stéphane Boudin, Delbée designed rooms for sensory impact, first and foremost, for clients, a critic observed, with "vaguely traditionalist inclinations and the lightest cultural baggage."[2]

After Delbée's death, his widow sold the apartment, furnished, along with the couple's country house, to Jansen's premier Spanish client, Bartolomé March Servera. The March family retained the apartment for 15 years before dispersing its contents, including the trompe l'oeil doors, at Christie's Monaco in 1999.

TWO OF FIVE INLAID EBONY DOORS

The Wrightsman Galleries

The Metropolitan Museum of Art

New York City

W HEN WRITING HIS AUTOBIOGRAPHY, THE ONETIME DIRECTOR of the National Gallery of Art in Washington, D.C., John Walker, titled the chapter about Jayne and Charles B. Wrightsman "Collecting in Partnership." Although the description well defines the pair as a team, there is little doubt that when it came to 18th-century French decorative arts, Jayne Wrightsman spearheaded the couple's connoisseurship and eventual influence in the field. Through years of studying actual objects, photographing them, and mentally filing away every fact, detail, and note attained through comparisons, she gained knowledge unrivaled by most museum curators. Once the couple's collection had been formed, it was inevitable that she would wish to share that achievement. Thus was born the Wrightsman Galleries of the Metropolitan Museum of Art.

Boudin's close association with Jayne Wrightsman ensured Jansen's participation in the formulation of such galleries. Through his eyes, she had been able to see beyond a specific object and take in a whole interior. In the manner of a tutor, he guided her understanding of proportion and balance and instructed her in details such as the differences between trimmings of the Louis XV period and those manufactured during the reigns of Louis XVI, Napoleon I, and Napoleon III. In fact, the Wrightsman-sponsored work at the Metropolitan Museum

OPPOSITE: PAAR ROOM AS INSTALLED BY JANSEN

of Art actually began with the installation of new draperies and trimmings for the museum's existing French period rooms in the early 1960s. The Frenchman was not the final voice Wrightsman sought in her studies, but his connections in the world of galleries and museums greatly expanded her horizons. Jayne and Charles Wrightsman used his initial proposal, formulated with curators, as the plan for new galleries within the famous Manhattan museum.

Discussion regarding the museum spaces began in the late 1950s, although serious planning did not start until the early 1960s. Boudin proposed an initial layout, which included what is known as the Paar Room, a large interior made up of some of the circa-1765–72 paneling he had acquired in 1934 from the Paar Palace in Vienna. He had sold sections of this paneling to the collector Sir Philip Sassoon that same year for inclusion in his London townhouse at 25 (later 45) Park Lane. When that residence was scheduled for demolition in the mid-1950s, Boudin reacquired the woodwork for Jansen's stock. With plans for the galleries at the Metropolitan Museum well under way by 1963, Jansen sold the paneling to the Wrightsmans. For these, the Paris firm created a pair of window surrounds and a doorway to accommodate an expanded installation of the period paneling. The firm also restored the woodwork's original pale blue finish and gilded detailing. Jansen also designed a ceiling ornament, basing its design on features shown in early photographs of other rooms in the Paar Palace.[1]

Scrutinizing the installation of the galleries that would bear both her and her husband's names, Jayne Wrightsman wrote in 1966 to a then-ailing Boudin to keep him abreast of the progress. "The Palais Paar Room will be a dream once we get the windows finished and the curtains up," she wrote. "Useless to say, you and I forgot to order the hardware for the windows (we always manage to forget one thing!). So Claude [Mandron, Boudin's nephew] is standing over the man with a gun in his back to have him make the necessary door handles in a hurry. I hated the chimney we chose–too small and too shallow to hold even a candlestick. We must have been drinking daiquiris the day we chose that. Happily the museum possessed a very beautiful one in the same marble but somewhat larger, so for once luck was on our side."[2]

Jayne Wrightsman informed Boudin that the neighboring room, composed of circa-1736–52 paneling acquired from Hôtel Pillet-Will in Paris, was "magnificent."[3] This space is now known as the Varengeville Room. Its gold and white paneling, attributed to Nicolas Pineau, was a later addition to Hôtel de Varengeville, which had been built in 1704 by Jacques Gabriel for Charlotte-Angélique Courbin, Marquise de Varengeville.[4] The Rococo woodwork was sold in the last quarter of the 19th century to Count Frédéric-Alexis-Louis Pillet-Will, a regent of the Bank of France, for inclusion in the hôtel particulier he was building at 29 rue du Faubourg Saint-Honoré.[5] The paneling again was sold, through auction, in early 1963, reunited with other architectural elements of Hôtel de Varengeville, and acquired by the Wrightsmans, who gave it as a gift to the Metropolitan Museum of Art. Additional woodwork was manufactured by Jansen and added to the antique paneling, in order to increase the gallery's overall size for display and public accessibility purposes.

The beautiful Cabris Room, with its gold and white paneling made circa 1777, was commissioned from the most fashionable Paris artisans by Jean-Paul de Clapiers, Marquis de Cabris, and his wife, the former Louise de Mirabeau, for their townhouse in Grasse, France. The

Detail of Paar Room

CABRIS ROOM

Wrightsmans had acquired this room in 1957 from the noted art dealers Duveen Brothers and had Jansen install it in their dining room at 820 Fifth Avenue.[6] Boudin and the Wrightsmans likely envisioned this particular set of paneling one day becoming part of the Wrightsman Galleries, and it did so in 1972.[7]

"We can't think what in the world to do with the huge gallery leading into the rooms [at the Metropolitan Museum]," Jayne Wrightsman noted to

Boudin in a letter that no doubt allowed the dying man to feel still involved with the life of his friend and client. "We are trying different ideas and I shall write to ask you your choice."[8] For this space, Jansen provided various scale drawings for elaborate white and gold cornices and indicated that the walls would be painted in imitation of marble. Perhaps more austere than originally envisioned or hoped for by Boudin, the completed space nonetheless conveyed a regal formality

PAAR ROOM

without competing with the 18th-century paneled rooms to which it led, a concern of both the Frenchman and Jayne Wrightsman.

Jayne Wrightsman personally directed the placement of some of her many magnificent acquisitions in these rooms. Most of these had royal provenance and already were celebrated in a five-volume set of books on the Wrightsman collection, published in 1965 and written by Sir Francis J. B. Watson, the director of the Wallace Collection in London. Among the most ambitious articles was one of 92 carpets woven for the Grand Gallery of the Louvre between 1669 and 1680. Furniture included fauteuils, bergères, chaises, canapés, consoles, commodes, and bureau plats, including seminal works by Georges Jacob, Jacques-Jean-Baptiste Tilliard, Guillaume Beneman, and Jean-Henri Riesener.[9] Many of these acquisitions were advised upon and encouraged by Sir Francis Watson and Pierre Verlet, the

193

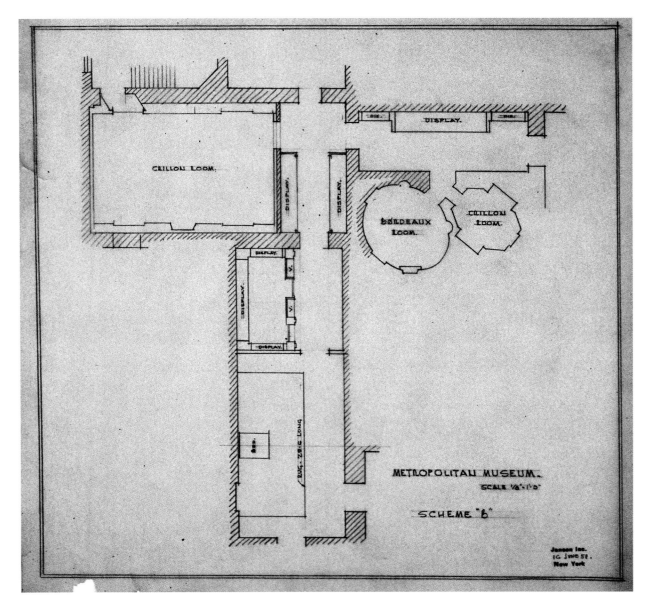

REINSTALLATION PLAN FOR EXISTING FRENCH PERIOD ROOMS, 1958

conservator of decorative arts at the Louvre, and it was an astounding cache. As described by John Russell in *The New York Times,* "The Wrightsmans have given the Met tables and chairs that are unsurpassed in the history of French cabinetmaking . . . all the more . . . complete with paneling, sculptures in low relief, doors and over-doors, windows and chimney pieces."[10]

"The work in the new rooms at the Metropolitan Museum is proceeding at a snail's pace!" Jayne

Wrightsman wrote to Boudin. "The Lord alone knows when they will be opened. But they do look very beautiful."[11] The galleries, however, did open on schedule in 1969, two years after Boudin's death. Harold A. Eberhard Jr., who had been a designer at Jansen's New York office, took over for Boudin in the further development of the galleries. He worked in collaboration with the legendary interior decorator Henri Samuel, who had worked in the rue Royale establishment in the

PROPOSALS FOR WINDOW TREATMENTS FOR EXISTING FRENCH PERIOD ROOMS, 1962

1920s. The last gallery to be added to the Wrightsman rooms was a Louis XIV state bedchamber in 1987; it was designed by Samuel. This interior served as both a visual and physical bridge between earlier museum gifts by J. P. Morgan, Louis Untermeyer, and others and the Wrightsmans' concentration on Louis XV and Louis XVI.

The Wrightsman Galleries remain today as initially planned by Jansen, in collaboration with Jayne and Charles Wrightsman and the curators of the Metropolitan Museum of Art. From the beginning, these spaces were not intended to serve as period rooms; they did not replicate the actual layout of any 18th-century house, nor did their furnishings—individually, or together—replicate arrangements documented in a specific period inventory, drawing, or painting.[12] Instead, these rooms are elegant backdrops for a rich collection of fine and decorative arts assembled, for the most part, by the Wrightsmans. This clarification should not devalue the importance of the period architectural elements, which remain an equally important focus for admiration and study as one of the finest public collections of 18th-century French high-style design. Unintentionally, these same fragments now serve as a rare surviving example of the multifaceted work of Maison Jansen.

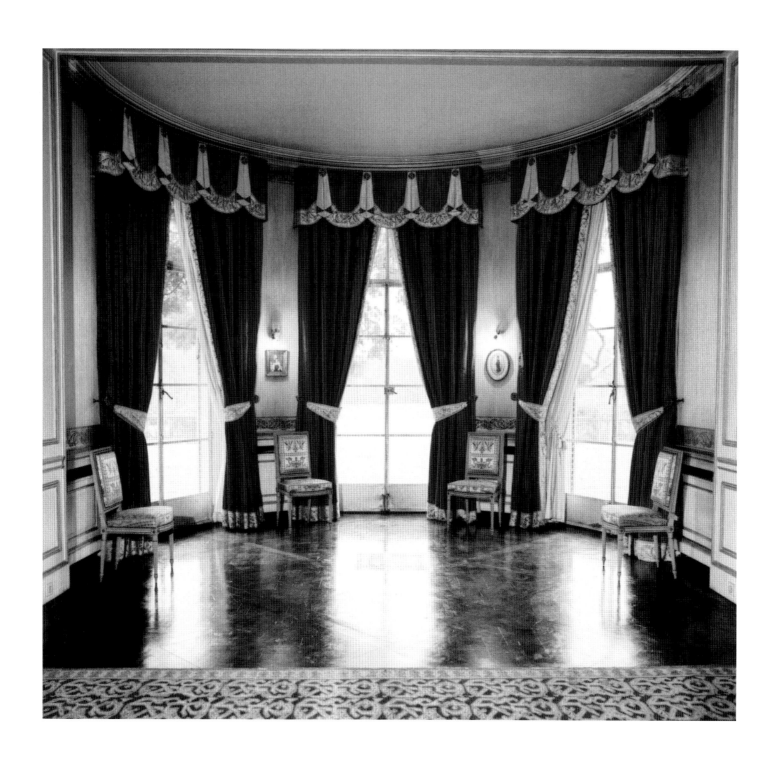

King Leopold III and
Princess Lilian of Belgium

Domaine d'Argenteuil

Ohain, Belgium

A STATELY COUNTRY HOUSE NEAR THE CITY OF WATERLOO, Domaine d'Argenteuil is among the last expressions of Jansen's influence on the taste of the Belgian royal family, for which the Paris firm had worked since the 1890 renovation of Château de Laeken.[1] It was one of Stéphane Boudin's favorite projects, and he began decorating it in 1959 as a home for former king Leopold III, his second wife, Princess Lilian, and their three children.[2] As he had with clients such as the Duchess of Windsor, Jayne Wrightsman, and Jacqueline Kennedy, the decorator developed a special bond with the princess, a beautiful brunette, serving as both tutor and friend. "[He was] a very nice, reserved man, always wearing a[n] immaculate dark suit," the couple's youngest child, the journalist Esmeralda de Rethy, recalled. "My mother used to spend a great deal of time with him discussing ideas, colors, etc. Then, he would stay for lunch with us."[3] As for the princess, she saw Boudin as nothing less than a confidant and "friend, steady and true."[4]

The French-inspired buff brick and limestone house was the centerpiece of 353 wooded acres at the edge of the forest of Soignes, not far from the site of Napoleon's defeat by the British in 1815. Built in 1929, it was designed by William Adams Delano of Delano & Aldrich, a prestigious New York architecture firm responsible for some of the most

OPPOSITE: BAY OF GRAND SALON ADDED BY BOUDIN

distinguished houses on the East Coast.[5] It had been commissioned by William Hallam Tuck, an American chemical engineer and dye-company executive who had served in both the British and American armies, and his Belgian wife, Hilda.[6] Tuck was a leader of war relief efforts in Belgium, Finland, and Japan and served as the director general of the International Refugee Organization. After World War II, the estate was acquired by the Belgian government.

Leopold III, who was given permission to use the title of king as a courtesy after his abdication, and Princess Lilian moved to the former Tuck residence after leaving the royal palace at Laeken amid suspicions that they were unduly influencing his son King Baudouin. Acceding the throne in 1934, after his father, Albert I, died during a mountain climbing expedition, Leopold (1901–1983) embarked on what proved to be an unlucky reign. A year later, he was the driver in an automobile accident that killed his very popular first wife, Astrid.[7] In 1941, he secretly wed the daughter of a former Belgian government minister, Mary Lilian Baéls (1916–2002), and once the marriage was revealed, the king became the object of much criticism; Lilian was not only a commoner, but she was believed to have Nazi supporters as friends. Bowing to public pressure, the king announced that she would become a princess of Belgium instead of his queen.

Facing German occupation in World War II, Leopold bravely refused to retreat to England to establish a government in exile. Instead, he surrendered and was held prisoner at Château de Laeken, unfortunately providing the indelible image of a conquered leader. The day after the Normandy invasion in 1944, the king, his wife, and his children were taken prisoner to Germany, and his brother, Charles, became prince regent in his absence. The royal family eventually was freed in May 1945, but charges that the king had col-

laborated with the Nazis, which were investigated and later dismissed, led them to settle in Switzerland. Concerns lingered about his conduct during the war, and when Leopold went back to Belgium in 1950, he faced a divided country and riots opposing his return to the throne. On August 11, 1950, he passed his powers and authority to his teenaged son Baudouin; a year later, the prince was crowned king.

Domaine d'Argenteuil provided a new beginning for the ex-monarch. The longstanding relationship between the Belgian royals and Maison Jansen was called into play once more as Boudin worked with Princess Lilian to create a residence befitting both formal entertaining and private family life. The Frenchman sought to relieve the house of what he deemed as largely out-of-scale English architectural details—the high-roofed house recalled a manor in Normandy, but its interior architecture followed 18th-century English models—and replace them with models based on the Louis XV and Louis XVI designs favored by Jansen. (To some observers, this remodeling seemed a kind of revenge for Napoleon's defeat 144 years before.) The overall decorative concept, however, was not unlike those Jansen formulated for other clients. Indeed, schemes for the formal dining room and a new loggia for the house's grand salon mirrored parallel projects in the French ambassador's residence in Washington and the Kennedy restoration of the White House, respectively.[8]

The princess and Boudin decided on a cheerful yellow for the small library on the ground floor; the existing pine paneling was painted three shades of yellow with additional glazes used to distress its appearance. On the floor was placed a mid-18th-century Savonnerie carpet, its ivory ground ornamented with a pattern of drapery and floral garlands of pinks, greens, and golds. For the primary seating area in front of the

SMALL LIBRARY

GRAND SALON

fireplace, Boudin selected a comfortable yellow-velvet-upholstered sofa, a gilt and lacquer low table, and two deep armchairs of chocolate brown velvet. Additional chairs, which were informally arranged about the room, were variously covered in yellow silk satin or green cut velvet. At the four arched windows that overlooked the garden, panels of ivory and yellow silk brocade were tied back with matching tassels. Chests, tabletops, and the mantel displayed framed photographs of family gatherings intermingled with formal portraits of world leaders. Cheerful and inviting, it was a family room, used by the royal couple and their children on a daily basis. Esmeralda de Rethy remembered it as "my favorite . . . a place where we would always sit through the day."[9]

Next to the library was the grand salon, which represented Boudin's most dramatic transformation of the house's interior. As designed by Delano & Aldrich, the room was much in keeping with the Americanized ideal of an English great hall. A large stone mantelpiece, flanked by doors, faced three equally large windows opening onto a grass terrace that spanned the rear of the central block of the house and led to the park. The length of the room was further pronounced by the presence of two large chandeliers. Visually austere, the grand salon was less a destination than a passageway. Boudin began his reinterpretation by replacing the heavy mantelpiece with a white marble and gilt bronze Neoclassical example of smaller scale and much finer proportions. He continued by gilding portions of the

FORMAL DINING ROOM

wainscot to unite the room's architectural details with bronze ornaments of the new mantelpiece. An Empire chandelier of patinated and gilt bronze replaced the pair of fixtures that remained from the Tuck family's tenure, a substitution that reinforced the center of the room as its focus. Opposite the mantelpiece, a large central window was removed and replaced by a deep, one-story, semicircular bay with three sets of glazed exterior doors that recalled the garden facade of the king's former home, Château de Laeken. Serving almost as a small stage, this demilune addition created a sense of ceremony for those coming from or going to the adjacent grass terrace and surrounding park.

Boudin lined the walls of the grand salon with white silk moiré, which was trimmed above the chair rail, below the cornice, and vertically in the room's corners by a wide, finely woven tape with a scroll pattern woven in pink, gold, and ivory. This border also trimmed the red velvet draperies and valances of the windows. The use of the tape mirrored the Frenchman's coinciding design for the oval Blue Room of the White House. The incorporation of sconces mounted above gilt-framed pictures, a Boudin hallmark, further reinforced the connection between these two iconic Jansen interiors of the early 1960s. The furniture in the grand salon was largely Directoire and

DETAIL OF THE PRIVATE DINING ROOM

Empire, another detail that echoed the Blue Room. Exceptions were contemporary sofas, upholstered in red velvet, which stood at either side of the fireplace and along a far wall. Marble-topped pier tables, crowned by 19th-century royal portraits, were arranged on either side of the fireplace, and additional color was provided by the pink and red silk lampas that was used to upholster parcel gilt Empire chairs. The overall composition of the grand salon was formal, befitting the room's function, yet it had little of the rigidity that might be expected of the audience chamber or reception room of a royal residence. Domaine d'Argenteuil, after all, was a country house and constructed on a much more human scale than Château de Laeken.

Out of the Tucks' formal dining room, which was located on the other side of the grand salon, Boudin created a very feminine, less formal living room. Here he relied on the blue-gray and ivory palette that he had

used frequently in the 1930s for clients such as Olive, Lady Baillie, again with multitonal glazing of the existing paneling; the cool pastel scheme showcased Princess Lilian's striking olive complexion and dark hair. This emphasis on lightness led to the revamping of the existing mantelpiece through the removal of baronial carving from its central tablet. No longer a dominant focus, the mantelpiece was surmounted by a portrait of Princess Lilian as a sportswoman, with golf club in hand.[10] The majority of the chairs and sofas were upholstered in silks in various pastel shades of blue and purple, close in tone to the painted walls; dark wood tables and ebonized pedestals were strategically placed along the room's perimeter to frame artwork and seating areas.

As Domaine d'Argenteuil was the official residence of a former king, whose position required some degree of grand entertaining, a new wing was added to the house to accommodate a dining room in the Louis XVI taste. Similar to Boudin's decorative scheme for the formal dining room of the French ambassadorial residence in Washington, its walls were framed by carved wood panels, pilasters, and cornice, all painted various shades of moss green and highlighted with gold leaf. The paneling was designed around three large tapestries depicting hunting scenes; made in the early 18th century, they were assigned to the studio of Gaspard van der Borght, a Brussels designer whose patrons included William III of England and the first Duke of Marlborough. Two of the tapestries framed the mantel breast, and the third was placed on another wall, between the room's two doors.[11] White-painted Directoire chairs with yellow velvet upholstery accompanied the large mahogany banqueting table, over which was suspended a 24-candle gilt and patinated bronze Empire chandelier. The room's five windows received a standard Jansen treatment of multitab valances adorned with delicate metallic woven tapes.

Boudin's work in the other rooms of the house was far less formal, emphasizing its primary role as a family residence. In the small oval dining room, he removed the shelves from the American Colonial Revival niches to accommodate a pair of Louis XVI–style carved alabaster urns; the addition of these vertical objects helped to counteract the dominant horizontality of the interior architecture. On the walls, which were painted a neutral ivory, the decorator displayed a collection of more than 40 blue and gold porcelain plates, each bearing the Audubon-like image of a bird. Made in Belgium between 1829 and 1869, the plates were hung in three tiers by Boudin, which balanced the room's proportions, drawing the eye up and down, as opposed to across. Dramatically simple in its decoration, this smaller family dining room was furnished with austere Restauration-style chairs, a mahogany dining table, and a pair of green-painted, curule-based serving tables that had been made in the Jansen ateliers. For a sitting room on the second floor, Boudin applied green velvet to the walls and used a somewhat whimsical green and ivory striped silk at the windows, the latter's pattern reminiscent of the tented room that he had created decades before for Lady Mendl's Circus Ball. Red velvet club chairs complemented a large sofa of similar color. A Louis XV–style bergère and fauteuil, upholstered in ivory damask, could be easily moved about, making the room an intimate and inviting space for reading or quiet conversation.

What Stéphane Boudin accomplished for the royal couple is conveyed in an excerpt from a letter that Princess Lilian wrote to Brigitte Boudin de Laage de Meux, following her father's death in 1967: "During

LIVING ROOM

the years he brightened our halls through his sense of beauty and harmony, and through his heart," the princess wrote. "I have often told him that I wondered whether he realized the importance of his talents to create a framework, to lay a foundation for happiness."[12] That foundation—a combination of formality and comfort—served as the family's residence for more than 40 years. Prince Alexandre Emmanuel, the couple's son, defined Domaine d'Argenteuil as the residence in which his mother "invested the most energy and spirituality. In a way it was like a signature."[13]

King Leopold III died in 1983, his wife 19 years later. Following her death, the interiors that Boudin created were disassembled, with a large number of items being sold at public auction through Sotheby's, Amsterdam. Domaine d'Argenteuil reverted to the Belgian state, which subsequently sold it.[14]

MR. H. WINSTON. DISPLAY WINDOWS.

Harry Winston, Inc.

718 Fifth Avenue

New York City

J ANSEN REMAINED A MOSTLY RESIDENTIAL DESIGN FIRM INTO THE 1960s. Among its few known commercial endeavors was the redesign of 718 Fifth Avenue for the society jeweler Harry Winston. This commission was brought about through Winston clients Jayne and Charles B. Wrightsman, who were recognized as Jansen's greatest American patrons by the beginning of the decade.

Harry Winston (1896–1978) began his career on the West Coast at age 15. His early years were spent selling jewelry with his father to oilmen in small-town saloons and bars. At age 19, he moved to New York with a couple thousand dollars and established Premier Diamond Company. By 1932, his business had become Harry Winston, Inc. and soon was based in a townhouse at 7 East 51st Street, at which time his name was heralded throughout the world. Among Winston's greatest business coups was the acquisition of Evalyn Walsh McLean's collection of jewelry, which included the famous Hope diamond, which the Colorado mining heiress had purchased from Cartier. He gave the famous gem to the Smithsonian Institution in 1958, and the gesture garnered even greater prestige and publicity for his firm. Following the opening of a California gallery, Winston began plans for a major expansion of his New York enterprise.

Formerly the Steuben Glass Building, 718 Fifth Avenue was designed in the mid-1930s by the architectural firm of Charles A. Platt, in collaboration with Steuben designer John

OPPOSITE: APPROVED DESIGN FOR NEW DISPLAY WINDOW CONFIGURATION, 1963

STEUBEN GLASS GALLERY IN 1937

ADVERTISEMENT ANNOUNCING THE OPENING OF HARRY WINSTON, INC., ON 5TH AVENUE, 1959

Monteith Gates. With 3,800 glass blocks incorporated into a stylish yet restrained Art Moderne facade, the building was heralded as one of New York's great new structures when it opened in 1937. But time and fashion quickly changed. Following World War II, and more specifically the construction of Skidmore, Owings & Merrill's glass-skinned Lever House in 1952, the Steuben building's once-celebrated architecture suddenly became antiquated, a dangerous thing for a company that promoted innovation in design. Corning Glass, Steuben's parent company, purchased a site directly across the street in the late 1950s and hired Harrison, Abramovitz & Abbe to design a more modern, International-style high-rise that provided greater rental space. Once the new Steuben building was opened in 1959, the old gallery was sold to Harry Winston. Following a suggestion by the Wrightsmans, Winston solicited the assistance of Stéphane Boudin during one of the Frenchman's frequent New York visits. Boudin no doubt dictated the change of the building's facade to 18th-century French, as well as offered the services of Jansen's Paris headquarters and the Manhattan office and its director, Paul Manno.

MR. H. WINSTON. GILT BRONZE ORNAMENT ON.
STAINLESS STEEL GATE BET.
FOYER & SALON.

DRAWING OF EMPIRE-STYLE ORMOLU FIGURE TO CAP GATES TO MAIN SALON

Using the talents of one of its Paris-based architects, Jacques Regnault, Jansen envisioned a French urban structure, with ornamented travertine facing and windows and doors adorned with iron. The surviving drawings prepared within the Rue Royale offices included a three-bay configuration for the Fifth Avenue side, with iron railings installed in the second-story windows and a grand arched entrance formalized with parcel-gilt iron gates. For the side street facade, Regnault devised 10 bays, with a street-level gallery of nine arched windows. The approved Jansen design for the new facade was finished on March 10, 1959,

although Harry Winston's purchase of the building was not publicly announced for 10 more days.[1] When completed, the Winston building was applauded by the Fifth Avenue Association—an AIA-recognized group of civic leaders and architects intent on acknowledging good design—as the best "job of alteration" of an existing structure for 1960.[2]

The formality introduced to the exterior was continued inside. After passing through the entrance gates, customers were received in an elegant domed foyer with cantered corners and marble floors. They then proceeded through another gate, made of steel and

APPROVED ELEVATION DRAWING, C. 1959

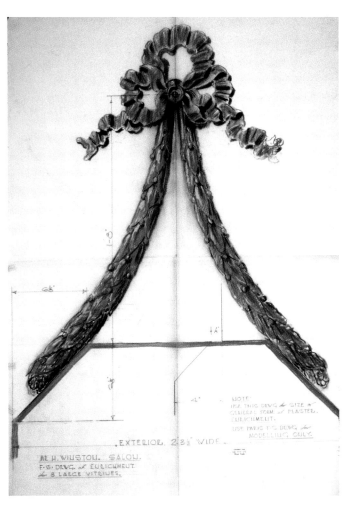

DRAWING OF ORMOLU MOUNTS FOR VITRINES IN MAIN SALON,
C. 1959

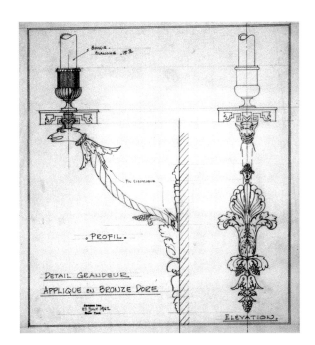

ELEVATION DRAWING FOR PROPOSED APPLIQUÉ, 1962

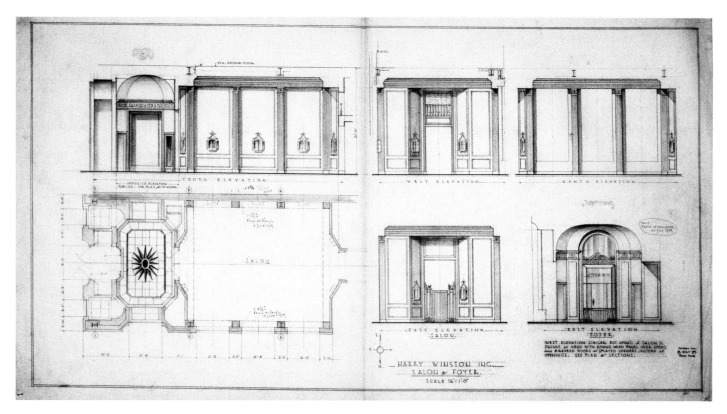

ELEVATION DRAWINGS OF SALON AND FOYER

framed by a pair of gilded Napoleonic sphinxes, into the large main salon, with arched windows opening onto 56th Street. The overall theme was classical, with delicate tables and groupings of chairs arranged about the salon for individual viewings of jewelry. Doors were upholstered in gray leather with gilt nailheads. Windows were draped in elegantly trimmed silk. Jansen designed certain key pieces of furniture, including ormolu-adorned vitrines.

Jansen also redesigned the existing staircase, which was given a simple bronze-toned railing. The walls were painted to resemble inlaid panels of cream-colored marble. On an upper floor, Jansen created an office for Mr. Winston, with Louis XV–style boiserie.

Jansen, Inc., provided additional designs for Harry Winston in the early 1960s. These included the redesign of the front display windows, which had intimate exhibition cases for the display of individual pieces of jewelry.

Harry Winston, Inc., remains at 718 Fifth Avenue. Under the leadership of Ronald Winston, Harry's son, the Jansen contributions to the firm's identity have been preserved and, in some cases, copied for other Winston galleries around the world.

1959

Mildred and Charles Allen Jr.

THE NEW YORK APARTMENT OF CHARLES ALLEN JR., THE FOUNDER of the investment securities firm of Allen & Company, Inc., and his second wife, Mildred, at 2 East 67th Street, is typical of the work accomplished by Jansen in the 1950s and early 1960s. It included rooms of painted paneling, silk draperies with elaborate passementerie and tab-edged valances, and a spectacular array of 18th-century furniture and art objects. The apartment, which served as an elegant backdrop for business entertaining, was a definitive example of Jansen's post–World War II bread-and-butter business.

The Bronx-born Allen (1903–1994) was considered one of the most powerful men on Wall Street; at one time he was worth $500 million and held controlling interests in Warner Bros. Pictures, Columbia Pictures, a Mexican drug manufacturer, and America's most profitable shipbuilding firm. A former stock exchange messenger boy and high-school dropout, he had founded Allen & Company, then a bond trading business, shortly before the depression, in partnership with his two younger brothers. In the ensuing years, he was known for his profitmaking abilities and canny investment hunches. After his divorce from his first wife, the former Rita Friedman—as Rita Allen, she was a noted theatrical producer, like their daughter Terry Allen Kramer—Charles Allen married Mildred Haas (1908–1997).[1]

OPPOSITE: VIEW OF LIBRARY FROM HALL

MILDRED ALLEN

Located at the corner of 67th Street and Fifth Avenue, in a 1928 apartment building designed by Rosario Candela, the entrance hall or gallery of the Allen residence had four single and two double doors opening off of it.[2] Jansen designed elaborate pediments of mirrored glass and gilt-bronze trelliswork for the single doors (the doors were made in the Paris ateliers). The double doors retained plain surrounds. Other additions included a new ceiling with a lighted recessed oval center and a white marble mantelpiece with a Louis XVI–style giltwood mirror.

Through one set of the hall's double doors was the salon, which overlooked Central Park. A corner room, with four broad windows, its walls were covered with fragments of 18th-century French paneling, interspersed with new moldings. The wall color was a soft water green, what Gérald Van der Kemp, a former

curator of Versailles, remembered to be Boudin's favorite color.[3] A pair of built-in display cases framed the mirror-topped mantelpiece along the east wall. Lined in light orange silk, these cases contained a collection of 18th-century French porcelains that included Chantilly and St. Cloud white figural pieces, ormolu-mounted tobacco jars, and a wide range of vases. Also displayed here were impressive mid-18th-century Meissen polychrome figures from romanticized pastoral settings and some important Meissen imitations of Japanese Kakiemon porcelains. Suspended from the ceiling was a rock crystal chandelier, which provided light to the numerous seating areas meticulously arranged about the room by Boudin and Mrs. Allen.[4]

Mildred Allen demonstrated her precision as a collector when a suite of Louis XV chairs signed by ébéniste Mathieu Criard for the salon first arrived in New York. She wrote to Boudin in Paris: "Just saw mobilier [set] at Brown Warehouse and was shocked to see fresh green and white paint and shiney [sic] glaz . . . also stain damage on every upholstered back . . . evidently set not examined before shipping."[5] She continued by noting she had called in a leading expert to examine the finish of the set of furniture, which revealed "a former stripping of the original painting and or gilding of the frames . . . I am terribly disappointed . . . and feel I cannot be happy with the set . . . I am checking arrangements to return it to Paris but I would appreciate your comments . . . devotedly, Mildred Allen."[6] The ever-diplomatic Boudin responded with an informative and soothing response that was surely one of many:

> You do not doubt, I am sure, of the interest that
> I take in your house . . . [which is] looking like a
> very great success for which you kindly said also

SALON

SALON

SALON DETAIL

MANTEL WALL OF DINING ROOM

your satisfaction . . . It is always a pity to send a mobilier covered in poor material and plain as it does not [show well] . . . but according to the difficulties of customs, if covered in new silk it would . . . [cost] an impossible amount of duty as being all modern . . . What I can assure you is that the chairs have always been painted and were never stripped. But the paint that was on them had, in course of times, been . . . so coarsely touched up that we had to "scratch" (if that is English) it to find the original colour underneath and to clean to depth of the sculpture . . . This being done we reglazed the color as we always do to hide the effect of "scratching" and to harmonize it with the room and the material . . . I can assure you that so far nothing has been done that I have not seen . . . should you be in trouble let me know and I will try to soften my wife and doctor to let me jump over earlier [than scheduled] . . . There is nothing that I would hate more that [sic] to displease the most delicate and charming customer I have.[7]

DINING ROOM

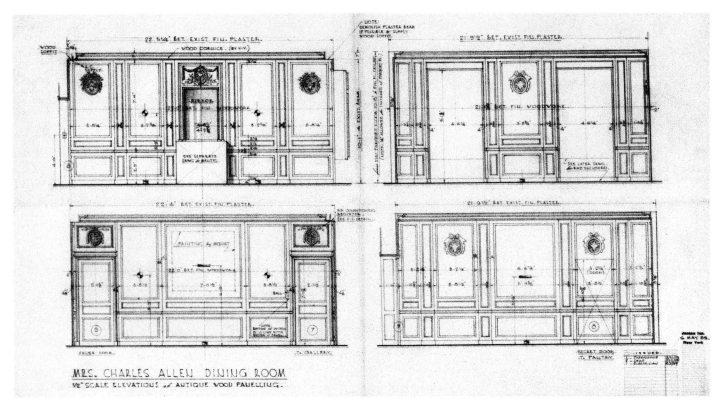

MRS. CHARLES ALLEN DINING ROOM
½" SCALE ELEVATIONS OF ANTIQUE WOOD PANELLING.

ELEVATION DRAWINGS FOR THE DINING ROOM

The most magnificent room of the apartment was the nearly square dining room, lined with characteristic Boudin-directed distressed period paneling from Paris, in three related shades of blue. The room's palette was dictated by one of the series of large canvases of water lilies by Claude Monet, which was placed over a Louis XVI–style gray-painted console table, presumably made by Jansen's ateliers in Paris. The 18th-century mahogany and ormolu dining table was surrounded by oval-back Louis XVI–style chaises en cabriolet, painted white and upholstered with a fine striped silk from Paris. Twenty-four of these chairs were made for the apartment.

For Mildred Allen's private library, Jansen designed new paneling in the Louis XV taste and painted it primrose yellow. Lighted by a delicate Baltic Neoclassical chandelier of green glass and gilt metal—personally selected by Boudin—the room had a handsome green onyx and white marble Louis XVI–style mantelpiece as its central focus. Between the windows of this intimate space stood a Louis XVI ormolu-mounted ebony writing table, signed by Louis Moreau, a piece that was representative of the more restrained lines of French furniture design just prior to the 1789 revolution.

Mildred Allen worked with the designers at Jansen from 1959 through the late 1960s, and her appetite for new proposals for window treatments, carpets, and other decorative features remained constant. After her death, the contents of the apartment were sold by Sotheby's New York.

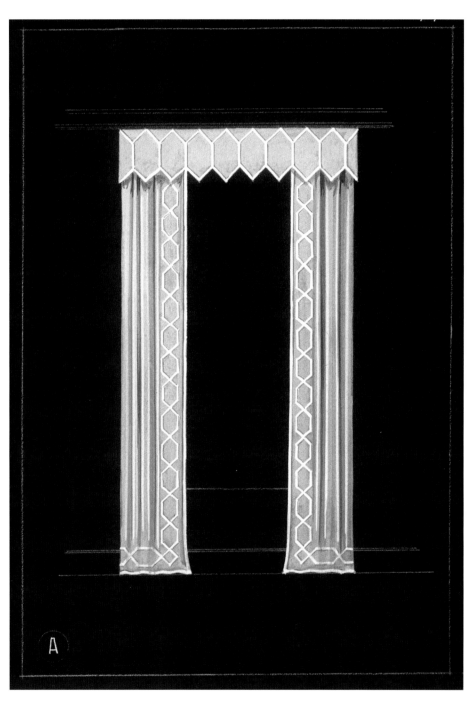

PROPOSAL FOR WINDOW TREATMENT FOR MRS. ALLEN'S BEDROOM

Moufida and Habib Bourguiba

Palace of Carthage

Carthage, Tunisia

HABIB BOURGUIBA (1901[1]–2000) WAS CALLED THE SUPREME Warrior and the Great Combatant by his people.[1] Having fought 30 years for Tunisia's freedom from French colonization—battles that left him at times in exile and at others in prison—he became president of the country in 1957. One of the most pro-Western of all Arab leaders, Bourguiba sought to develop Tunisia through industry and tourism, opposed militant Islam, abolished polygamy, and granted women the right to vote. In seeming contradiction to his historical role in leading his country's fight for independence from France, Bourguiba greatly admired French history and culture.

Much of this admiration began during the mid-1920s, when Bourguiba, who grew up under French colonial rule, studied political science and law in Paris. Amid discussions with fellow students from Morocco and Algeria regarding nationalism and independence, he took in the architecture, as well as the fine and applied arts, of France. In 1927 he also married, as his first wife, French Catholic widow Mathilde Le Fras Lorrain (1892–1976), who took the name Moufida after her conversion to Islam.[2] When Bourguiba became president of Tunisia and acquired his own governing stage, he sought to emulate the grandeur and style of French palaces he had visited and admired during his college years. Though defined as a pragmatist,

OPPOSITE: HABIB BOURGUIBA'S OFFICE

VIEW FROM THE THEATER STAGE

THEATER WITHIN PALACE

he recognized the importance of pomp and pageantry for conveying strength and leadership. Therefore, he commissioned Jansen and Pierre Delbée to decorate the interiors of the new presidential residence in La Marsa, a seaside suburb of Carthage, north of the capital, Tunis. Overlooking the Mediterranean, the Arab-Andalusian-style mansion was designed by the Tunisian architect Olivier-Clément Cacoub after Bourguiba declined to move into the palace of Muhammad al-Amin, the Tunisian king he had overthrown.[3] President Bourguiba lived in the new palace until he, too, was ousted, 30 years later.

The greatest of Jansen's interiors for the Palace of Carthage, which was built on the site of a French colonial official's house, was the two-story-high cabinet room furnished in the Empire style.[4] Parcel-gilt wainscoting, pilasters, and pedimented doors framed panels of specially woven Genoese velvet with the national crest of Tunisia as a central motif. At the center of the room was a large, oblong mahogany conference table, surrounded by more than two dozen white and gold Empire-style chairs, all upholstered in gold damask and trimmed in actual military braid; additional armchairs and side chairs were placed against the walls. From the center of the white and gilt ceiling was suspended a specially made 48-light, two-tier chandelier; smaller ormolu and crystal fixtures were suspended from the room's corners. Along with busts of Tunisian worthies such as Hannibal, St. Augustine, Jugurtha, and Ibn Khaldun that were displayed in the broken pediments over each door, a life-size portrait of President Bourguiba reigned from the walls.

Borrowing from Versailles, specifically the Queen's Theater in the gardens of the Trianon, Delbée also designed a modern underground performance hall for the palace. Configured as an oval, the theater had balconies and tiers adorned with parcel-gilt balustrades, blue velvet-upholstered railings, and marbleized wainscoting. Up to 300 guests could enjoy opera, ballet, and other stage performances in this 18th-century-inspired theater. In 1962 the president's lavish marriage to his second wife, Wassila ben Ammar, took place there.

Although Jansen publicly defined the president's office as Directoire, thus associating it with France's short-lived system of governance by five directors in the late 18th century, the room's decor indisputably was representative of the later imperialistic taste of the Empire period.[5] Delbée based his design on Napoleon's library at the Château de Compiègne. Walls framed by pilasters and wainscoting of Cuban mahogany were crowned by a continuous garland of ormolu. Coffered doors and bookcases were similarly adorned. Mounted between pilasters topped with Empire-style gilt-metal capitals were panels of silk of the same rich emerald green color as the upholstery of the room's mahogany chairs. Less the office of an elected official than an emperor, the grandiose interior became a more appropriate backdrop for Bourguiba when he was appointed president for life in 1975.

The Palace of Carthage continues to be the official residence of the president of Tunisia. Its interiors have changed slightly over the years, but many of Jansen's installations remain in place.[6]

CABINET ROOM

Nicole and Hervé Alphand

The French Ambassador's Residence

WASHINGTON, D.C.

A RGUABLY THE MOST BEAUTIFUL OF WASHINGTON'S AMBASSADORIAL
residences is a neo-Tudor stone-and-brick house that the architect Jules
Henri de Sibour designed for William Walton Lawrence, a Pennsylvania-born
tycoon who made his fortune in the manufacture of paints and varnishes.[1]
Built in 1910, it soon became the home of millionaire mining engineer John
Hays Hammond, who sold the property to the French Republic for $450,000 shortly before
his death in 1936.[2] Stéphane Boudin and Jansen decorated the house for Ambassador Hervé
Alphand and his wife Nicole, beginning in 1960; a 1961 electrical fire delayed completion of
the project until early summer 1963.

Son of a French ambassador to the USSR, Hervé Alphand (1908–1994) began his career
as the youngest inspector of finance in the history of France; within five years, Alphand, then
just 27, was providing financial advice to the Turkish government. Soon after France's occupation by Hitler in 1940, he arrived in the United States as an economics expert representing
the Vichy government, though he quickly abandoned this post to join Charles de Gaulle's
government in exile as its director of economic affairs. Alphand served as France's ambassador to the United Nations before accepting the Washington post in 1956. Shortly after
arriving in the capital, he divorced his first wife, Claude, and married Nicole Bunau-Varilla

OPPOSITE: EMPIRE SALON

FRONT FACADE

(1917–1979), the ex-wife of a French playboy.[3] Elegant and stylish, she was immediately seen as a political asset. Time magazine described the former fashion model as "a tawny blonde . . . bronzed by the sun of Bar Harbor summers and Palm Beach winters."[4] By the time of John F. Kennedy's inauguration in January 1961, Nicole Alphand was the capital's star hostess and included among her friends the new first lady as well as

Jansen's premier American client, Jayne Wrightsman.[5]

The Jansen decor for the Alphands, for the most part, was formulaic, because public scrutiny of government residences then—as now—constricted the degree of ambassadorial luxury. Few architectural modifications were made to the building; the Jansen contributions were almost exclusively restricted to paint, textiles, and furniture arrangement.

Dining room

SALON DU BOIS

An exception to such restraint was the lowering of the ceiling in the Salon du Bois or main reception room, an alteration Boudin felt necessary to balance the interior's overall proportions. For this room's very English oak paneling, he chose a softly textured, heavily distressed finish of ivory paint. In front of the existing Louis XV marble mantelpiece, Boudin placed a pair of off-white velvet Lawson-style loveseats and two damask-upholstered fauteuils. The straight-falling silk drapery panels at the windows were of similar color to the walls and topped by sculpted valances, and a pair of silk-covered round tables in Boudin's favored shade of water green flanked the mantel breast. There were two additional seating areas in the room, each a characteristic Jansen mix of Louis XV chairs and contemporary sofas. Blue and white Chinese porcelain vases were used as lamp bases, complementing the large red, blue, and green Turkish carpet that presumably was a holdover from an earlier decorative scheme.[6] Likely it was the transformation of this important and highly visible room that led *Time* magazine to describe the redecorated mansion as having a "light, airy look."[7] It was a far cry from the dark English manor house interior to which Washington's diplomatic corps had been accustomed.

The main hall was brightened, too, its oak staircase and balustrade receiving an off-white pickling. Existing gilt-bronze nine-light sconces capped with stylized rays of laurel leaves provided lighting. Against the off-white walls Boudin arranged Louis XIV–style chairs and a sofa upholstered in Renaissance-style crimson-on-ivory silk. Three matching contemporary needlework carpets covered the wood parquet floor, and a wall-mounted antique Gobelin tapestry, representing Africa, hung at the top of the staircase. From Leeds Castle to the White House, Boudin was known for dictating a set palette of colors for each room he designed, a palette that included the flowers he considered appropriate decoration for the space, so he probably was instrumental in devising the monumental flower arrangements that Nicole Alphand used in this grand hall, which intermixed silk and natural blossoms. Perhaps more fitting as a backdrop for an opera, these dramatic arrangements were among the most talked-about additions to the social sphere of Washington's Camelot era.

This sense of the theatrical was somewhat carried over into the Empire salon, a space that had been established in the 1930s as an imposing visual translation of France's strength before the official outbreak of World War II. Boudin seems to have viewed the unchanged room—with its Napoleonic furniture—as too serious for the 1960s. In a gesture that was a domestic-scale version of Marc Chagall painting the ceiling of the Napoleon III–era Opéra Garnier in Paris, Boudin selected brightly colored 20th-century still lifes by Henri Matisse and Pierre Bonnard that countered the severity of the drawing room's imperialistic theme. Walls were lined with white satin, which also was used for window draperies and as upholstery for some of the chairs; for each use a variation of a red and ivory key-patterned silk tape was made, the largest serving as borders for the walls above the chair rail and below the cornice.[8] From the Matisse still life Boudin borrowed a light blue for upholstery of two contemporary sofas and additional Napoleonic side- and armchairs placed about the room. A rich green from the Bonnard was repeated in the cut velvet for a pair of Empire fauteuils and decorative bolsters for the sofas. Once again, the Boudin trademark of a fabric-covered round table was included—near the Matisse, this time using crimson velvet. The finished room was a celebration of French culture, with Boudin giving it a less period and more evolutionary sense of style.

For the more personal and private Salon Gris, the sunroom at one end of the mansion's first floor, Boudin masked the dark red brick and stone walls with white paint and established a black, white, and gray color scheme accented with chartreuse. Sofas of light gray silk stood in front of the fireplace; a silk twill of similar color was made into straight curtains that covered the room's three walls of windows. A black-lacquered baby grand piano occupied one corner. On it stood one of a series of black wood and ceramic lamps with white silk shades of varying sizes, strategically placed along the perimeter of the room like contemporary sculpture. As in the main reception room, sofas and chairs were gathered into conversation areas and here upholstered in black velvet, black and white silk twill, or green and white fern-patterned damask. A solid green-gray silk was used for a round table. Gilt-bronze faux bamboo tables with black lacquer tops, made by the Jansen ateliers, received neat arrangements of white alabaster smoking equipage.[9] Uniting all of these elements was a diamond-patterned black-on-white woven carpet. The sunroom was one of the most handsome contemporary confections created by Boudin in the postwar years.

The popular Alphands were noted for their lively dinners, for which they received few "regrets" and to which Nicole Alphand invariably wore a gown by Pierre Cardin.[10] The ambassador's appreciation of fine wines was well known in Washington, and in 1963 the Alphands' annual entertainment and housekeeping budget was $80,000. As would be expected, the dining room received the Jansen firm's greatest attention. The existing Neoclassical paneling was glazed in multiple shades of green, with gold denoting the capitals, the fluting of pilasters, and the intricacies of the cornice;

the palette and some of the architectural detailing are reminiscent of Boudin's decor for the dining room of King Leopold III of Belgium and his wife, Princess Lilian, at Domaine d'Argenteuil. A set of seven 18th-century allegorical paintings once displayed in the Petit Trianon at Versailles were restored by Jansen and hung on the walls. These were illuminated by gilt-bronze picture lights, which served as the only electric lighting in the room during dinners. Ivory silk draperies identical to those in the main reception room framed the windows, making the overall composition somewhat reminiscent of Boudin's white and green dining room for Leeds Castle. Louis XV–style side chairs with ivory-painted frames and gold silk velvet upholstery stood around the room and oval dining table. A green-on-ivory Bessarabian-inspired contemporary carpet defined the center of the room, set like an island within beige wall-to-wall carpeting. A Louis XIV sunburst clock was suspended over the mantel, against a 16-panel looking glass modeled after an 18th-century trompe l'oeil garden folly.

Among Boudin's more innovative contributions to the dining room was the introduction of multiple round tables for formal dinners, an intimate formula for entertaining that received greater attention when it was adopted by his other notable Washington clients, the Kennedys. Outfitted with Boudin's favored gold-trimmed Porthault linens and Baccarat crystal, the tables could seat from four to 15 each and were used at large dinners and luncheons, with a maximum of 60 people being served.

The Alphand interiors lasted intact through the 1960s. Today, the house still serves as the residence of France's ambassadors to the United States, but only the dining room remains representative of Jansen and the work of Boudin.

SUNROOM, OR SALON GRIS

1961–67

Jacqueline and John F. Kennedy

THE WHITE HOUSE

WASHINGTON, D.C.

Jansen's work at the White House in the 1960s for President and Mrs. John F. Kennedy has been given near-iconic status in the history of American decorative arts and design. It is doubtful that any later occupant of 1600 Pennsylvania Avenue had, or will have, the freedom to redefine the presidential stage to such an extent as did the Kennedys. These interiors are part of a mythical legacy, the backdrop to the martyred president's administration and political ambitions. For Jansen, and specifically for Stéphane Boudin, these same interiors represented somewhat of a swan song. It was Boudin's greatest postwar commission and the firm's most celebrated American work.

As with so many of Jansen's accomplishments in the post–World War II United States, the White House project was initiated by Jayne Wrightsman, the wife of oil millionaire Charles B. Wrightsman and a dedicated and eager student of Stéphane Boudin. In 1959 she introduced Boudin to Jacqueline Kennedy, then the wife of the junior senator from Massachusetts. At the end of her letter of introduction, Wrightsman postscripted a wise observation: "some day she may be First Lady." Boudin became both a confidant and tutor for Kennedy, initially advising her on the decoration of her Georgetown townhouse. They communicated in every way possible, from telegrams to telephone calls, letters, and the occasional cartoon via the first lady's talented hand. Boudin attended the exclusive 1962 White House dinner in honor

OPPOSITE: RED ROOM, 1962

235

THE QUEENS' SITTING ROOM, HOUSE & GARDEN, OCTOBER 1967

of André Maulraux, the French minister of culture; his invitation was addressed simply to "Monsieur Boudin." Jacqueline Kennedy eventually hung on his every word and photographed him—she had been a professional news photographer in her youth—in the executive mansion as he guided pictures from one wall to another or initiated grand new schemes for as-yet-untouched rooms.[1]

Often working behind the scenes of the Kennedys' famous restoration of the White House, Boudin, in collaboration with the staffs of Jansen's New York and Paris offices, redecorated both public and private rooms. He sometimes collaborated with the restoration's official chairman, Henry Francis du Pont, the founder of Winterthur Museum and the leading authority on American period furniture, as well as with the often-confrontational society decorator Sister Parish.[2] However, Boudin reigned as chief tastemaker for the project from the beginning, winning out when challenged by differing opinions through his personal friendships with Jacqueline Kennedy and Jayne Wrightsman.

Boudin's vision for the White House was based on European palaces and English country houses, an approach well suited to the executive mansion. Its architect, James Hoban, based his Georgian design on 18th-century models, among them a Dublin house built in 1745 for first Duke of Leinster.[3] However, the Frenchman's most eccentric and ambitious proposals—such as white and gilt paneling in the State Dining Room or, for the East Room, the incorporation of 18th-century tapestries commissioned by Louis XVI for presentation to George Washington—were passed over for more conservative schemes deemed acceptable to the American public by President and Mrs. Kennedy.[4]

The State and ground-floor rooms often borrowed details from previous Jansen commissions, including the library and dining room of Leeds Castle, which served as inspirations for their White House counterparts. The distressed blue-and-white scheme of the paneled Vermeil Room, named for a 1956 bequest of French and English gilt-silver collected by Boudin client Margaret Thompson Biddle, was based on that of Lady Baillie's bedroom at Leeds Castle. Schemes and arrangements for the Red Room and Entrance Hall copied aspects of Boudin's recognized but not publicly acknowledged contributions to Empress Josephine's country house, Malmaison, near Paris. The Red Room, with its cerise textiles woven with gold medallions and scrollwork, was the most successful of

RESTORED TREATY ROOM ON THE SECOND FLOOR, C. 1963

Jansen's White House rooms in terms of public approval. For this Empire-style interior, Boudin personally directed "ancient documents of seat trimmings, made around 1812"[5] for reproduction purposes by the American textile manufacturer Scalamandré.[6]

Among other important Boudin-designed rooms were the Victorian-inspired Treaty Room, the neighboring, semiformal Yellow Oval Room, and the Oval Office. The green and red Treaty Room had the

greatest influence on American historians and decorators, emphasizing a stronger, bolder palette for post–Civil War period interiors than had previously been explored in North America. The Yellow Oval Room—almost exclusively furnished with painted as opposed to gilded Louis XVI furniture—was simple, if not democratic, especially in comparison to the gilt-laden interpretations of succeeding presidential administrations. This second-floor reception room has

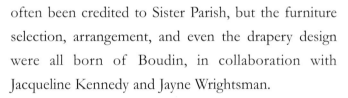

ONE OF TWO PROPOSALS SUBMITTED FOR THE RED ROOM

AN ALTERNATIVE PROPOSAL FOR SECOND FLOOR TREATY ROOM

often been credited to Sister Parish, but the furniture selection, arrangement, and even the drapery design were all born of Boudin, in collaboration with Jacqueline Kennedy and Jayne Wrightsman.

The Oval Office scheme evolved over two years, and its red, white, and blue palette was a restatement of the decorator's original concept for the Treaty Room, which was rejected by the first lady. For the president's office, Boudin's initial grand vision included elaborate off-white silk draperies and valances, reigning above a pair of thronelike gilt armchairs that had been purchased in Paris for the Blue Room by James Monroe. His final scheme, as refined with the Kennedys, was more contemporary and less formal, with stark white walls, a blood red carpet, straight-falling plain white silk curtain panels suspended from polished steel rods, and blue leather upholstery for the existing suite of cane-back armchairs; the two sofas before the fireplace were

to have had either white cotton slipcovers or red leather upholstery. President Kennedy never used the Boudin-decorated office, as its installation took place at the time of his assassination.

Boudin's masterpiece for the White House was his Napoleonic transformation of the oval Blue Room. He resisted the temptation to redefine the room as a sitting or drawing room, choosing to respect its traditional configuration as a formal reception room where the American presidents and their spouses stood to receive guests. Based on the Music Room of the Residenz in Munich—a Neoclassical palace that was the seat of the kings of Bavaria until 1918—Boudin's decorative scheme consisted of off-white striped silk walls, blue silk draperies, white and gold wainscoting, and Boudin's hallmark velvet-draped round table in the center. The French textile manufacturer Tassinari & Chatel's meticulous reproduction of an early-19th-century blue fabric

OVAL OFFICE, AS DECORATED BY BOUDIN

DETAIL OF BLUE ROOM UPHOLSTERY FABRIC

with white-to-gold eagle, laurel wreath, and lightning bolt patterning covered the Pierre-Antoine Bellangé gilt chairs Boudin had at one time envisioned for the Oval Office and which he arranged along the perimeter of the room. Also made in France, the trimmings for both the draperies and chairs consisted of ivory and rich purple silk, woven as a floral-patterned tape for the former and twisted to form an intricate, ropelike gimp for the latter.

Jayne and Charles Wrightsman presented a number of important decorative elements to the Blue Room, the complete decoration of which they underwrote. Encouraged by Boudin, who discovered the items, the Wrightsmans donated a pair of early-19th-century French torchères with winged female figural supports. These were complemented by four gilt- and patinated-bronze sconces, circa 1825, which were mounted on the piers separating the three doors at the room's north end and the three windows to the south; these sconces were positioned above portraits of early presidents, in a manner characteristic of Boudin. Lastly, Jansen devised electrified candle branches for an existing pair of Monroe-era, cannon-base candlesticks on the

mantelpiece. As arranged, these various period lighting fixtures created a rhythmic patterning that helped to unite uneven sections of wall created by doorways, windows, and the fireplace. The final addition was an Empire chandelier of gilt-bronze and crystal. It was specially wired by Jansen's Paris workshop to light from within in an effort to preserve the original candle arms, which remained untouched. As Jacqueline Kennedy noted in a thank-you letter to Boudin, the completed Blue Room was praised even by Gérald Van der Kemp, then the curator of the royal palaces at Versailles, who was described as "green with envy."[7]

As the former first lady recalled in 1980, "The Blue Room was Boudin's masterpiece."[8] It was the most dramatic of the White House interiors created by Jansen, and it was also the most controversial aspect of the otherwise well-received Kennedy-era restoration of the mansion. Boudin's decor for the space was likely too dramatic for the often-conservative presidential stage. It was an unusually personal public space, reflective of the idealism and somewhat romanticized sense of history embraced by both President and Mrs. Kennedy.[9] Criticized as being overly French, the room was probably more accurately too intertwined with the ethereality of the Camelot years. Boudin's scheme all the same represented the highest level of skill and talent, including an unrivaled understanding of period design vocabularies, sensitivity to proportion, and comprehension of ceremonial needs; his design for the Blue Room has yet to be equaled by succeeding decorators and historians for this White House room (let alone other imitators).

In writing to Jacqueline Kennedy following her husband's assassination in November 1963, Boudin regretted that "now our wonderful days are ended."[10] However, although his clients were no longer in

RESTORED BLUE ROOM

residence, there was still work to be completed. The officially retired and ailing Boudin, along with Paul Manno and Jansen's New York office, continued to work at the White House into the Johnson administration, mostly completing Kennedy-initiated projects, such as new draperies for the East Room and State Dining Room. Jansen's decor remained largely unchanged through the early 1970s, but it was inevitably replaced as a result of wear and redefined ambitions for the mansion's interior.[11] When this volume went to press, only the intimate Queens' Sitting Room, with its blue and white upholstered walls, survived intact.

1965–66

Barbara and William S. Paley

I N 1965, William S. Paley, the chairman of CBS, and his second wife, Barbara, known as Babe, purchased a 20-room apartment at 820 Fifth Avenue, a 1916 limestone building overlooking Central Park.[1] This spacious apartment, which was long a centerpiece of Manhattan's society firmament, evolved with the talents of many decorators, including Billy Baldwin, Sister Parish, Albert Hadley, and Stéphane Boudin, who had worked for the high-powered couple since the early 1950s.[2] "Not content with just one decorator," wrote biographer Sally Bedell Smith, "the Paleys enlisted four to design one of the most elegant apartments in New York."[3] Contrary to how unique this situation might seem, a scenario of multiple decorators was common practice for the time, and it was perhaps almost characteristic of Babe Paley and her numerous residences; the many offerings allowed her to choose from, if not appreciate and combine, the talents of individual decorators.[4] Suggesting confidence and security in her own judgment, this approach supported Jansen, Inc., director Paul Manno's classification of Babe Paley as "one of the very few women in the world to have been truly born with a sense of good taste."[5]

Following his 1922 graduation from the University of Pennsylvania, Bill Paley (1901–1990), the son of Russian Jewish immigrants, took responsibility for his family's tobacco-company advertising and thereby became interested in the burgeoning radio industry. First as a client,

Opposite: Gallery

SALON

Salon

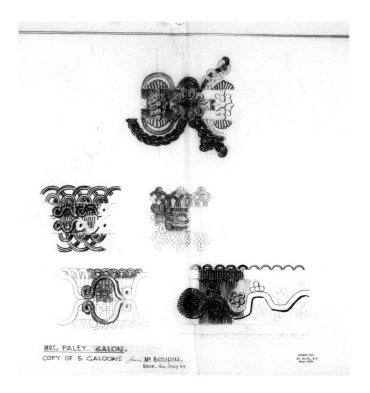

DRAWING OF FIVE GALOONS FOR SALON WINDOW TREATMENTS

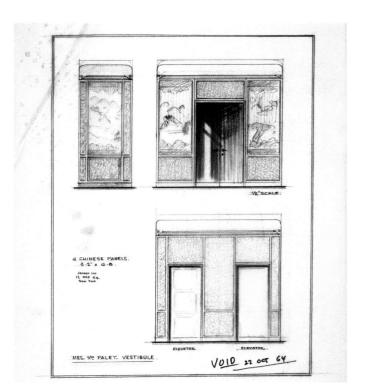

PROPOSED VESTIBULE, 1964

then as partner, and finally as controlling shareholder of the United Independent Broadcasters Network (later the Columbia Broadcasting System), Paley transformed both the company and the medium through advertising and innovative programming. Acquiring not only additional affiliates, but also unrivaled talents such as singer Bing Crosby and newsman Edward R. Murrow, he made CBS radio a multimillion-dollar empire before expanding into television in 1939. As avid a collector of fine art as he was of talent for CBS, he supported the formation of New York's Museum of Modern Art in 1929; nearly 50 years later, Paley was the largest contributor to the creation of the Museum of Television and Radio. Four days after his 1947 divorce from best-dressed socialite Dorothy Hart Hearst, he married Barbara Cushing Mortimer (1915–1978), an iconic fashion plate who had been an editor at Vogue magazine.[6] Socially astute, impeccably dressed, and notably

well-connected—one of her sisters married a son of Franklin Delano Roosevelt, and the other became the second Mrs. Vincent Astor—she "devoted her life to creating a perfect world for her husband."[7]

Although the finished decoration of the Paleys' Fifth Avenue apartment was rightfully credited to Parish-Hadley, Jansen's contributions were significant enough to stand on their own. For example, the elevator hall has been assigned to both Parish-Hadley and Jansen, but a small model of the room, which exists in the collection of a Jansen employee, identifies Jansen as its creator. Walls were papered in a mottled finish of caramel and bronze, covered by sheets of glass held in place by ormolu rosettes. Along both sidewalls were serpentine, built-in benches with hidden compartments for the storage of umbrellas, a solution suggested by the highly organized Babe Paley. Jansen also designed the room's stylish spherical bronze doorknobs, which

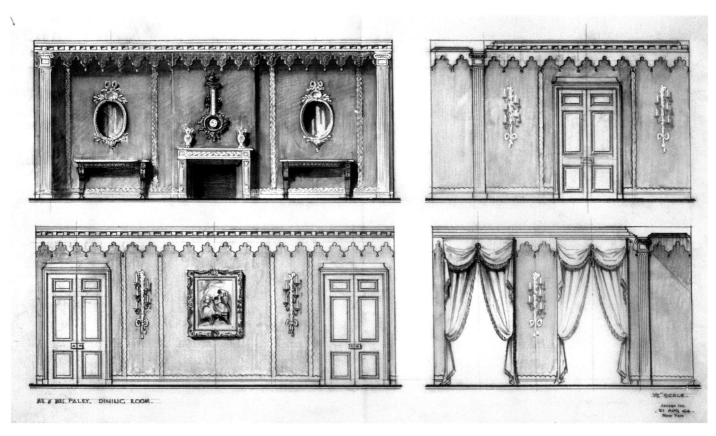

Proposals for the dining room, c. 1964

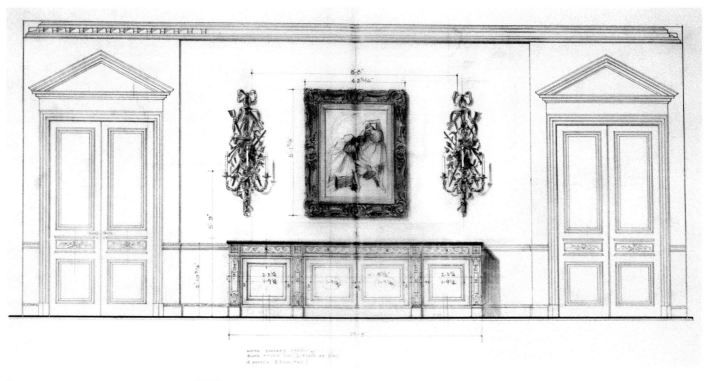

Proposal for the dining room, c. 1965

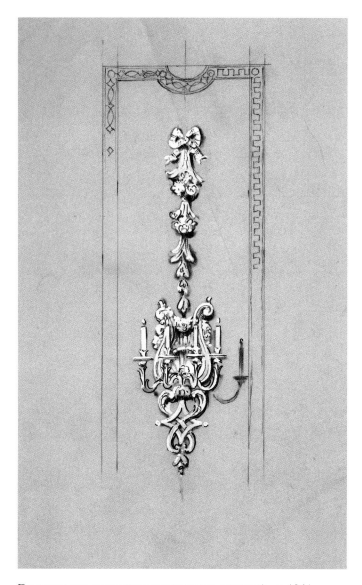

DRAWING FOR PROPOSED DINING ROOM APPLIQUÉ , C. 1964

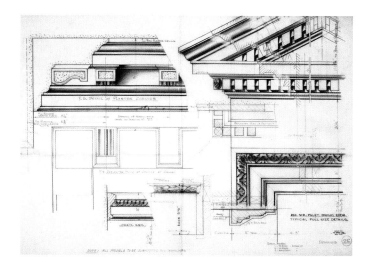

DRAWINGS FOR THE DINING ROOM'S GEORGIAN-STYLE CORNICE AND DOOR SURROUNDS, 1964

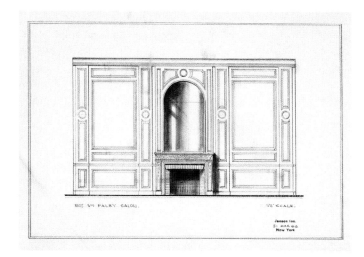

ELEVATION DRAWING FOR SALON MANTELPIECE AND WALL

were produced in the Paris ateliers. The overall scheme was one of several proposals submitted by Jansen's Manhattan office on behalf of Boudin. Drawings for three other Jansen schemes survive. These include green upholstered walls, capped by Boudin's characteristic continuous valance; Chinese scenic panels with wainscoting; and a coved ceiling that may have been intended to receive a trompe l'oeil sky.

Measuring 44 feet long, the entrance hall or gallery of the apartment was divided into three bays. The walls were made up of floor-to-ceiling, pilaster-adorned bookcases and cabinets, defining the Paleys' collection of rare books as the central focus of the apartment while giving them a prominence as significant as the couple's renowned collection of paintings and sculpture. With the recessed positioning of the upper portion of the casework, as well as the narrowing of shelves, the cabinets enhanced the height of the space. For the floor, 18th-century Italian wood parquet consisting of two different patterns was installed. In the

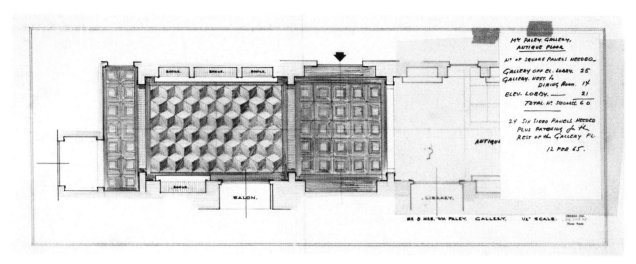

PLAN FOR INSTALLATION SHOWING TWO PATTERNS OF 18TH-CENTURY ITALIAN WOOD PARQUET FLOORING

central bay was a grid of 25 squares of concentric bands of dark and light woods, and within the end bays were energetic compositions of mixed woods in a trompe l'oeil pattern that mimicked linenfold paneling. The depth-defying end sections of the floor magnified the hall's size, but Boudin's true genius was in having a different, more subdued pattern for the room's middle section. This break relieved the space from appearing solely as a passage and provided a subtle delineation of the center of the room as the space for greeting and bidding farewell to guests.

An officially retired, ailing Boudin dictated his vision for the Paley salon or living room to Jansen, Inc., basing it on a Louis XV example in the Musée Carnavalet, a 16th-century mansion in Paris that had been home to the hostess and writer Madame de Sévigné.[8] Seemingly simple in its overall composition of framed tiers of square and rectangular panels, bordered by piers with unadorned rondelles, the wall treatment actually was complex. Characteristic of all paneling designed and produced by Jansen, there were subtle differences in the scale of the moldings used to frame the large central panels and those that lay above

and below. The panels that would receive a mirror, a painting, or a decorative bracket with a porcelain ornament were assigned a slightly broader molding profile and thus a subtly greater importance.

For the dining room, Jansen proposed a series of options. The favored color scheme appears to have been blue and white, with one proposal dominated by another variation of Boudin's characteristic room-encompassing valances. This proposal was followed by one of which the Paleys eventually selected a variation: an Adamesque scheme with large architectural panels picked out in white, as well as large matching appliqués at either side of the mantel breast, the doors capped by Georgian-style pediments with dentil detailing.

With the completion of the elevator hall, as well as the installation of the woodwork and plaster ornament for the entrance hall, salon, and dining room, Jansen's role in the decoration of the Paley apartment came to an end. In recognition of Boudin's established vocabulary that included distressed, pastel-pigmented paneling, it is presumed that similar historically directed schemes were envisioned for this residence. Surviving miniature models executed for this commission suggest just such paint treatments and identify placement of carpets and key works of art from the Paley collection. But because of his increasing ill health and advancing age, Boudin was no longer able to work with the Paleys in person, a limitation that altered his influence on their apartment. At the same time, concurrent design work being done by other decorators at the couple's Long Island estate, Kiluna Farm, indicated that Babe Paley perhaps wanted something more contemporary in composition than what the Frenchman initially proposed. In any event, the apartment at 820 Fifth Avenue was turned over to Parish-Hadley, Inc.

Albert Hadley revised the Jansen-designed entrance hall, selecting a crisp, uniform cream color for the woodwork. For the salon, he cancelled the large sheet of mirrored glass intended for over the fireplace in favor of a mid-18th-century looking glass with a highly sculpted gilt frame. He also glazed the paneling in five shades of vibrant yellow. In another deviation from Boudin's plan, Hadley selected an earth-toned Louis XVI mantelpiece, less formal than the white painted wood example presumably envisioned by Jansen, Inc. "Palazzo Paley is finished at last, and I like it a lot," wrote Jayne Wrightsman to a dying Boudin in Paris. "[Babe] ended by painting the drawing room bright, bright yellow which I think is a success, as the pictures look marvelous on it."[9]

Though not a complete representation of Jansen's work, the Paley apartment documented a reality of the period, wherein not one but several creative individuals partnered to decorate an important residence. Wrightsman's letter to Boudin about the apartment's completion is telling. By assessing the finished residence a success and assigning the color selection to the owner, she rightfully extended subtle praise to Boudin for having created the elegant architectural envelope while adhering to the Jansen practice that the firm's designers should not take credit away from the client.

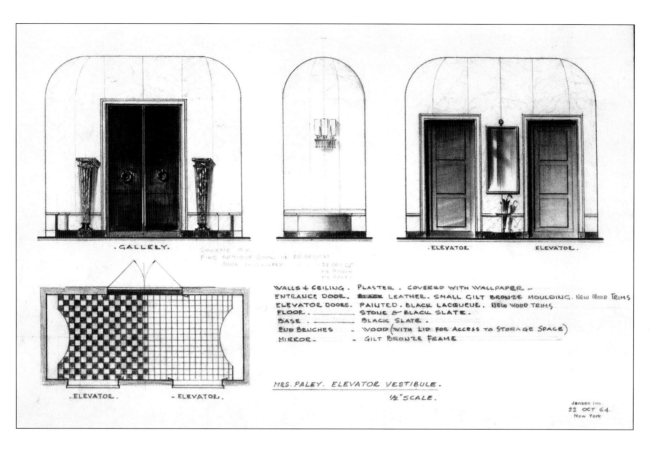

WALLS & CEILING . PLASTER . COVERED WITH WALLPAPER .
ENTRANCE DOOR . ~~BLACK~~ LEATHER . SMALL GILT BRONZE MOULDING . NEW WOOD TRIMS
ELEVATOR DOORS . PAINTED . BLACK LACQUEUR . NEW WOOD TRIMS
FLOOR . _____ STONE & BLACK SLATE .
BASE . _____ BLACK SLATE .
END BENCHES - WOOD (WITH LID FOR ACCESS TO STORAGE SPACE)
MIRROR - GILT BRONZE FRAME

MRS. PALEY. ELEVATOR VESTIBULE.
½" SCALE.

Janson Inc.
22 OCT 64.
New York

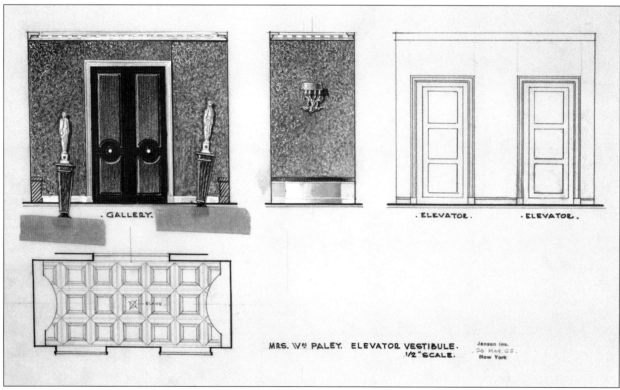

MRS. Wm PALEY. ELEVATOR VESTIBULE.
½" SCALE.

Janson Inc.
20 MAY. 65.
New York

TOP AND ABOVE: PROPOSED AND APPROVED DESIGN FOR THE ELEVATOR HALL

Shah Mohamed Reza Pahlavi and Shahbanou Farah of Iran

The 2,500th Anniversary of the Empire

PERSEPOLIS, IRAN

OFTEN-OVERLOOKED ASPECTS OF JANSEN'S DECORATIVE WORK are designs for special events. Called upon by hosts and hostesses for numerous occasions, including weddings and debutante balls, Jansen provided elegant and dramatic pageants and backdrops. This highly profitable sideline added to the firm's coffers while enhancing its reputation and public recognition. Stéphane Boudin is known to have begun his career at Jansen with designs for banquets and special exhibition displays; his designs for Lady Mendl's 1938 Circus Ball was his most celebrated such endeavor. Pierre Delbeé was equally famous for these creations, which included theater stage sets. The most spectacular of these temporary commissions was a four-day, multimillion-dollar series of parties, dinners, and parades that marked the 2,500-year anniversary of the founding of Persia and was hosted by Shah Mohamed Reza Pahlavi of Iran and his third wife, Shahbanou Farah.[1]

Representative of the shah's desire to celebrate the history of his country, as well as an opportunity for him to align his dynasty, only two generations old, with the storied history of Persia, the event required almost a decade of initial planning and subsequently utilized all of Jansen's resources. Indeed, the scale of this celebration was larger than what the firm, alone, could fulfill. In 1969, Pierre Delbée, the president of Jansen at the time, negotiated a

OPPOSITE: MODEL FOR THE PROPOSED CITY OF TENTS, AS DISPLAYED AT 9 RUE ROYALE

TESTING THE GRAND BANQUETING TENT IN PARIS BEFORE SHIPMENT TO IRAN

partnership with Maison Leleu, a celebrated purveyor of luxurious French modern design since the 1920s. Whether this joining of forces was necessary for the complexities of the ambitious project or to ensure that the then financially strapped Jansen could retain the favor of the shah, this partnership was, in the end, responsible for the elaborate and highly publicized spectacle. As a result, Leleu became part of Maison Jansen.

The celebration began on October 12 in Persepolis, four hundred miles southeast of Tehran, and ended on October 16 with the dedication of the Shahyad Tower and Persian History Museum in Tehran.[2] Serving as the primary backdrop were the ruins of Persepolis, the ancient capital of Darius I, founder of the Persian Empire, which had been destroyed by Alexander the Great. There were numerous arrival ceremonies for visiting heads of state, two parades, two large banquets, and various smaller celebrations. Among the guests were kings and queens, crown princes and pretenders, and sultans and grand dukes representing more than 60 nations, including Denmark, Greece, Monaco, Thailand, Spain, Afghanistan, and Japan.[3] England's Prince Philip arrived with his daughter, Princess Anne; Ethiopia's Emperor Haile Selassie was accompanied by his diamond-collared Chihuahua. Added to this imposing list of royalty were numerous government officials, ranging from Marshal Tito of Yugoslavia to the prime ministers of Yemen and Korea to the first lady of the Philippines, Imelda Marcos. The United States sent Vice President and Mrs. Spiro T. Agnew.

The major feature of the Persepolis celebration was a tent city, a star-patterned cluster of 54 circular pavilions

DETAIL OF ORIGINAL MODEL, SHOWING THE HELICOPTER PAD AND GRAND BANQUETING TENT

Original model for the Persepolis celebration, c. 1970

INTERIOR OF THE GRAND BANQUETING TENT DURING INSTALLATION

that would house the most important guests.[4] They were arranged along five avenues that symbolized the five continents participating in the event and banked by acres of temporary gardens.[5] Forty-two feet in diameter and nearly 20 feet in height, each tent was actually a prefabricated, air-conditioned guest house composed of a sitting room, two bedrooms with single beds, two bathrooms, and a service room for a maid or other staff member.[6] Their plywood structures were covered in sand-colored sailcloth that had been trimmed with Jansen's characteristic Baroque-style tabs or tongues of contrasting light blue; each tent had a recessed red entrance. The interiors were decorated in different styles,

ranging from Louis XVI to contemporary. Included in the decoration was a presentation portrait of the tent's primary occupant made by Iranian carpet weavers using official photographs as models. The bathrooms were outfitted with Porthault towels and equipped with colognes and perfumes supplied by leading French firms.[7] The tent for the shah and shahbanou was furnished with marble bathtubs and gilded fixtures.[8]

At the center of the tent city was a multilevel fountain, modeled after those in the gardens of Versailles. At night, the dramatically lighted jets of water served to join the contemporary tented city with the illuminated monumental ruins of Persepolis beyond. It also

VIEW OF THE GRAND BANQUETING TENT IN PARIS

visually drew guests to a processional walkway that culminated at the entrance to the Tent of Honor and Grand Banqueting Tent, located about five hundred feet farther on. The shah and his wife used the Tent of Honor to greet each nation's delegation. The decoration of the tent, which measured 34 feet in diameter, was sumptuous: walls of red Italian silk damask that were finished with a continuous gold-trimmed valance reminiscent of that employed in the Blue Room of the White House, and eight Empire-style chandeliers made of ormolu and Bohemian crystal hanging from an elegantly gathered ceiling of golden voile. The floor was covered with cerise moquette, a smooth woven wool

fabric, completing the illusion of the room as a large jewel box. The finishing touch was an array of gemlike Rococo furniture, appliqués, and mirror-adorned sections of paneling in white and gold.

The Grand Banqueting Tent measured a little more than 223 feet long by nearly 79 feet wide. Here the walls were covered draped with blue faille, a slightly rib-textured silk. Along one wall stood the 187-foot-long serpentine banqueting table, lavishly decorated with scroll-patterned gold embroidery. The backdrop for this table consisted of elaborate white fringed swags, festoons, and canopy-capped doorways of gold-embroidered blue velvet. Behind the shah's chair was

SITTING ROOM FOR A GUEST TENT

Sitting room for a guest tent

BEDROOM IN A GUEST TENT

an embroidered and bejeweled representation of a peacock, the symbol of the monarchy. The ceiling was made of pink silk, carefully folded to form a templelike coffered pattern. From each of the 12 coffered recesses was suspended a gilt- and patinated-bronze triple-tier chandelier with stylized branches in the form of acanthus leaves. Bathed in the light of these chandeliers were approximately 40 round tables paired with Louis XIV–style curule-base chairs upholstered in sky blue velvet.

In this space, the shah and shahbanou hosted two banquets, the largest and most important taking place during four and half hours on the evening of October 14, the shahbanou's 33rd birthday. A specially commis-

sioned blue and gold Limoges dinner service bearing the crest of the Iranian imperial family set the stage for a multicourse meal prepared by Maxim's. (The Paris restaurant closed its Rue Royale dining room for 15 days to travel to Persepolis and prepare for the celebration.) The menu consisted of quail eggs stuffed with caviar, followed in succession by crayfish mousse; roast lamb with truffles; roast partridge stuffed with foie gras and truffles; and, finally, oporto glazed figs with raspberries.[9] The 92 serving platters were anchored by taxidermy peacocks, their tail feathers spread and surrounded by dozens of cold quail in aspic. Jaime Peñafiel, a Spanish journalist, later described this banquet as an "expression of the most absolute luxury . . .

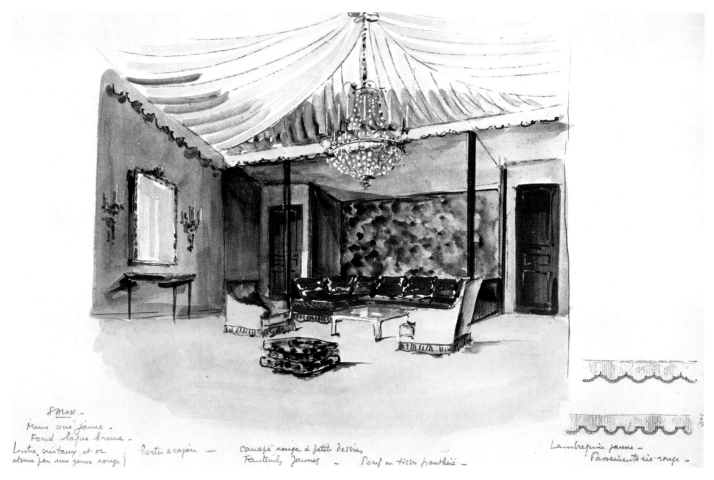

SALON –
Mens une jaune –
Fond laque brune –
Lustre cristaux et or   Portes acajou –   Canapé rouge à petit dessins
stone par une gaine rouge)   Fauteuils jaunes   –   Pouf en tissu panthère –   Lambrequin jaune –
                                                                                                          Passementerie rouge –

SCHEMATIC DRAWING FOR A SITTING ROOM AT THE CENTER OF A GUEST SUITE

[and] the most complete refinement. It was the greatest of all the parties of the century and it is very possible that a similar one is never organized again."[10]

Following the banquet, guests proceeded to viewing stands facing the Persepolis ruins, to watch a fireworks display by Jacques Quiry. "From the tomb in the mountainside overlooking the ruined palaces where he ruled 500 years before Christ, the voice of Darius the Great spoke in the dark, but in French. Andre Castelot, France's eminent historian, recounted the glories of Xerxes and the last days of the Persian Empire," wrote Cyrus Kadivar, a historian. "The columns of Persepolis were bathed in white light then gradually they turned red and the sound of fire mixed with the drunken orgy of Greek soldiers. It was the sacking of Persepolis by Alexander all over again. The guests were thrilled and applauded."[11] The next day's program consisted of tours of the ruins, led by the shah and shahbanou, followed by an extravagant theatrical parade that illustrated the history of Persia.

The banquet on October 15 also was held in the Banqueting Tent, which had been reconfigured and redecorated overnight as a less-formal dining room. Inserts of printed paisley-patterned cotton were placed against the walls, and contemporary banquettes and chairs upholstered in similar fabrics allowed for informal mingling among guests. Tables were draped in lavender and yellow.

SCHEMATIC DRAWING FOR THE INTERIOR OF THE GRAND BANQUETING TENT

SCHEMATIC DRAWING FOR THE TENT OF HONOR

Schematic drawing for outdoor communal seating areas

Following the 1971 celebration, the shah envisioned the tent city serving as reception buildings for tourists traveling to see the ancient ruins, to be operated by Club Méditerranée.[12] This did not come to pass before he was deposed in 1978. However, the Islamic fundamentalist government that succeeded him revived interest in using the tent city to encourage tourism in 2001. Praising the beauty and craftsmanship of the 30-year-old structures, an Iranian tourist at the time wryly noted, "We haven't even been able to build a proper door in the past 20 years."[13] Today, the tourism proposal remains just that, as so much of what the tent city symbolized is what the current government sought to abolish. Politically sensitive and increasingly tattered, this second series of ruins at Persepolis will, for however long it survives, be seen as an unrivaled example of imperialism.

ERECTION OF THE TENT OF HONOR, WITH PIERRE DELBÉE AND PIERRE DESHAYS STANDING AT CENTER

1963–1975

Bartolomé March Servera

MONG JANSEN'S MOST PROLIFIC CLIENTS WAS THE SPANISH banking family March, for whom Stéphane Boudin, Pierre Delbée, and Carlos Ortiz-Cabrera each worked. The primary patrons were Juan March Ordinas (1880–1962), recognized through most of the 20th century as Spain's wealthiest citizen, and his youngest son, financier and philanthropist Bartolomé March Servera (1917–1998). For these men, Jansen created elegant palaces befitting Medici princes and Bourbon kings in Madrid, Mallorca, and elsewhere, and they also staged numerous spectacular events, including family weddings. As March's grandson, Alfonso Fierro March, assessed in 2005, "after the Shah of Iran, my grandfather was the most important client of the House of Jansen in the 1960s and 1970s."[1]

The enduring relationship between Jansen and the March family began with Bartolomé March, son of Juan March, who was a politician, entrepreneur, and banker—he founded Banco March. The elder March's near-unrivalled authority in the national and international affairs of post-revolutionary Spain no doubt led to his personal patronage of Maison Jansen, then the recognized tastemaker for Europe's figural as well as real powerbrokers.

The grandest of the March residences was Palacio March in Palma de Mallorca, the capital of Mallorca, one of the Balearic Islands off the southeastern coast of Spain. This

OPPOSITE: TOP VIEW OF ENTRANCE HALL AT SA TORRE CEGA, CALA RATJADA

Entrance hall at Sa Torre Cega, Cala Ratjada

Renaissance-inspired, sand-colored, stucco-and-terracotta-tiled, three-story mansion was built between 1939 and 1944 on the site of the former Santo Domingo Convent. Situated between La Seo, Palma's 14th-century cathedral, and its parliament building—visually representing the March family's iconic social and political standing in Spain—the residence commanded some of the most spectacular views of the island and the Mediterranean Sea. The house was designed as a backdrop for a growing collection of fine and decorative arts—the music salon was painted by José María Sert—much of which was vetted and arranged by Jansen's president Stéphane Boudin.

The firm's greatest contributions came in the mid-1960s, under the auspices of Juan's youngest son, Bartolomé. It was the son who expanded and refined the family's art holdings, contributing manuscripts and maps from the 1400s to the 1700s, an important collection of ivory, as well as significant works by 20th-century modern and contemporary artists such as Henry Moore, Eduardo Chillida, Salvador Dalì, Javier Corberó, and others. Bartolomé worked with Boudin's successor Pierre Delbée, and soon thereafter, Carlos Ortiz-Cabrera, to update the interior decor.

Another March residence on the island of Mallorca was Sa Torre Sega, built in 1911 in Cala Ratjada. Delbée designed most of the work, although among the most striking additions was Ortiz-Cabrera's Pop Art–inspired trompe-l'oeil floor of blues and white within the residence's two-story Italianate foyer. Forming an optical illusion of either a convex or concave floor elevation—depending on where one stood—the overall composition was based upon 16th-century Italian Baroque patterns for inlaid floors and garden pathways. But what made the March commission more modern and less of a historical restatement was the

vibrancy of the palette, which had the intensity of a then-contemporary neon sculpture. Dramatic and awe-inspiring, the illusion was further enhanced when one looked down from the surrounding gallery, seeing the celebrated design framed by bands of intense sunflower yellow, blue, and white concentric-square patterned tiles on the second-story floor. The success of this and other designs at Sa Torre Cega is said to have led to Carlos Ortiz-Cabrera's promotion "to the position of director of the New York branch of the firm."[2] The English landscape architect Russell Page laid out the gardens here, which included a number of important sculptural works.

In 1965, Bartolomé March commissioned Jansen to decorate his official Madrid residence, formerly the Palacio Sotomayor, in the posh residential section known as Miguel Angel and inspired by the 18th-century Casa del Labrador in Aranjuez, Spain. Pierre Delbée oversaw the more traditional decoration of this great house. Delbée's main stair hall was nothing less than imposing, and it set the tone for other rooms. The ceilings were of distressed plaster, varying in color from warm ivory to cool white. The floor was of diagonally placed white marble squares, with inset X-form black tiles accentuating the grand scale of the space. Rich claret-colored velvet walls were trimmed in specially woven decorative silk tape and illuminated by electrified wall-mounted antique oil lamps. The walls were covered with 19th-century nautical paintings, which followed the orderly upward procession of bronze-clad white marble steps.

Among the most famous rooms was the main salon with walls and draperies of ivory silk, trimmed in red and ivory Grecian key–patterned decorative tapes reminiscent of Boudin's scheme for the Empire Salon of the French ambassador's residence in Washington

ENTRANCE HALL AT MIGUEL ANGEL HOUSE, MADRID

created just a few years earlier. Crimson-upholstered Louis XVI–style fauteuils and gilt-bronze and eglomisé-ornamented tables were intermixed with contemporary chairs and sofas covered in luxurious water green silk-pressed velvet. During the day, the setting was light and cheerful with sun streaming in through floor-to-ceiling French doors opening onto a private brick courtyard. By night, the richly tailored wall treatment became an appropriately formal backdrop for entertaining as well as for the display of art masterpieces. Throughout the room, Delbée and March arranged priceless works of fine and decorative

arts, among them landscape paintings by Francisco Goya and by his contemporary Antonio Carnicero (1748–1814), under which was placed a magnificent pair of console tables by French Baroque furniture maker André-Charles Boulle (1642–1732).

Opening off the main salon was a large, rectangular, formal dining room, with distressed Louis XVI woodwork in various shades of green. Upholstered, oval-back Louis XVI-style painted and gilded chairs were positioned around a mahogany extension pedestal-base table, presumably made in Jansen's Paris ateliers. A delicate Baltic neoclassical chandelier with

LIBRARY AT MIGUEL ANGEL HOUSE, MADRID

pleated silk shades was suspended from the ceiling. With its somewhat staid decor, the dining room was less representative of Jansen of the 1960s than of the firm's design vocabulary from previous decades; the original paneled treatment of walls, the initial chair selection, and choice of lighting fixture duplicated those of earlier commissions, including the prewar London residence of the Audrey and Hon. Peter Pleydell-Bouverie and the postwar New York City apartment of the Mildred and Charles Allen. Indeed, it seemed more reflective of the Boudin aesthetic than the modern taste Delbée espoused. It is probable that a more conservative, historically based decor was sought by the March family for their Spanish capital residence—thus Delbée harkened back to what the Paris firm was best known.

Perhaps the grandest of the March Madrid interiors designed by Jansen was the library, in which Delbée referenced the Napoleonic libraries at Malmaison and the royal palace at Compiègne. Although the firm had used such historical models as inspiration in designing interiors for other clients, as in the office of Tunisian president Habib Bourguiba, none of those prior commissions rivaled the scale or level of detail of this monumental two-story room. Rich, highly polished mahogany Ionic columns, pilasters, and cornices with finely chased ormolu mounts defined double tiers of bookcases as an uninterrupted succession of temples, sheltering thousands of rare historical volumes collected and coveted by the March family, including the rare Medinacelli collection of 17,000 volumes, now deemed a national treasure by the Spanish government.

Throughout the main floor, Delbée devised intimate alcoves for reading, study, and occasional conversation, as well as special cabinets for smaller collections of cameos, medals, and coins. Chairs upholstered in dis-

tressed red and brown leather complemented the aged Moroccan leather bindings of books, and imperial emerald green silk velvet-covered Empire méridiennes. Suspended from the ceiling for illumination of the lower floor were four Empire-style gilt-bronze chandeliers of eight lights with delicate anthemia and acanthus leaf decoration. Eight smaller versions of these fixtures provided light for the upper gallery, which was framed by a bronze balustrade.

Also for the Madrid residence, Jansen designed an elegant interior swimming pool that emulated Versailles' famous Hall of Mirrors. Bronze-colored mottled mirrored glass formed a trompe-l'oeil gallery of archways on three walls, with the fourth having actual windows to an exterior garden. The floor was laid with intricate mosaics modeled on ancient Roman examples, including a dolphin motif, and polychrome classical busts projected from wall-mounted decorative brackets. Forged iron chaises, based on the Roman *lectus*, or reclining couch, were mixed with polychrome porcelain garden seats in imitation of stacked pillows.

The March family also sought out Jansen for the design of special events and dinners. This largely overlooked aspect of the firm's repertoire was called upon by clients worldwide prior to World War II. Jansen designed iconic parties for the majority of its most important clients, including Lady Mendl at Villa Trianon and Lady Baillie at Leeds Castle. For the Duke and Duchess of Windsor, a specially designed banqueting table in the shape of the letter W was devised for a variety of Jansen-conceived social events at their rented house, La Cröe, on the French Riviera. Specially designed dinner services, linens, and other equipage were also created, with each event given a special and unique identity by Jansen's artisans. Such grandeur continued in the postwar years with less frequency and for a smaller coterie of clients.

SWIMMING POOL COMPOUND, WITH CEILING CLOSED, AT MIGUEL ANGEL, MADRID

There were a number of such special events for the March family. The reception in Palma to the April 11, 1970, wedding of Bartolomé March's daughter, Leonor March Cencillo—the groom was Francisco Javier Chico de Guzmán y Girón, Marqués de las Amarillas, heir to the Duque de Ahumada—Jansen conjured a setting inspired by 18th-century French prints and paintings documenting lavish entertaining by the Bourbon kings. Specially configured tables, floral arrangements, and place settings were based on documented designs for Louis XV and his son and heir.

That event was soon followed by the June 27, 1970, wedding in La Seo of Leonor's sister, Marita, to Alfonso Fierro Jiménez-Lopera, an heir to the Fierro banking fortune. Jansen draped the rooms and garden walls of Palacio March with seemingly endless swags and jabots of blue silk taffeta. Dinner was served in the villa's courtyard, the stone columns of which were wrapped in ivy vines intermixed with blue hydrangea. Potted artificial trees made of polished steel bore fruit of clear glass globes protecting miniature electric bulbs. Round tables were covered with blue silk of a lighter hue than used on the walls. Around these tables were placed a Jansen standard—blue velvet-upholstered Louis XIV–style curule-based chairs, the same chairs used a year later for the Shah of Iran's celebration at Persepolis. The grandeur of the event was matched by an international guest list, which

275

PATIO AT PALMA DECORATED FOR THE WEDDING OF MARITA MARCH AND ALFONSO FIERRO JIMÉNEZ-LOPERA

included ambassadors from England, France, and Italy, as well as members of society's elite from Spain and South America. *The New York Times* dubbed the event "the last great wedding on the Iberian Peninsula."[3]

The connection of the March family to Jansen was further enhanced when Bartolomé March acquired two properties owned in France by Suzy and Pierre Delbée. These included both the couple's Paris apartment, which was purchased fully furnished, and Delbée's country house.

Jansen's work for the March family continued through the 1970s and included work performed by Delbée for Marita March de Fierro, and her husband at their apartment in Madrid.

PALACIO MARCH ON LEFT WITH LA SEO CATHEDRAL AT RIGHT

DINING ROOM OF MARITA MARCH DE FIERRO AND ALFONSO FIERRO JIMÉNEZ-LOPERA, MADRID

P ART OF THE LORE ASSOCIATED WITH JANSEN IS THE BELIEF THAT the firm designed and manufactured every piece of furniture included in a commission. This was obviously not the case. Jansen did design and make furniture—as well as paneling for rooms, lamps, chandeliers, and even decorative metalwork—in its famous ateliers. Much of this work fell under the heading of reproductions, as Jansen frequently was called on to expand an existing set of 10 Louis XV chairs to 12, provide an exact mate for a late-18th-century commode, or extend a suite of antique wall panels intended for an alcove to encompass a large modern living room. Occasionally, there was a contemporary object to be made for a client, such as a small, two-tiered telephone table on miniature casters, a design that was originally created so that the husband or wife of a couple who rarely spoke to each other could pass the receiver between themselves. So admired was the original of this table that additional examples were made for many of Jansen's clients, including the Duchess of Windsor.[1] Yet in its more than a century of existence, in the many apartments, townhouses, villas, and palaces that it decorated, Jansen also included chairs, tables, and other works designed and manufactured by furniture makers such as François Linke, Jean-Michel Frank, and T. H. Robsjohn-Gibbings (1905–1976). The firm also enhanced existing designs created by others, redefining them through altered scale

OPPOSITE: SET OF LOUIS XVI-STYLE STOOLS, C. 1965

A VARIATION OF JANSEN'S GILT-BRONZE SIDE TABLE DESIGN.
TABLES WERE PRODUCED IN MANY SIZES WITH MAHOGANY,
ROSEWOOD, OR LACQUER PANELS.

or ornamentation. Among the most famous examples of such copying was that of the Thebes stool no. 2, which was designed by Leonard F. Wyburd (1866–?) for Liberty & Company of London around 1885. In the mid-20th century, Jansen reinterpreted Wyburd's take on an ancient Egyptian three-legged seat, replacing its Arts and Crafts polished wood (usually walnut or oak) with exotic red and black lacquer finishes, sometimes highlighted with gold leaf. Another popular design by the firm was an oblong or oval rolling dining table with legs made of gunmetal adorned with polished brass rings in a modernistic interpretation of bamboo; the surface of the table was typically of a shiny dark gray or black laminate.[2] Immensely popular with many Jansen clients, the table was noted for its ingenuity. Not only could it be set in the butler's pantry or kitchen and then rolled into position elsewhere in a house or apartment, making it doubly attractive to clients with smaller residences, some models could be divided in two and collapsed into a pair of matching demilune consoles. Cora Caetani, the director of the Jansen boutique in Paris, used one of these in her dining room, together with black-painted Napoleon III ballroom chairs upholstered in sulfur-yellow silk, a colorful geometric Charles X carpet, and satin-striped tone-on-tone white wallpaper.[3]

Another application of Jansen's furniture-design prowess was the Jansen Collections, which were put into production in 1972 by the firm's director Pierre Deshays. Intended to be sold to the general public, this line of chairs, tables, cabinets, and desks offered luxurious finishes that ranged from black lacquer to malachite, from ivory inlay to ormolu mounts. Not quite the exclusive pieces unique to a particular commission or famous client, these pieces of furniture nonetheless demonstrated the level of luxury associated with the house of Jansen.

On these pages is a collection of Jansen designs, spanning from 1900 to the 1970s. They are included here not as a complete record of the firm's creativity but instead as an introduction to the hundreds of thousands of designs and proposals that Jansen produced.

An example of Jansen's personalized trompe-l'oeil pieces

Louis XV-style commode with elaborate faux finish. Boudin is credited with having revived the art of faux bamboo finishes and trompe-l'oeil painting in the 1930s for clients such as Lady Baillie.

Palm-supported console table, c. 1940

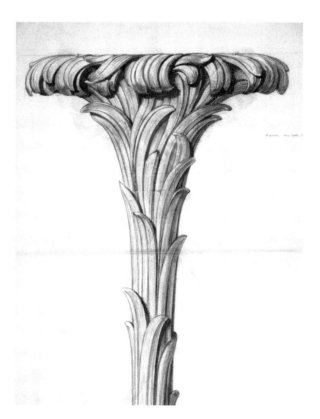

Detail of drawing for a plaster torchere, c. 1940

Fleur-de-lis console table, c. 1940

Small console table, c. 1938

GLASS AND BRONZE CONSOLE TABLE ATTRIBUTED TO GASTON SCHWARTZ

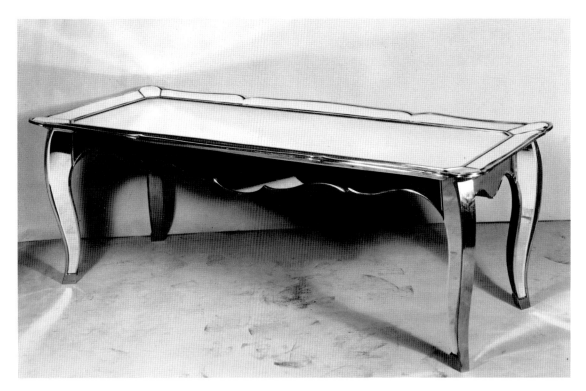

MIRRORED-GLASS VENEERED COFFEE TABLE, C. 1940, DESIGN NO. '12061'

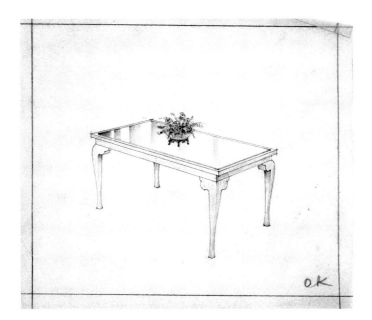

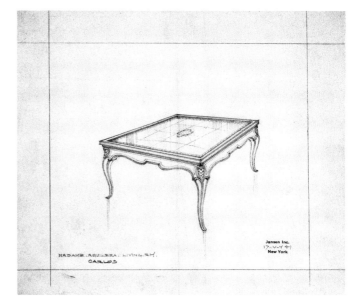

ABOVE AND RIGHT: DRAWINGS FOR GLASS-TOPPED COFFEE TABLES, C. 1960.

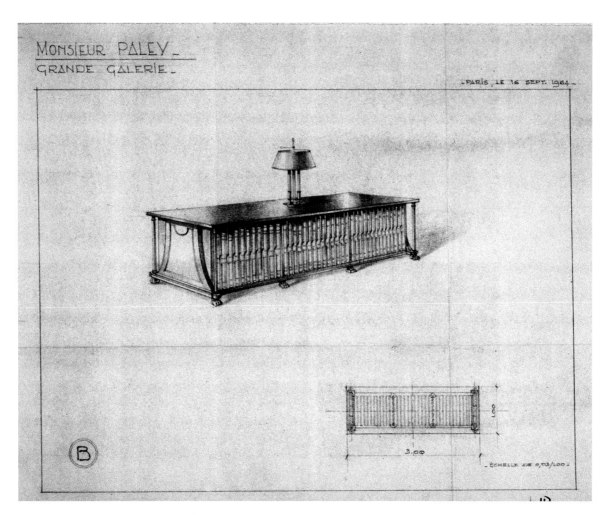

DRAWING FOR A FOLIO CASE, C. 1964

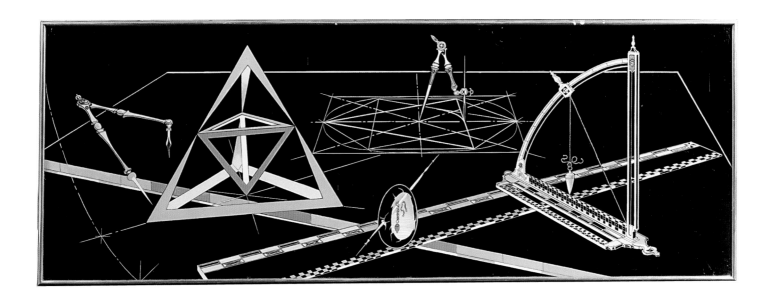

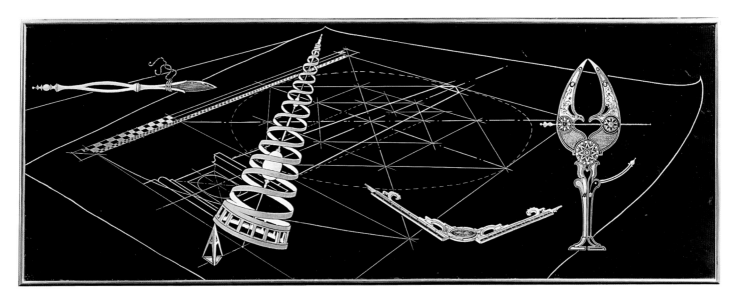

DETAILS OF TOPS FOR OCCASIONAL TABLES (OPPOSITE) WITH PAINTED SCAGLIOLA INSETS

PAIR OF TWO-TIERED OCCASIONAL TABLES WITH BRASS MOUNTINGS, C. 1965

GILT-BRONZE TABLE AND STOOL, C. 1960

BRONZE AND GLASS OCCASIONAL TABLE, C. 1965

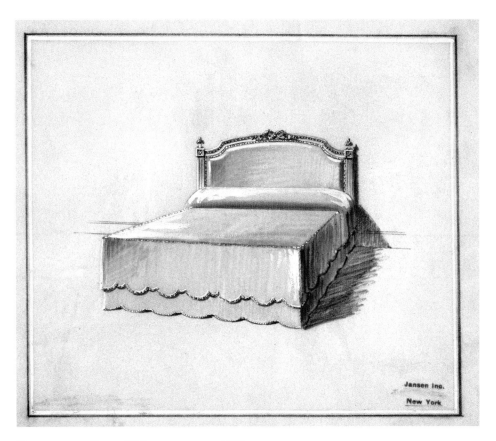

DRAWING FOR LOUIS XVI-STYLE BED, C. 1965

DRAWING FOR BED FOR HENRY FORD II, C. 1964

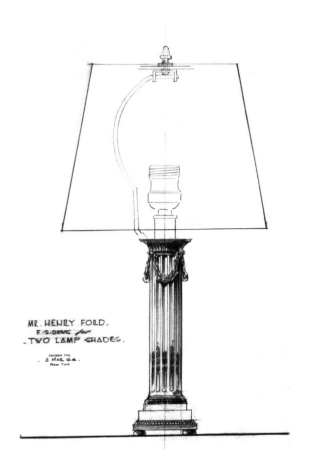

DRAWING FOR LAMPSHADE FOR HENRY FORD II, C. 1964

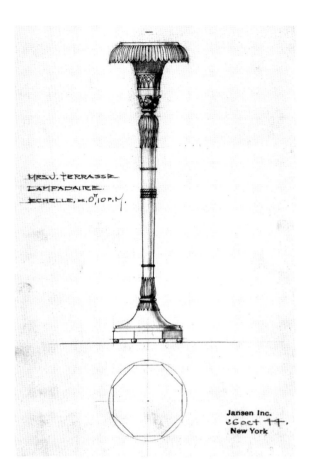

DRAWING FOR GILT-BRONZE LIGHTING FIXTURE, C. 1944

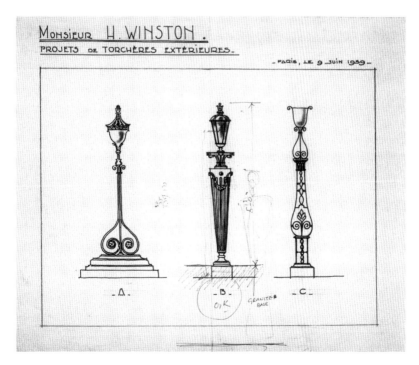

DESIGNS FOR EXTERIOR TORCHERES FOR HARRY WINSTON, INC., 1959

ORMOLU-MOUNTED LOUIS XVI-STYLE PEDESTAL

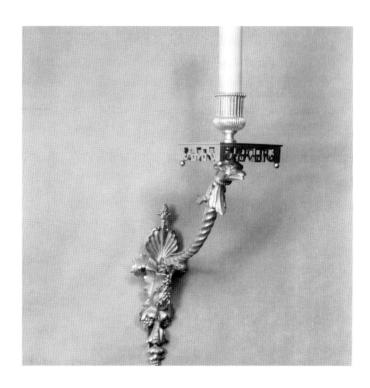

GILT-BRONZE SCONCE DESIGNED FOR THE ALLEN'S NEW YORK
APARTMENT, C. 1959

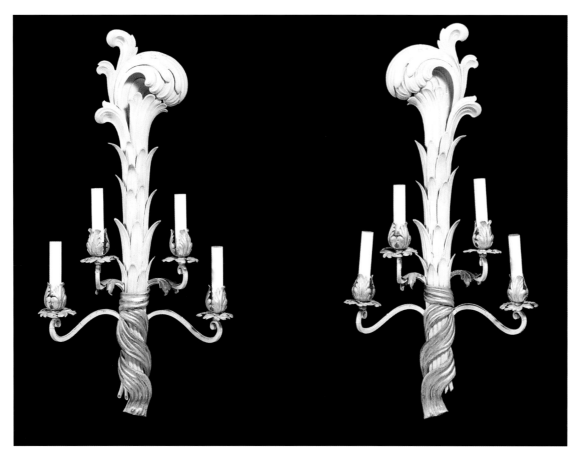

PAIR OF POLYCHROME-DECORATED SCONCES IN THE FORM OF ACANTHUS BRANCHES, C. 1965

POLYCHROME-DECORATED SCONCE, C. 1965

CIRCA 1885
KING WILLEM III
ROYAL PALACE
AMSTERDAM, NETHERLANDS

CIRCA 1890
KING LEOPOLD II
CHÂTEAU DE LAEKEN
BRUSSELS, BELGIUM

CIRCA 1890
HELENE AND ETIENNE VAN ZUYLEN
    VAN NYEVELT VAN DER HAAR
86 AVENUE DU BOIS
PARIS, FRANCE

CIRCA 1890
HELENE AND ETIENNE VAN ZUYLEN
    VAN NYEVELT VAN DER HAAR
IL PARADISO
NICE, FRANCE

CIRCA 1895
HELENE AND ETIENNE VAN ZUYLEN
    VAN NYEVELT VAN DER HAAR
KASTEEL DE HAAR
HAARZUILENS, NETHERLANDS

CIRCA 1902
KING EDWARD VII
BUCKINGHAM PALACE
LONDON, ENGLAND

CIRCA 1912
STEPHANIE AND MAURICE STIFFTER
    (AUNT AND UNCLE OF ARTIST TAMARA
    DE LEMPICKA)
ST. PETERSBURG, RUSSIA

1920
BANQUE DE FRANCE
1 RUE DE LA VRILLI PRE
PARIS, FRANCE

CIRCA 1920,
DAME NELLIE MELBA
LONDON, ENGLAND

CIRCA 1920
ALFONSO GOMEZ MENA
VEDADO
CALZADA STREET AND AVENUE OF THE
    PRESIDENTS
HAVANA, CUBA

1925
CARL AND EDITH VAN SLYKE WEEKS
SALISBURY HOUSE
4025 TONAWANDA DRIVE
DES MOINES, IOWA, USA

CIRCA 1927
COUNT AND COUNTESS DE REVILLA
    DE CAMARGO
502 17TH STREET
HAVANA, CUBA

CIRCA 1930
MR. AND MRS. CARLOS GUINLE
BOTAFOGO BOULEVARD
RIO DE JANEIRO, BRAZIL

CIRCA 1930
MR. AND MRS. OTTO EDUARDO
    BEMBERG
BUENOS AIRES, ARGENTINA

1931
COMPAGNIE DE NAVIGATION SUD
    ATLANTIQUE
L'ATLANTIQUE (1ST CLASS GRANDE
    SALON)
FRANCE

1931
WALDORF-ASTORIA HOTEL
PEACOCK ALLEY; JANSEN SUITE
NEW YORK CITY, USA

1932
BARON ROBERT DE ROTHSCHILD
23 AVENUE MARIGNY
PARIS, FRANCE

1932
COMPAGNIE GENERALE
    TRANSATLANTIQUE
NORMANDIE (COUTANCES SUITE)
FRANCE

1933
NANCY AND RONALD TREE
DITCHLEY PARK
ENSTONE, CHIPPING NORTON,
    OXFORDSHIRE, ENGLAND

CIRCA 1933
OLIVE, LADY BAILLIE
GROSVENOR SQUARE
LONDON, ENGLAND

1934
PRINCE REGENT PAUL OF YUGOSLAVIA
BELI DVOR
BELGRADE, YUGOSLAVIA

CIRCA 1934
SIR PHILIP SASSOON
25 PARK LANE
LONDON, ENGLAND

CIRCA 1934
SIR PHILIP SASSOON
PORT LYMPNE
LYMPNE, ENGLAND

CIRCA 1934
EDWARD, PRINCE OF WALES
ST. JAMES'S PALACE
LONDON, ENGLAND

1935
LADY HONOR AND SIR HENRY
    CHANNON
5 BELGRAVE SQUARE
LONDON, ENGLAND

1935
OLIVE AND SIR ADRIAN BAILLIE
LEEDS CASTLE
MAIDSTONE, KENT, ENGLAND

CIRCA 1935
SOLVEIG AND FRANCIS FRANCIS JR.
CHÂTEAU SOLVEIG
GLAND, SWITZERLAND

CIRCA 1935
ZEFIRA AND DANIEL NESSIM CURIEL
VILLA CURIEL
42 GABALAYA ST.
CAIRO, EGYPT

CIRCA 1935
COCO CHANEL
29 RUE DU FAUBOURG SAINT-HONORÉ
PARIS, FRANCE

CIRCA 1935
HELENA RUBINSTEIN
MOULIN DE BREUIL
COMBS-LA-VILLE, FRANCE

1936
KING EDWARD VIII
BUCKINGHAM PALACE
LONDON, ENGLAND

CIRCA 1936
LILIAN AND ALFONSO FANJUL JR.
HAVANA, CUBA

1937
HELENA RUBINSTEIN
24 QUAI DE BETHUNE
PARIS, FRANCE

1937
ALBERT PROUVOST
LE VERT BOIS
FRANCE

1937
MARCEL BOUSSAC
CHÂTEAU DE MIVOISIN
FRANCE

1938
LADY ELSIE AND SIR CHARLES MENDL
VILLA TRIANON
BOULEVARD ST. ANTOINE
VERSAILLES, FRANCE

1938
THE DUKE AND DUCHESS OF WINDSOR
CHÂTEAU DE LA CR`E
CAP D'ANTIBES, FRANCE

1938
CIE SUD ATLANTIQUE
PASTEUR
FRANCE

1938
THE DUKE AND DUCHESS OF WINDSOR
24 BOULEVARD SUCHET
PARIS, FRANCE

CIRCA 1938
MONA AND HARRISON WILLIAMS
IL FORTINO
CAPRI, ITALY

CIRCA 1938
ANTENOR PATINO
PARIS, FRANCE

CIRCA 1938
JORGE ORTIZ LINARES
PARIS, FRANCE

1939
FRENCH GOVERNMENT
NEW YORK WORLD'S FAIR
FLUSHING, QUEENS, NEW YORK, USA

CIRCA 1939
AUDREY AND HON. PETER PLEYDELL-
    BOUVERIE
THE HOLME, REGENT'S PARK
LONDON, ENGLAND

CIRCA 1940
HATTIE CARNEGIE AND JOHN ZANFT
1113 FIFTH AVENUE
NEW YORK CITY, USA

CIRCA 1940 LEONOR AND JUAN ALBERT
    MARCH ORDINAS
PALACIO MARCH
PALMA DE MALLORCA,
SPAIN

1942
AVA RIBBLESDALE
420 PARK AVENUE
NEW YORK, USA

1942
BANK OF ROMANIA
BUCHAREST, ROMANIA

CIRCA 1942
MR. AND MRS. GEORGE GREGORY
903 PARK AVENUE
NEW YORK CITY, USA

CIRCA 1942
BANK OF GERMANY
BERLIN, GERMANY

1944
EUTIMIO FALLA BONET
LA IGLESIA DE REMEDIOS
    (RESTORATION)
REMEDIOS, CUBA

CIRCA 1946
HARTA AND FRITZ MANDL
AVENIDA ALVEAR
BUENOS AIRES, ARGENTINA

CIRCA 1946
TAWFIKA AND CHERIF MOHAMMED
    SABRY
CAIRO, EGYPT

CIRCA 1946
ELIZABETH AND NINO LO SAVIO
825 FIFTH AVENUE
NEW YORK CITY, USA

CIRCA 1946
MARGARET THOMPSON BIDDLE
PARIS, FRANCE

CIRCA 1946
SUSAN AND CARLOS GUINLE JR.
RIO DE JANEIRO, BRAZIL

CIRCA 1946
GEORGIA AND EDWARD BEMBERG
NEW YORK CITY, USA

1947
ROBERTA AND ROBERT GOELET
845 FIFTH AVENUE
NEW YORK CITY, USA

1947
JAYNE AND CHARLES B. WRIGHTSMAN
513 NORTH COUNTY ROAD
PALM BEACH, FLORIDA, USA

CIRCA 1947
ROBERTA AND ROBERT GOELET
CHAMP SOLEIL
BELLEVIEW AVENUE
NEWPORT, RHODE ISLAND, USA

CIRCA 1948
LANCÔME BOUTIQUE
PARIS, FRANCE

CIRCA 1948
OMAR CHIRINE BEY
VILLA CURIEL
42 GABALAYA ST.
CAIRO, EGYPT

CIRCA 1948
MARGARET THOMPSON BIDDLE
NEW YORK CITY, USA

CIRCA 1950
ANITA AND ROBERT R. YOUNG
FAIRHOLME
NEWPORT, RHODE ISLAND, USA

CIRCA 1950
OLIVE, LADY BAILLIE
HARBOURSIDE
NASSAU, BAHAMAS

CIRCA 1950
MARGARET THOMPSON BIDDLE
LES EMBRUNS
SAINT-JEAN-CAP-FERRAT, FRANCE

CIRCA 1950
BARONESS RENEE DE BECKER
820 FIFTH AVENUE
NEW YORK CITY, USA

CIRCA 1950
ANITA AND ROBERT R. YOUNG
THE TOWERS
PALM BEACH, FLORIDA, USA

1952
GIANNI AGNELLI AND PAMELA
    CHURCHILL
LA LEOPOLDA
VILLEFRANCHE-SUR-MER, FRANCE

1952
THE DUKE AND DUCHESS OF WINDSOR
MOULIN DE LA TUILERIE
VALLJE DE CHEVREUSE, FRANCE

CIRCA 1952
KING LEOPOLD AND PRINCESS LILIAN
CHÂTEAU DE LAEKEN
BRUSSELS, BELGIUM

1954
THE DUKE AND DUCHESS OF WINDSOR
4 ROUTE DU CHAMPS D'ENTRAINEMENT
PARIS, FRANCE

CIRCA 1954
MARGUERITE AND GEORGE TYSON
LES ORMES, 4040 52ND ST. NW
WASHINGTON, D.C., USA

1955
JAYNE AND CHARLES B. WRIGHTSMAN
820 FIFTH AVENUE
NEW YORK CITY, USA

CIRCA 1955
GLORIA AND FRITZ MANDL
AVENIDA ALVEAR
BUENOS AIRES, ARGENTINA

CIRCA 1956
MR. AND MRS. STAVROS NIARCHOS
L'HOTEL DE CHANALEILLES
PARIS, FRANCE

1957
SUZY AND PIERRE DELBÉE
AVENUE FOCH
PARIS, FRANCE

CIRCA 1957
LORD GEOFFREY-LLOYD
77 CHESTER SQUARE
LONDON, ENGLAND

CIRCA 1958
BARBARA AND WILLIAM S. PALEY
KILUNA FARM
LONG ISLAND, NEW YORK, USA

CIRCA 1958
METROPOLITAN MUSEUM OF ART
WRIGHTSMAN GALLERIES/FIFTH
    AVENUE
NEW YORK CITY, USA

1959
MILDRED AND CHARLES ALLEN JR.
2 EAST 67TH STREET
NEW YORK CITY, USA

1959
KING LEOPOLD AND PRINCESS LILIAN
DOMAINE D'ARGENTEUIL
OHAIN, BELGIUM

1959
HARRY WINSTON, INC.
718 FIFTH AVENUE
NEW YORK CITY, USA

1959
C. Z. AND WINSTON GUEST
1 SUTTON PLACE
NEW YORK CITY, USA

CIRCA 1959
ANITA AND ROBERT R. YOUNG
FIFTH AVENUE
NEW YORK CITY, USA

1960
FRENCH AMBASSADOR'S RESIDENCE
2221 KALORAMA ROAD NW
WASHINGTON, D.C., USA

CIRCA 1960
HABIB BOURGUIBA
PRESIDENTIAL PALACE
CARTHAGE, TUNISIA

1961
HON. PAMELA AND LELAND HAYWARD
1020 FIFTH AVENUE
NEW YORK CITY, USA

1961
JACQUELINE AND JOHN F. KENNEDY
THE WHITE HOUSE
WASHINGTON, D.C., USA

1963
C. Z. AND WINSTON GUEST
TEMPLETON
ROSLYN, NEW YORK, USA

CIRCA 1963
ANNE AND HENRY FORD II
NEW YORK CITY, USA

CIRCA 1963
ANNE AND HENRY FORD II
30 BEVERLY ROAD
GROSSE POINTE, MICHIGAN, USA

CIRCA 1963
HON. PAMELA AND LELAND HAYWARD
HAYWIRE
MOUNT KISCO, NEW YORK, USA

CIRCA 1963
MRS. DOROTHY JOHNSTON KILLAM
LA LEOPOLDA
VILLEFRANCHE-SUR-MER, FRANCE

CIRCA 1963
DRUE AND HENRY J. HEINZ II
1 SUTTON PLACE
NEW YORK CITY, USA

CIRCA 1964
ALAN J. LERNER
NEW YORK CITY, USA

CIRCA 1964
ALEXANDRE (SOCIETY HAIRDRESSER)
BOULEVARD LANNES
PARIS, FRANCE

1965
MARITIN AND BARTOLOME MARCH
    SERVERA
PALACIO MARCH, MIGUEL ANGEL
MADRID, SPAIN

1965
BARBARA AND WILLIAM S. PALEY
820 FIFTH AVENUE
NEW YORK CITY, USA

CIRCA 1965
MRS. (ANITA) ROBERT R. YOUNG
MONTSORREL
PALM BEACH, FLORIDA, USA

1966
MARITIN AND BARTOLOMÉ MARCH
    SERVERA
13 CONQUISTADOR
PALMA DE MALLORCA, SPAIN

CIRCA 1966
HELAINE AND VICTOR J. BARNETT
EAST 72ND STREET
NEW YORK CITY, USA

CIRCA 1967
AILSA MELLON-BRUCE
960 FIFTH AVENUE
NEW YORK CITY, USA

CIRCA 1968
SHAH OF IRAN
NIAVARAN PALACE
TEHRAN, IRAN

CIRCA 1968
MRS. WATSON BLAIR
834 FIFTH AVENUE
NEW YORK CITY, USA

1969-72
ZIUTA AND J. JAMES AKSTON
LA RONDA
444 NORTH LAKE WAY
PALM BEACH, FLORIDA
(ARCHITECTURAL DESIGN AND CONCEPT
    BY PIERRE DELBÉE)

1970
MARITIN AND BARTOLOMÉ MARCH
    SERVERA
APARTMENT, CASTELLANA
MADRID, SPAIN

CIRCA 1970
MARITIN AND BARTOLOMÉ MARCH
    SERVERA
CASA MARCH (TORRE CEGA), CALA
    RATJADA
MAJORCA, SPAIN

CIRCA 1970
BARTOLOMÉ MARCH SERVERA
OFFICES OF URALITA
MADRID, SPAIN

CIRCA 1970
MARITA AND ALFONSO FIERRO
PUERTA DE HIERRO
SOMONTES, SPAIN

CIRCA 1970
MARITA AND ALFONSO FIERRO
APARTMENT, CASTELLANA
MADRID, SPAIN

1971
SHAH OF IRAN/2,500TH ANNIVERSARY
    OF EMPIRE
ANCIENT RUINS AT PERSEPOLIS
PERSEPOLIS, IRAN

CIRCA 1972
ALFONSO FIERRO
HOTEL VILLA MAGNA
MADRID, SPAIN

INTRODUCTION

1. Claude Mandron to James Abbott, interview held in Paris, February 5, 1999.

2. The rue Royale address later became the home of Musée Bouilhet-Christofle and the main showroom of the silver company Christofle.

3. Antoinette Berveiller and Gérard Bonal, eds., *Jansen Décoration* (Paris: Société d'Etudes et de Publications Economiques, 1971), 15.

4. Pauline C. Metcalf, ed., *Ogden Codman and the Decoration of Houses* (Boston: Boston Athenaeum/D. R. Godine, 1988), 80.

5. Simas was noted for his Art Nouveau faience tiles, many of which were produced in association with Sarreguemines, the French ceramics manufacturer. He also created advertising art for the cookie manufacturer Lefèvre-Utile.

6. "Decoration, Antiquités: Jansen," 1922, an article on the Jansen firm from an unidentified publication. Collection of Brigitte Boudin de Laage de Meux, Paris.

7. Published in the magazine *The Decorative Furnisher,* the article listed Fred Esturge, Roger Sherman, and Richard Bennett Jr., as the managing partners of this American annex. With at least two of the three men having law degrees, Esturge, Sherman, and Bennett administered the establishment of a number of businesses in New York. They were not associated with Maison Jansen specifically or directly.

8. *The New York Times,* October 26, 1915, p. 19: "Commodore Morton F. Plant's former home at 25 West Fifty-fourth Street, near the Rockefeller residences, has been claimed for business. The property, which consists of a five-story American basement dwelling on a lot of 25 by 100, has been leased by William B. May & Co. as brokers to Jansen, Inc., art dealers, of Paris. Extensive alterations to the premises will be made by the lessees." Jansen, Inc. appears to have moved from this location within the year, although it continued to maintain a gallery of antiques in its subsequent business address of 1 East 57th Street, as well as at 42 East 57th Street.

9. "Decoration, Antiquités: Jansen," 1922, p. 5.

10. Ibid.

11. Although completed, the ship, *Pasteur,* did not serve its intended role as a passenger liner until after World War II.

12. Samir Raafat to James Abbott, e-mail communication, May 6, 2005. Raafat is considered the leading authority regarding the social and architectural histories of modern Egypt.

13. News clipping titled "El Titular de la Firma, Jansen Arribará Mañana," undated (c. mid-1950s), includes ". . . y el ex rey Faruk," in a listing of Stéphane Boudin's clients. Collection of Brigitte Boudin de Laage de Meux. Boudin did travel to Egypt more than once, as his daughter noted one trip when the deco-

rator was accompanied by his wife. Brigitte Boudin de Laage de Meux to James Abbott, interview held in Paris, February 4, 1999.

14. Among the sources to make reference to Edward VII's patronage of Jansen is Berveiller and Bonal, *Jansen Décoration,* 16.

15. Letterhead also noted the following: "DIRECTORS: STEPHANE BOUDIN (FRENCH). OLIVER FORD (BRITISH)." Collection of Brigitte de Laage de Meux, Paris.

16. Claude Mandron to James Abbott, interview held in Paris, February 5, 1999.

17. Brigitte Boudin de Laage de Meux to James Abbott, interview held in Paris, January 27, 2000.

18. Claude Mandron to James Abbott, interview held in Paris, February 5, 1999.

19. Meyer (1898–1979) married Bella Lehman. Their Jansen-decorated apartment was located in the Hotel Carlyle in New York City.

20. This credit is based on recollections of Jansen employees Paul Manno and Albert Ernandez, as well as Brigitte Boudin de Laage de Meux, as told to James Abbott in 1999 and 2000. On June 21, 1937, Schwartz sent a letter to Jansen, Inc.'s director, Chaillou, to clearly describe the details of the Château Solveig commission for publication in a magazine. The fact that the letter came from the then former president of the firm, and accompanied his highly detailed descriptions of the house's rooms, further attests to his being the creator of the decoration. This letter is in a private collection.

21. This woodwork was sold back to Maison Jansen when the Sassoon residence was demolished in the mid-1950s. It was subsequently acquired by Jansen clients Jayne and Charles Wrightsman and later donated by them to the Metropolitan Museum of Art.

22. Gabrielle van Zuylen, *Gardens of Russell Page* (New York: Stewart, Tabori & Chang, 1991), 26.

23. Lady Baillie's London residence eventually was demolished to make way for a new American embassy.

24. Janet Flanner, "Handsprings across the Sea," *The New Yorker,* January 15, 1938.

25. Ibid., 64.

26. Claude Mandron to James Abbott, interview held in Paris, February 5, 1999.

27. At the same time, Elsie de Wolfe (Lady Mendl) had been asked to present redecorating concepts for Fort Belvedere, Edward VIII's favorite country house.

28. Brigitte Boudin de Laage de Meux to James Abbott, interview held in Paris, January 27, 2000.

29. Claude Mandron to James Abbott, interview held in Paris, February 5, 1999.

30. Ibid.

31. Children of Victoire Camille Gautier and Alexandre Boudin: Cecile, born 1885; Stéphane, born 1888; André, born 1891.

32. Brigitte Boudin de Laage de Meux to James Abbott, interview held in Paris, February 4, 1999.

33. Jayne Wrightsman to James Abbott, interview held in London, August 28, 2000.

34. Paul Manno to James Abbott, interview held in New York, April 23, 1996.

35. Claude Mandron to James Abbott, interview held in Paris, February 5, 1999.

36. Boudin's wife traveled to Austria and Egypt with her husband. Brigitte Boudin de Laage de Meux to James Abbott, telephone conversation, April 30, 2004.

37. Paul Manno to James Abbott, interview held in New York, April 23, 1996.

38. Brigitte and her husband opened in 1972 the last Jansen boutique in Geneva, Switzerland, with the permission of then Jansen president Pierre Deshays. It closed in 1983. Brigitte Boudin de Laage de Meux to James Abbott, telephone conversation, April 30, 2004.

39. The painter Eugène Boudin (1824–1898) was not a relation of Stéphane Boudin.

40. La Chatellerie was purchased by Boudin in 1948 and sold in 1955. Rochebonne, a smaller house of white stone built into a hillside, with terraced gardens, was sold by Boudin's wife and daughter after his death in 1967.

41. Etienne Drian (1885–1961), a popular society artist patronized by Jansen clients such as the Duchess of Windsor, Audrey Pleydell-Bouverie, and Lady Mendl, also was the former owner of an old mill near Paris that Boudin decorated as a country house for the Windsors.

42. Albert Ernandez to James Abbott, interview held in Paris, January 28, 2000.

43. Ibid.

44. Benoist F. Drut to James Abbott, e-mail communication, September 15, 2004. Drut interviewed Françoise Siriex, a former assistant to designer André Leleu, on September 12, 2004. In this interview, Siriex identified Poubelle as "the son of Mr. [Eugène] Poubelle, [the chief of police in Grenoble and Paris] who invented the garbage can in France, also known as 'poubelle' [in 1884]." Per Siriex, the younger Poubelle was in charge of the drawing studio of Jansen, prior to if not also after World War II.

45. Albert Ernandez to the author, interview held in Paris, January 28, 2000.

46. *Five Centuries of French History Mirrored in Five Centuries of French Art, New York World's Fair, 1939, Pavillon de la France* (France: Groupe de l'Art Ancien, 1939), 7.

47. Claude Mandron to James Abbott, interview held in Paris, February 5, 1999. As Stéphane Boudin's nephew and a former employee of Jansen, Mandron knew the inner workings of the firm. He witnessed the protective shifting of furniture from one department to another during the German occupation of France.

48. Carlos A. Rosas, "When Louis Quinze Conquered New York," *Quest* (November 1996):69.

49. Alfred Fabre-Luce, *Journal de la France, août 1940–avril 1942* (Paris: Imprimerie JEP, 1942), 144–45. This quotation was discovered by the author in Dominique Veillon's *Fashion under the Occupation* (Oxford, UK: Berg, 2002), 36.

50. This paneled room remained in locked storage until the mid-1970s, after which it vanished. Serge Robin and Brigitte Boudin de Laage de Meux to James Abbott, interview held in Paris, January 27, 2000.

51. Allied debriefing of Stéphane Boudin, September 26, 1944. Collection of Brigitte Boudin de Laage de Meux.

52. Boudin acquired this automobile from Pierre Delbée. Brigitte Boudin de Laage de Meux to James Abbott, interview held in Paris, February 4, 1999.

53. Brigitte Boudin de Laage de Meux to James Abbott, interview held in Paris, January 27, 2000.

54. Cora Maria Antinori, Patrician of Florence (1896–1974), was the daughter of Marchese Piero Antinori and his wife, Nathalie Fabbri. She married, in 1920, Don Michelangelo Caetani de Sermoneta.

55. Daughter of a Belgian banker and a Rothschild heiress, Baroness Renée Lambert (1899–1987) was the former wife of Baron Paul de Becker-Remy (1897–1953). She and her distant cousin and lover, Goldschmidt-Rothschild (1899–1987), moved during World War II to New York, where they sold furniture and art objects and became successful real estate investors. Her former home in Brussels, which was decorated by Jansen, is now the British embassy.

56. John Walker, *Self-Portrait with Donors: Confessions of an Art Collector* (Boston: Little, Brown, 1974), 255.

57. Ibid.

58. Ibid.

59. Stéphane Boudin to Brigitte Boudin, May 24, 1954, collection of Brigitte Boudin de Laage de Meux.

60. Jacqueline Kennedy to Stéphane Boudin, March 8, 1963, collection of Brigitte Boudin de Laage de Meux.

61. Jayne Wrightsman to James Abbott, interview held in London, August 28, 2000.

62. Arthur Bennett Kouwenhoven to James Abbott, interview held in Savannah, Georgia, November 10, 2004.

63. "Paris, New York, Buenos Aires, Milan" are listed on the letterhead included in an April 27, 1967, statement sent to Lady Baillie at Lowndes House, Lowndes Place, London. Apparently Buenos Aires was reestablished as a Jansen satellite in the mid-1960s, but this time as a franchise boutique.

64. According to Paul Manno and Arthur Bennett Kouwenhoven, "Plain Grounds," by Katzenbach and Warren, Inc., served as the palette for most of Jansen, Inc.'s work. The three-by-four-inch "pocket" booklet included a "complete current collection of plain clay grounds, including the approved Williamsburg Colors." Author's collection.

65. Arthur Bennett Kouwenhoven to James Abbott, telephone interview, February 1, 2005.

66. Leon Amar to James Abbott, interview held in Palm Beach, February 2003.

67. Leon Amar to James Abbott, e-mail communication, February 19, 2005.

68. Ibid.

69. In 1972 and 1973, Ortiz was listed in display advertisements published in *The New York Times*. The October 26, 1973, ad, p. 29, says, "Jansen, Inc./Carlos Ortiz, Director/25 E. 55 St." In 1974, Ortiz moved, but he advertised the same information in a multiple display advertisement, noting Jansen, Inc.'s new address as "55 East 57 Street"; see the September 29, 1974, issue, p. 418.

70. Françoise Arnaud to James Abbott, e-mail communication, February 21, 2005.

71. Benoist F. Drut to James Abbott, e-mail communication, September 15, 2004. Drut interviewed Françoise Siriex, a former assistant to designer André Leleu, on September 12, 2004.

72. Ibid.

73. Ibid.

74. Pierre Deshays, interview published with the introduction of the Jansen Collections, c. 1972. Courtesy of Liz O'Brien, New York.

75. Ibid.

CHÂTEAU DE LAECKEN

1. Jacqueline Kennedy to Stéphane Boudin, March 8, 1963, collection of Brigitte Boudin de Laage de Meux.

2. Though designed by Wailly (1729–1798), the plans of what was originally called Château de Schonenberg were executed by architectural contractor Louis Montoyer (1749–1811).

3. Some of the furniture, whose cabinetmakers included Jean-Joseph Chapui, used the then-pioneering technology of steam-bent and laminated wood. Napoleon's second wife, Marie Louise, used the château as her residence in 1811, when the emperor sent her on a state tour.

4. The king chose to live at Laeken, reportedly, because Château de Stuyvenberg was too full of memories of his late wife. As a result of this change of addresses, Stuyvenberg became known for its use as a dower residence by the widowed queens Elisabeth (widow of Albert I and mother of Leopold III) and Fabiola (widow of Baudouin).

5. "A Royal Palace Burned," *The New York Times*, January 2, 1890, p. 1.

6. "King Leopold's Gift," *The New York Times*, May 1, 1900, p. 10.

7. After the restoration of Château de Laeken, Girault (1851–1932) also designed the Musée du Congo (now the Royal Museum for Central Africa) for Leopold II.

8. "Belgian Socialists' Attacks on Leopold," *The New York Times*, July 19, 1903, p. 19. It is possible that Jansen also worked on several other Belgian royal houses that were being built or remodeled at the time of the restoration of Château de Laeken, including Leopold II's villa at the seaside resort of Ostend and his house on the French Riviera, Villa Les Cèdres. The firm presumably decorated a house next door to Château de Laeken, which the king had built for his mistress, and later morganatic wife, Blanche Delacroix, Baroness de Vaughan, as well as two houses in France

that she shared with the king, Château de Balincourt, near Arrenville, and Château de Lormoy, near Longpont-sur-Orge.

9. "Leopold's One Hope Hangs on Operation," *The New York Times*, December 14, 1909, p. 10. Among the many items controversially sold by the king were paintings by Turner, Millet, Ingres, and Carolus-Duran.

DE REVILLA DE CAMARGO

1. Another niece, Lillian Gomez Mena, consolidated the family's financial and social positions by marrying the Cuban sugar king Alfonso Fanjul Sr.

DITCHLEY PARK

1. Churchill famously replied that if she were his wife, he would drink it.

2. In 1917, Nancy Keene Perkins married Ronald Tree's first cousin Henry Marshall Field, who died five months later after a botched operation to remove his tonsils. In 1948, a year after she and Tree divorced, she married her longtime lover, Lt. Col. Claude Granville Lancaster; they divorced in 1951. In 1947, Ronald Tree married, as his second wife, Marietta Peabody FitzGerald (1917–1991), who became a member of the United Nations Commission on Human Rights.

3. Robert Becker, *Nancy Lancaster: Her Life, Her World, Her Art* (New York: Alfred A. Knopf, 1996), 192.

4. Ibid., 204–5.

5. Ibid., 201.

6. Brigitte Boudin de Laage de Meux to James Abbott, interview held in Paris, January 27, 2000. The Boudin trimmings company produced tapes, galloon, fringe, and tassels for a number of important Jansen commissions. It also manufactured trimmings for the palace restorations at Versailles, specifically the Royal Theatre. This specific relationship has been misinterpreted in other histories to mean that Stéphane Boudin and Maison Jansen were involved with these important restorations. According to de Laage, it was André Boudin, Stéphane's younger brother and head of the Boudin firm, who actually was involved at Versailles.

7. Becker, *Nancy Lancaster*, 201.

8. Claude Mandron to James Abbott, interview held in Paris, February 5, 1999.

9. Seymour Egerton, seventh Earl of Wilton (1921–1999)

10. Sir David Wills (1917–1999). At the time the house was sold to Sir David, many of its Boudin-era contents were sold back to Nancy Lancaster.

BELI DVOR

1. Although this aesthetic interest may have been a personal preference, the Yugoslavian royal family was intimately connected with England, through marriage as well as education. The prince regent's sister-in-law Marina was married to Prince George, Duke of Kent, a brother of the Duke of Windsor; and King Alexander I's widow, the former Princess Marie ("Mignon") of Romania, was a great-granddaughter of Queen Victoria.

2. Prior to becoming the first king of Yugoslavia in 1929,

Alexander (1888–1934) was known as the king of the Serbs, Croats, and Slovenes.

3. Robert Rhodes James, ed., *Chips: The Diaries of Sir Henry Channon* (London: Phoenix Press, 2003), 285.

4. Ibid.

5. Ibid.

SOLVEIG AND FRANCIS FRANCIS

1. Dated June 13, 1937. Private collection.

2. Office memorandum, possibly a draft for a press release, 1937. Stamped on reverse: "Jansen Inc., New York." Private collection.

3. Francis' thrice-married mother, Evelyn Bostwick, was the daughter of Jabez Abel Bostwick, a founding partner of Standard Oil. Francis' elder half-sister was Marion "Joe" Carstairs (1900–1993), a crossdressing champion speedboat racer who romanced Marlene Dietrich and Tallulah Bankhead.

4. Gustave Peyrot (1885–1962) and Albert Bourrit (1878–1967).

5. In 1989, Château Solveig and its interiors were used as settings for the movie *Nouvelle Vague* (released 1990), by director Jean-Luc Godard.

6. As of 2005, the present owner of the house had embarked on a full-scale restoration.

LADY HONOR AND HENRY CHANNON

1. Robert Rhodes James, ed., *Chips: The Diaries of Sir Henry Channon* (London: Phoenix, 2003), 38.

2. Their wedding, at St. Margaret's Church, Westminster, was attended by the former king of Greece.

3. Chips Channon represented Southend-on-Sea, continuing the Guinness family's representation of the constituency in Parliament, which lasted without a break from 1912 to 1997.

4. James, *Chips,* 38.

5. The remainder of the house had been assigned to Dolly Mann, a London decorator, and Gerald Wellesley, seventh Duke of Wellington, an architect and close friend of Channon.

6. James, *Chips,* 37.

7. Queen Mary visited 5 Belgrave Square on July 17, 1936. Per the diary of Chips Channon, the queen stayed in the room for "quite twenty minutes," admiring the impressive decor, especially the small black dining room.

8. The dining room, plus the two smaller anterooms, cost the Channons £6,000, at the time approximately $30,000.

9. James, *Chips,* 38.

THE HON. LADY BAILLIE

1. Lady Baillie's only sibling was the Hon. Dorothy Wyndham Paget (1905–1960), a prominent owner of racehorses, including Straight Deal, which won the 1943 Derby. Unlike her elegant elder sister, she was "inordinately shy, largely through an aversion to men. Usually dressed in a large grey overcoat that came down almost to her ankles. . . . To avoid being accosted by strangers, the racing press and almost anybody else, she surrounded herself with a bevy of female secretaries" (Roger Mortimer et al., *Biographical Encyclopaedia of British Flat Racing* [London: Macdonald and Janes, 1978], 436). She owned the famous Ballymacoll Stud, a horse farm near Dunboyne, Ireland.

2. Named for an aunt who had died in childhood, Olive Baillie was exceedingly well connected. An uncle was married to Gertrude Vanderbilt Whitney, the founder of the Whitney Museum of American Art. Her mother's sister was Dorothy (Whitney) Straight Elmhirst, a cofounder of *The New Republic* magazine and the New School for Social Research. Her first cousins included John Hay Whitney, who became a U.S. ambassador to the Court of St. James's; Joan Whitney Payson, owner and president of the New York Mets baseball team; and the American stage and film actress Beatrice Straight. Her maternal grandfather, William Whitney, declined to stand as the Democratic candidate for the United States presidency in 1892. She also inherited money from her great-uncle Oliver Hazard Payne, a partner in Standard Oil.

3. "Leeds Castle, Centuries Old, Will Be Occupied Again," *The New York Times,* March 13, 1927, p. XX10.

4. *Leeds Castle, Maidstone, Kent* (Kent, UK: Leeds Castle Foundation, 1996), 25.

5. Jayne Wrightsman to James Abbott, interview held in London, August 28, 2000. Wrightsman spoke of Lady Baillie's fondness for lists for every aspect of her life.

6. David A. H. Cleggett, *History of Leeds Castle and Its Families* (Kent, UK: Leeds Castle Foundation, 1994), 209.

7. Lady Baillie's daughters, both from her first marriage, were Pauline Katherine Winn (1920–1983) and Susan Mary Sheila Winn (1923–2001). She also had one son, Gawaine Baillie (1934–2003), who succeeded his father as seventh baronet.

THE *PASTEUR*

1. The *Ile de France* was 43,450 tons; the *Normandie* was 83,423 tons.

2. Brigitte Boudin de Laage de Meux to James Abbott, interview held in Paris, January 27, 2000.

3. These photographs were owned by Brigitte Boudin de Laage de Meux, but following her 2004 death, they disappeared.

AUDREY AND HON. PETER PLEYDELL-BOUVERIE

1. It had previously been the home of Sir George Dance (1858–1932), a theatrical producer known as the Napoleon of touring companies, and his wife, Grace.

2. *Time,* December 5, 1938.

3. She had no children by any of her three marriages but adopted a son, Jeremy James, after her divorce from Pleydell-Bouverie.

4. Paul Phipps married, in 1909, Nora Langhorne, the youngest sister of Lizzie Langhorne Perkins, Nancy Tree's mother.

5. Allied debriefing of Stéphane Boudin, September 26, 1944. Collection of Brigitte Boudin de Laage de Meux.

6. John Cornforth, *London Interiors from the Archives of Country Life* (London: Aurum Press, 2000), p. 153.

7. After Pleydell-Bouverie's departure, the house became the property of Bedford College, London University. In 1984 it was sold, reputedly to a member of the Kuwaiti royal family, and turned back into a private home. Her country house, Julians, presently is owned by her son, Captain Jeremy James.

HATIE CARNEGIE AND JOHN ZANFT

1. The 15-story apartment building was constructed in 1928, to the designs of architect Emery Roth.

2. Arthur Bennett Kouwenhoven to James Abbott, interview held in Savannah, Georgia, November 11, 2004.

3. Christian Dior's so-called New Look held no appeal for Carnegie, however, and she had no interest in adapting it for her clientele, calling it disfiguring and lacking in romance.

4. The couple also had a Revolutionary-era farm of 117 acres near Red Bank, New Jersey, which Carnegie purchased in 1937 after selling her house in Deal, a resort on the Jersey shore.

5. Carnegie preferred off-white rooms at home and on her business premises because they did not distract from a woman's clothing.

6. The Windsors, however, eventually were discomfited by the glare of the mirrored top of their dining table and soon replaced it with one of polished wood.

7. Born in humble circumstances as Ann Crowell (d. 1975), Woodward was a fashion model and sometime showgirl when she married banking heir and racehorse owner William Woodward Jr. in 1943. She shot her husband to death in 1955, reportedly mistaking him for an unknown intruder. Despite the fact that Long Island's monied communities were being plagued by a particularly persistent burglar at the time, most observers believed that Ann Woodward was responsible for her husband's murder. A burglar named Paul Wirths admitted that he had been in the Woodward's house that night and heard the shots. After a lengthy and much-publicized trial, she was exonerated and eventually committed suicide.

AVA RIBBLESDALE

1. "Americans Getting Best English Houses," *The New York Times,* September 3, 1911, p. C2. Ava Astor remodeled and redecorated the house at a reported cost of $50,000. ("Coronation to Draw 100,000 Americans," *The New York Times,* March 19, 1911, p. 13.) In 1944, after Lady Ribblesdale moved to New York, Regent's Lodge, which is located at 146 Park Road, became the Islamic Cultural Centre and London Central Mosque.

2. Vincent Astor was definitely the couple's child, but the parentage of their daughter, Alice, was much debated. The rumors were considered justified when it was reported that John Jacob Astor IV's will made no provision for his 10-year-old daughter.

3. The king reportedly thought that Lord Ribblesdale looked like a Regency aristocrat come to life. It was an observation with which many observers agreed, particularly after the unveiling of a dashing portrait of Lord Ribblesdale by John Singer Sargent in 1902.

4. However, she continued to be listed as Lady Ribblesdale in the New York City telephone directory and was widely known in New York society as Lady Rib.

5. The Coromandel screen that was likely the one used in the living room brought $5,750.

LYDIA AND GEORGE H. GREGORY

1. "Four Renters Pick Park Avenue Units," *The New York Times,* April 16, 1941, p. 42.

2. "George S. Gregory," *The New York Times,* May 7, 1983, p. B10. Involved in real-estate development in the United States and France, Gregory was the president of Gregory-Roth-Schenker Corporation and received the Legion of Honor in 1957 for helping to construct 10,000 prefabricated houses in France following World War II. In the 1950s, his firm was a partner in a plan, ultimately thwarted, that would have demolished Carnegie Hall and replaced it with a 44-story office tower. A third son, Peter, was born after the family's relocation to New York City.

3. It reputedly was the tallest apartment building in the world when newly constructed. "Apartment Renting Season Now at Its Height," *The New York Times,* September 21, 1913, p. X10.

4. The Gregorys also were known for their art collection.

ROBERTA AND ROBERT GOELET

1. Grace Graham Wilson (1870–1953) was the wife of General Cornelius Vanderbilt III (1873–1942) and was a noted New York hostess. Mary (May) Goelet (1878–1937) was the wife of Henry Innes-Ker, eighth Duke of Roxburghe.

2. Robert Goelet was married three times: to Elsie Whelen (married 1904, divorced 1914), Fernanda Rocchi Riabouchinsky (married 1919, divorced 1924), and Roberta Willard (married 1925).

3. La Lanterne, a pavilion in the park of Versailles, has been a popular inspiration for architects of American country houses. Noted for being only one room deep, it gets its name from the fact that the windows of the front and rear facades are arranged directly opposite one another, so that the house can be seen through like a lantern. It once served as the country house of David K. E. Bruce, a U.S. ambassador to France in the 1950s.

4. Irene Aitken to James Abbott, Interview held in New York, January 14, 2004.

5. James Gordon Douglas Jr. (1908–1990) married, in 1966, as his fourth wife, Mary Lummus Krumling.

6. By her first marriage to George Washington Crawford, Annie-Laurie Aitken (née Warmack, 1899–1985) was the mother of heiress Martha "Sunny" von Bulow, whose mysterious lapse into a coma resulted in a celebrated attempted-murder trial in the 1980s. She married Russell Aitken (1910–2002) in 1957.

MARGARET THOMPSON BIDDLE

1. Located at 11 East 73rd Street, in a McKim, Mead & White mansion that was built in 1902 for the newspaper publisher Joseph Pulitzer, Biddle's New York apartment included a red-and-white tented dressing room that was reminiscent of the Duchess of Windsor's dressing room at Château de La Cröe. Elsewhere in

the rooms were sofas upholstered in leopard-print fabric and gilt-brass tables of the kind that had become a staple of the Maison Jansen enterprise.

2. "Margaret Biddle Is Dead in Paris," *The New York Times,* June 9, 1956, p. 17.

3. She married, in 1916, Theodore M. Schulze (1891–1936), an investment banker from St. Paul, Minnesota. They divorced in 1926, after having two children, Theodore and Margaret. Initial reports put her father's estate at $85 million, but two years later, appraisers assigned it a much lesser value.

4. She and Biddle had one child, a son, who was born in 1933 and died soon after birth.

5. The collection included caryatid candelabra by Paul Storr, Nymphenburg knight figurines, and a covered tureen that was a gift from Louis XV of France to Frederick the Great of Prussia. During the Kennedy administration, numerous items from the Biddle bequest were displayed on tables and mantelpieces throughout the state rooms of the White House. "First Lady Puts Treasure Items on View at White House Tours," *The New York Times,* February 26, 1961, p. 45.

6. Prior to becoming a dedicated Jansen client, Biddle worked with several decorators, including Ruby Ross Wood (1880–1950).

7. Soon after Biddle's death, rumors began to circulate that her death might have been linked to "L'Affaire Lacaze," a criminal scandal involving the widow of a Moroccan mining millionaire, a call girl, false accusations of procuring, and attempted murder. A 2004 article in *Vanity Fair,* written by the art historian John Richardson, revisited the case and strongly indicated that Biddle had been murdered.

8. Much of her art collection was sold at Galerie Charpentier in Paris on June 14, 1957. It included works by Corot, Gauguin, Monet, Van Dongen, and Matisse, and more than 14 Renoirs.

HARBOURSIDE, THE HON. LADY BAILLIE

1. In 1962, Huntington Hartford, the A&P Grocery heir, gave Hog Island a new name, Paradise Island, and began developing much of its 862 acres into a luxury resort.

JAYNE AND CHARLES B. WRIGHTSMAN

1. Jane Larkin changed the spelling of her first name to Jayne when she was a high school student.

2. John Walker, *Self-Portrait with Donors: Confessions of an Art Collector* (Boston: Little, Brown, 1974), p. 255.

3. Van Risamburgh, 1696–1766.

4. Etienne Meunier (dates unknown) was a master chair maker by 1732. He is recorded as having made pieces in both the Louis XV and Louis XVI styles.

5. Sir Francis J. B. Watson (1907–1992) was curator and later director of the Wallace Collection in London (1937–74). He produced the five-volume catalogue of the Charles B. Wrightsman Collection for the Metropolitan Museum of Art between 1966 and 1973. John Walker, *Self-Portrait with Donors,* p. 259.

6. Rita Reif, "Wrightsmans' Furniture Collection and Palm Beach Mansion to Be Sold," *The New York Times,* February 2, 1984, p. C1.

7. Peter C. Wilson, Introduction, *Property from the Collection of Mrs. Charles Wrightsman, Removed from her Palm Beach Residence,* Sotheby's, New York, Saturday, May 5, 1984.

8. Jayne Wrightsman to Madame Boudin, undated (1967). Collection of Brigitte Boudin de Laage de Meux.

MARGUERITE AND GEORGE TYSON

1. The architect of the house is unknown, but it was built by a prominent Washington contracting company, W. C. and A. N. Miller, which was responsible for many of the houses in neighborhoods such as Cleveland Park and Wesley Heights and at the time had two staff architects, B. F. Meyers and G. R. MacNeil. A son of Mary Beecher Longyear, a philanthropic Christian Scientist noted for funding of the study of ancient Hebrew religious manuscripts, Robert Dudley Longyear served as United States consul to Port-au-Prince, Haiti; Lucerne, Switzerland; Munich, Germany; and Marseilles, France.

2. Spelling of "mostes" as per Perle Mesta's memoirs.

3. The Johnsons and their two daughters were temporarily residing at the Wardman Park Hotel after having sold their house in a Washington suburb. Upon acquiring the house, the Johnsons renamed it The Elms, because, as the vice president stated, every time the house was described as a château or its Frenchness was emphasized, it lost him 50,000 votes back home in Texas.

4. J. B. West, *Upstairs at the White House: My Life with the First Ladies* (New York: Coward, McCann & Geoghegan, 1973), 299.

5. Until Mesta's appointment, American relations with Luxembourg were the responsibility of the U.S. ambassador to neighboring Belgium. Though many observers believed that Mesta had been selected for the post as a result of her prominence in the Democratic Party, she often pointed out that Luxembourg was a major producer of steel, which made her experience in the Pennsylvania steel industry as valuable as her skills as a political hostess.

6. She appeared in silent films such as *Port of Missing Men* (1914), *Aristocracy* (1914), *The Rise of Susan* (1916), and *A Parisian Romance* (1916).

7. She changed her political affiliation from Republican to Democrat in 1940.

8. Telephone interview with Elizabeth Ellis, May 12, 2005. It was presumably Boudin's redecoration of the Legation residence that a visiting reporter described as being executed in "a cozy modern style with striped upholstery and flowery drapes." (Flora Lewis, "Madame Minister to Luxembourg," *New York Times,* December 25, 1949, p. SM8.)

9. Marguerite Tyson's daughter, Elizabeth Ellis, has disputed this oft-told tale. It is possible, however, that a living room of the proper size was created to hold the carpet, because the Tysons had the house gutted and remodeled before moving in.

10. Perle Mesta, *Perle: My Story* (New York: McGraw-Hill, 1960), 211. Mesta's description of the silk used on the walls may have been a misinterpretation of what her sister and Boudin had actually purchased. Mesta was presumably not greatly involved with the decoration of the house, and she did not consider herself

to be a connoisseur of antiques. It is assumed that this silk was a modern adaptation or reproduction of an 18th-century document. Some sources describe it as brocatelle or imitation brocade.

11. George O'Brien, "France and Texas Contribute to Decor in the Johnsons' Washington Home," *The New York Times,* October 31, 1961, p. 24.

12. Ibid, p. 211.

13. Ibid.

14. It is also possible that Boudin advised Marguerite Tyson to avoid tapestries because of their propensity to absorb food odors.

15. Jacqueline Kennedy to Jayne Wrightsman, undated, John F. Kennedy Library.

16. After the house was sold, Perle Mesta and Marguerite and George Tyson took over a floor of a Washington apartment building and moved to it the Boudin decorations from Les Ormes.

17. "Johnson House Is Bought for Algerian Ambassador," *The New York Times,* May 9, 1964, p. 17.

SUZY AND PIERRE DELBÉE

1. Rubestück (1723-1782)

2. Souren Melikian, "Monaco Sales Show Up French Dilemma," The International Herald Tribune, 18 December 1999, p. 8.

THE WRIGHTSMAN GALLERIES

1. For greater detail, see *Period Rooms in The Metropolitan Museum of Art* (New York: Harry N. Abrams, 1996), 77–115.

2. Jayne Wrightsman to Stéphane Boudin, October 25, 1966. Collection of Brigitte Boudin de Laage de Meux.

3. Ibid.

4. Gabriel (1667–1742), the fifth of his family to bear the name Jean, was the premier architect of Versailles; his son, Jacques-Ange Gabriel (1698–1782), succeeded him in this office and became famed as the designer of the Petit Trianon.

5. In 1923, Coco Chanel took an apartment within Count Pillet-Will's hôtel particulier and employed Maison Jansen to decorate its primary rooms.

6. Duveen Brothers was counted among the world's finest art dealers from the late 19th century to the mid-20th, maintaining galleries in New York, London, and Paris. The firm is credited with bringing high-quality European old master paintings and decorative arts to America. Beginning with Joseph Duveen (1869–1939), the firm dominated the art world for half a century, advising some of America's most prominent collectors, including Henry Clay Frick, Henry Edwards Huntington, and Andrew Mellon.

7. Jansen eventually sold the early-19th-century green and white marble mantelpiece with carved eagle ornament to the White House for inclusion in the Yellow Oval Room. However, it presumably was deemed too small for that space, because after being slightly reconfigured, the mantelpiece was installed in the mansion's Family Dining Room, where it remains.

8. Jayne Wrightsman to Stéphane Boudin, October 25, 1966. Collection of Brigitte Boudin de Laage de Meux.

9. Georges Jacob (1739–1814), Jacques-Jean-Baptiste Tilliard (1723–1798), Guillaume Beneman (active 1785–92), and Jean-Henri Riesener (1734–1806).

10. John Russell, "Art: Rooms with a View to the Past," *The New York Times,* May 20, 1977, p. 72.

11. Jayne Wrightsman to Stéphane Boudin, October 25, 1966. Collection of Brigitte Boudin de Laage de Meux.

12. It is important to recognize that Jansen's installation of the 18th-century paneling did not conform to the original period room proportions. As noted in the text, additional doors, surrounds, and panels were added to satisfy the requirements for exhibition galleries. Thus, Jansen and their clients were not so much interested in period rooms as in period-style backdrops for the fine and decorative arts collections.

DOMAINE D'ARGENTEUIL

1. The house is occasionally, and incorrectly, called Château d'Argenteuil. That name properly belongs to the former Château de Meeûs, a 19th-century castle nearby that is now the Scandinavian School of Brussels (Ecole Reine Astrid), an international primary and secondary school.

2. Leopold III, King of the Belgians, married, in 1941, Mary Lilian Baéls. They had three children: Alexandre Emmanuel, Marie Christine, and Marie Esmeralda.

3. Princess Esmeralda of Belgium, aka Esmeralda de Rethy, to author, e-mail communication, September 13, 2004.

4. Princess Lilian of Belgium to Brigitte Boudin de Laage de Meux, October 25(?), 1967. Collection of Brigitte Boudin de Laage de Meux.

5. For most of his career, William Adams Delano (1874–1960) worked in partnership with Chester H. Aldrich (1871–1940). The firm was in operation from 1903 to 1935, at which time Aldrich resigned to become director of the American Academy in Rome. Their commissions included the Walters Art Gallery (now Museum) in Baltimore, Maryland, the Japanese Embassy in Washington, D.C., and the American Embassy in Paris.

6. A son of a Maryland judge, Tuck (1890–1966) became a close associate of Herbert Hoover during World War I, when he helped direct the Belgian war relief effort. He married Hilda Bunge (1895–1980), daughter of an Antwerp businessman.

7. As Duke of Brabant, the heir to the Belgian throne, Leopold married, in 1926, Princess Astrid of Sweden (1905–1935), a granddaughter of Oscar II of Sweden. She was popularly known as the Snow Princess because of her Scandinavian origins.

8. Princess Lilian was a friend of President John F. Kennedy from their youth, and she attended school in London with one of the future president's sisters in the late 1930s. She visited the White House in 1963 and saw the work Boudin was doing for the president and first lady. Princess Esmeralda to author, e-mail communication, May 13, 2004.

9. Princess Esmeralda to author, e-mail communication, September 13, 2004.

10. It also was a reminder that the former Mary Lilian Baéls had met the king on a golf course.

11. "Sotheby's: Princess Lilian of Belgium, Château d'Argenteuil," auction catalogue, September 22 and 23, 2003, Amsterdam, Holland, VAT Reg. No. NL 0016.56.624.B01, pp. 52–55.

12. Princess Lilian to Brigitte Boudin de Laage de Meux, October 25(?), 1967, collection of Brigitte Boudin de Laage de Meux.

13. Prince Alexandre Emmanuel of Belgium, as quoted in "Sotheby's: Princess Lilian of Belgium, Château d'Argenteuil," p. 14.

14. The house was sold to Jean-Marie Delwart, a businessman who planned turn the property into a wildlife study center. Princess Esmeralda to author, e-mail communication, January 8, 2005.

HARRY WINSTON, INC.

1. "Steuben Building on 5th Ave. Sold," *The New York Times,* March 20, 1959, p. 48.

2. Glenn Fowler, "Wright Museum Is Among Winners," *The New York Times,* May 22, 1960, p. R1.

MILDRED AND CHARLES ALLEN JR.

1. Born Mildred Gottlieb, she was previously married to Arthur Arndt and Marc Haas (1902–1990), a millionaire stamp collector. Although she eventually became Charles Allen's widow, at the time of his death she had been separated from him for a number of years.

2. Born in Palermo, Italy, Candela (1890–1953) immigrated to New York City in 1909. After attending architecture school at Columbia University, he became the city's premier apartment-house architect of the prewar period.

3. Gérald Van der Kemp to James Abbott.

4. Also known as Chevallier, Criard (c. 1724–1787) was a member of an illustrious French cabinetmaking family of Flemish origin that was known for its luxurious creations.

5. Mildred Allen to Stéphane Boudin, telegram sent via French Cable Company, September 12, 1959. Courtesy of Dr. and Mrs. Jerry Kessel, New York.

6. Ibid.

7. Stéphane Boudin to Mildred Allen, September 16, 1959. Courtesy of Dr. and Mrs. Jerry Kessel, New York.

PALACE OF MOUFIDA AND HABIB BOURGUIBA

1. Some sources give his birth date as 1903, but this appears to have been a clerical error made during his college years in France.

2. Bourguiba and his first wife divorced in 1961. A year later, in the Palace of Carthage, he married Wassila ben Ammar (1912–1999), whom he divorced in 1986.

3. E-mail correspondence with Prince Fayçal Bey of Tunisia, May 18, 2005.

4. Ironically, the cabinet room is now called the Salle de 7 Novembre, in honor of the date Bourguiba was overthrown by his prime minister.

5. Antoinette Berveiller and Gérard Bonal, eds., *Jansen*

Décoration (Paris: Société d'Etudes et de Publications Econo-miques, 1971), 136.

6. The rooms' present state can be seen at www.carthage.tn.

NICOLE AND HERVÉ ALPHAND

1. A onetime Yale football star, Sibour (1872–1938) was a half-American French viscount who became one of Washington's leading society architects, noted for exuberant houses in the French Eclectic style. Lawrence (ca. 1860–1916) founded the Pittsburgh paint company W. W. Lawrence & Co. in 1884 and became, in 1910, president of the National Lead Company. He married Jane Yuille (later Mrs. Philip Marshall Brown).

2. Hammond (1855–1936) helped develop the gold and diamond mining industries in South Africa and was a close associate of Cecil Rhodes. He later initiated hydroelectrical and irrigation projects in the United States and Mexico. A friend of several American presidents, Hammond was chosen to represent the United States at the coronation of George V of the United Kingdom in 1911. He married, in 1881, Natalie Harris. Their son John Hays Hammond Jr. invented radio remote control; their daughter, Natalie Hays Hammond, became a Broadway set designer.

3. Alphand married, in 1930, as his first wife, singer Claude Raynaud. Nicole Alphand was previously married to Etienne Bunau-Varilla, a son of the chief engineer of the Panama Canal.

4. "The Party Line," *Time,* November 22, 1963, 21–22.

5. *Life,* November 12, 1965.

6. According to *The New York Times* ("French Ingenuity and Chic Also Leave Mark on New York Home," February 7, 1959, p. 17), Alphand's first wife, Claude, later an interior decorator, was responsible for the ambassadorial residence's previous decor.

7. Ibid., p. 25.

8. An almost identical treatment of walls and windows was incorporated in a drawing room in Madrid, also designed by Jansen. This interior is illustrated on pages 48 and 49 of *Jansen Décoration* (Paris: Société d'Etudes et de Publications Econo-miques, 1971), 136.

9. Whimsical occasional tables like these were a frequent component of Jansen interiors of the 1950s and 1960s, as seen in the homes of the Duke and Duchess of Windsor, Margaret Thompson Biddle, and other clients.

10. "The Party Line," 22. After her husband stepped down as ambassador in 1965, Nicole Alphand, a member of the International Hall of Fame Best-Dressed List, managed Pierre Cardin's fashion company.

JACQUELINE AND JOHN F. KENNEDY

1. Jayne Wrightsman to James Abbott, interview held in London, August 28, 2000.

2. Dorothy May Kinnicutt (1910–1994). Married to banker Henry Parish II in 1931, she was a founder of the New York decorating firm Parish-Hadley Associates. She was known as Sister, a childhood nickname.

3. James Hoban (1762–1831).

4. Boudin's attempted gilding of the State Dining Room paneling is documented in a single photograph in the archives within the Henry Francis du Pont Winterthur Museum, Wilmington, Delaware. The proposed acquisition of 18th-century tapestries for the East Room was revealed by Jayne Wrightsman in an August 28, 2000, interview in London with the author and was subsequently backed up by 1961 correspondence between Wrightsman and Henry F. du Pont in the archives at Winterthur.

5. The color scheme also was used in the living room of Domaine d'Argenteuil for King Leopold III of Belgium and his wife, Princess Lilian.

6. Stéphane Boudin to Lorraine Pearce (Mrs. John Newton Pearce), curator of the White House, July 5, 1961. Courtesy Henry Francis du Pont Winterthur Museum, Museum Archives.

7. Jacqueline Kennedy to Stéphane Boudin, March 8, 1963. Collection of Brigitte Boudin de Laage de Meux. In the early 1960s, Jansen executed some interiors at Versailles, a series of rooms in a wing of the Grand Trianon that President Charles de Gaulle set aside for the use of presidents of France and visiting heads of state and other distinguished guests. The first official guest to stay was Prince Philip, Duke of Edinburgh, who arrived on December 20, 1966, though King Savang Vatthana of Laos had been the first actual guest to use the rooms, in July 1966, followed in October by King Mahendra and Queen Ratna of Nepal.

8. Martin Filler, "A Clash of Tastes at the White House," *The New York Times Magazine* (November 2, 1980):89.

9. A photographic portrait of Jacqueline Kennedy's successor, Lady Bird Johnson, taken in the room in December 1963, illustrates how this backdrop was perhaps better suited to those who commissioned it. Johnson appears overwhelmed by the decor and clearly uncomfortable serving as its focal point.

10. Stéphane Boudin to Jacqueline Kennedy, undated, late 1963. This line was quoted by Jacqueline Kennedy in her response to Boudin, dated January 12, 1964. Collection of Brigitte Boudin de Laage de Meux.

11. The Treaty Room decor remained intact until the administration of President George H. W. Bush. At that time, it was redecorated by the designer Mark Hampton, who privately regretted removing Boudin's influential Victorian scheme.

BARBARA AND WILLIAM S. PALEY

1. The building was designed by the New York architecture firm Starrett & Van Vleck.

2. Jansen decorated numerous rooms in the couple's Long Island house, Kiluna Farm, as well as Bill Paley's office at CBS headquarters.

3. Sally Bedell Smith, *In All His Glory: The Life and Times of William S. Paley and the Birth of Modern Broadcasting* (New York: Simon & Schuster, 1990), 453.

4. Jansen client Hattie Carnegie, for example, hired several decorators, including Hobe Erwin and Billy Baldwin, to work simultaneously on various rooms of her house in New Jersey.

5. Paul Manno to James Abbott, interview held in New York, April 23, 1996.

6. Dorothy Hart Hearst had previously been married to a son of publishing titan William Randolph Hearst. As for Babe Paley, she was the youngest daughter of Dr. Harvey Williams Cushing, a celebrated brain surgeon and neurophysicist.

7. Smith, *In All His Glory,* 334.

8. Marie de Rabutin-Chantal (1626–1696), Marquise de Sévigné, leased Hôtel Carnavalet from approximately 1677 until her death.

9. Jayne Wrightsman to Stéphane Boudin, October 25, 1966. Collection of Brigitte Boudin de Laage de Meux.

PERSEPOLIS

1. A representative of Jansen said of its designs for the celebration, "The shah gave us carte blanche." The price of the event is not recorded. Jansen's representative did allow that it would be around "the price of building a grand deluxe hotel on the site, which was the original project." *The New York Times* estimated the cost to be $100 million, which included numerous public-works projects associated with the celebration throughout the country, but a court official later said the actual four-day event cost $16.8 million. (Years later, Abdolreza Ansari, a former minister of the interior, said the price was approximately $22 million.) Jansen also oversaw the installation of temporary gardens with 50,000 carnations and 1,500 cypress trees, which were the work of the prominent French horticultural firm Truffaut. A yellow rose, called "Persepolis," also was bred for the occasion and planted in the gardens. The livery for 50 so-called courtiers was designed for the occasion by Lanvin. (John L. Hess, "Made in France—Persia's Splendorous Anniversary Celebration," *The New York Times,* October 5, 1971, p. 17).

2. Today, Persepolis is known as Takht-I-Jamshid.

3. As the shah later said, "the descendants of Charlemagne came to Persepolis to pay homage to the son of a corporal." (R.W. Apple, Jr., "Guns Displace the Grandeur That Was Persepolis," *The New York Times,* November 17, 1982, p. A2.

4. The tents were sewn by an industrial textile firm, Saint Frères.

5. Charlotte Curtis, "Tent City Awaits Celebration: Shah's Greatest Show," *The New York Times,* October 12, 1971, p. 39.

6. King Hussein of Jordan and his English wife, Princess Muna, the former Toni Gardner, gave the maid's room and its two cots to his sister, Princess Basma bint Talal, and her husband, Timoor al-Daghestani. (Charlotte Curtis, "A Persian Night of Kings, Queens, Sheiks, Sultans, and Diamonds," *The New York Times,* October 15, 1971, p. 43.

7. Society reporter Charlotte Curtis was not impressed, reporting that the tents had "all the charm of motel rooms everywhere." *The New York Times,* October 12, 1971.

8. Ibid.

9. Shahbanou Farah told Charlotte Curtis of *The New York Times* that she was disappointed that the food and the decor were not entirely Persian in theme. Curtis also reported that when the shah was criticized for the extravagance of the dinner menus, he angrily responded, "What am I supposed to do, give them bread

and radishes?"

10. Marta Rivera de la Cruz, ed., *Fiestas que hicieron historia* (Madrid: Temas de Hoy, 2001).

11. Cyrus Kadivar, "We Are Awake: 2,500-Year Celebrations Revisited," *The Iranian,* January 25, 2002.

12. *The New York Times,* October 5, 1971, p. 17. Twelve years after the Persepolis celebration, the tents were used as dormitories for teenage soldiers training for the Iran–Iraq war. (*The New York Times,* November 17, 1982, p. A2.)

13. Neil MacFarquhar, "Shah's Tent City, Fit for Kings, May Lodge Tourists," *The New York Times,* September 7, 2001, p. A4.

BARTOLOMÉ MARCH SERVERA

1. Alfonso Fierro to Mitchell Owens and Barry Cenower, interview in New York and e-mail communication, November 14, 2005

2 "A Little Palace Called Home," "Suzy Says," Chicago Tribune, March 26, 1972, p. E 11 The garden for the Cala Ratjada house was designed by Russell Page.

3 "Marita March Bride in Majorca," *The New York Times,* June 28, 1970, p. 63

FURNITURE

1. This design was copied and adapted by the American designer Karl Springer, whose celebrity clientele further popularized it.

2. This table also was copied and adapted by Karl Springer.

3. Thomas Kernan, the Duchess d'Ayen, George Dubois, and Jacqueline de Léon, *Nouvelles Réussites de la Décoration Française, 1960–1966: L'Interprétation Moderne des Styles Traditionnels* (Paris: Editions Robert Laffont, 1966), 164.

Books

Abbott, James A. *A Frenchman in Camelot: The Decoration of the Kennedy White House by Stéphane Boudin.* Garrison, New York: Boscobel Restoration, 1995.

———— and Elaine M. Rice. *Designing Camelot: The Kennedy White House Restoration.* New York: Van Nostrand-Reinhold, 1998.

Albrecht, Donald. *Glass + Glamour: Stueben's Modern Movement, 1930–1960.* New York: Museum of the City of New York/Harry N. Abrams, 2003.

Alexandre of Belgium. *Argenteuil: "Pour garder intacte la mémoire du domaine royal."* Brussels, Belgium: Alice Editions, 2005.

Baldwin, Billy, with Michael Gardine. *Billy Baldwin: An Autobiography.* Boston: Little, Brown, 1985.

Bartlett, Apple Parish, and Susan Bartlett Crater. *Sister: The Life of Legendary American Interior Decorator Mrs. Henry Parish II.* New York: St. Martin's, 2000.

Becker, Robert. *Nancy Lancaster: Her Life, Her World, Her Art.* New York: Alfred A. Knopf, 1996.

Berveiller, Antoinette, and Gérard Bonal, eds. *Jansen Décoration.* Paris: Société d'Etudes et de Publications Economiques, 1971.

Borrus, Kathy. *One Thousand Buildings of Paris.* New York: Black Dog & Leventhal, 2003.

Bowles, Hamish, et al. *Jacqueline Kennedy: The White House Years.* New York: The Metropolitan Museum of Art/Bulfinch Press, 2001.

Boyden, Martha, and Alessandra Vinciquerra, et al. *Russell Page: Ritratti di giardini italiani.* Rome: American Academy in Rome, 1998.

Bryan, J., III, and Charles J. V. Murphy. *The Windsor Story.* New York: Dell, 1979.

Cleggett, David A. H. *History of Leeds Castle and Its Families.* Maidstone, UK: Leeds Castle Foundation, 1994.

Collas, Phillipe, and Eric Villedary. *Edith Wharton's French Riviera.* New York: Flammarion, 2002.

Cornforth, John. *London Interiors from the Archives of Country Life.* London: Aurum Press, 2000.

Crook, J. Mordaunt. *The Rise of the Nouveaux Riches: Style and Status in Victorian and Edwardian Architecture.* London: John Murray, 1999.

De Fayet, Monique. *Comment Installer Son Intérieur en Louis XVI.* Paris: Éditions Charles Massin, 1963.

De Gramont, Sanche. *The French: Portrait of a People.* New York: G. P. Putnam's Sons, 1969.

The Duke and Duchess of Windsor. New York: Sotheby's, 1997.

Dwight, Eleanor. *Edith Wharton: An Extraordinary Life.* New York: Harry N. Abrams, 1994.

The Estate of Mrs. Charles Allen, Jr. New York: Sotheby's, 1997.

Gore, Alan, and Ann Gore. *English Interiors: An Illustrated History.* New York: Thames and Hudson, 1991.

Hampton, Mark. *Legendary Decorators of the Twentieth Century.* New York: Doubleday, 1992.

Higham, Charles. *The Duchess of Windsor: The Secret Life.* New York: McGraw-Hill, 1988.

Honour, Hugh. *Cabinet Makers and Furniture Designers.* New York: G. P. Putnam's Sons, 1969.

Hubert, Gérard. *Malmaison.* Paris: Editions de la Réunion des musées nationaux, 1982.

James, Robert Rhodes, ed. *Chips: The Diaries of Sir Henry Channon.* London: Phoenix Press, 2003.

King, Greg. *The Duchess of Windsor: The Uncommon Life of Wallis Simpson.* New York: Citadell Press, 1999.

La Décoration: Collection Connaissance des Arts. Paris: Librarie Hachette et Société d'Etudes et de Publications Artistiques, 1963.

La Décoration: Maisons de Vacances. Paris: Librarie Hachette et Société d'Etudes et de Publications Artistiques, 1964.

Leeds Castle, Maidstone, Kent. London: Philip Wilson Publishers, on behalf of Leeds Castle Foundation, 1996.

Madsen, Axel. *Chanel: A Woman of Her Own.* New York: Henry Holt, 1990.

Menkes, Suzy. *The Windsor Style.* London: Grafton, 1987.

Mesta, Perle, with Robert Cahn. *Perle: My Story.* New York: McGraw-Hill, 1960.

Metcalf, Pauline C., ed. *Ogden Codman and the Decoration of Houses.* Boston: Boston Athenaeum–Godine, 1988.

Mosley, Diana. *The Duchess of Windsor.* New York: Stein & Day, 1980.

Ogden, Christopher. *Life of the Party: The Biography of Pamela Digby Churchill Hayward Harriman.* Boston: Little, Brown, 1994.

Parish, Sister, Albert Hadley, and Christopher Petkanas. *Parish-Hadley: Sixty Years of American Design.* Boston: Little, Brown, 1995.

Payne, Christopher. *François Linke, 1855–1946: The Belle Epoque of French Furniture.* Woodbridge, UK: Antique Collector's Club, 2003.

Peck, Amelia, et al. *Period Rooms in the Metropolitan Museum of Art.* New York: The Metropolitan Museum of Art/ Harry N. Abrams, 1996.

Poole, Mary Jane, ed. *20th-Century Decorating, Architecture, & Gardens: 80 Years of Ideas and Pleasure from House & Garden.* New York: Holt, Rinehart & Winston, 1980.

Price, Roger. *A Concise History of France.* Cambridge, UK: Cambridge University Press, 1993.

Princess Lilian of Belgium: Château d'Argenteuil. Amsterdam: Sotheby's, 2003.

Property from the Collection of Mrs. Charles Wrightsman, Removed from her Palm Beach Residence. New York: Sotheby Parke Bernet, 1984.

Rubin, William, and Matthew Armstrong. *The William S. Paley Collection.* New York: The Museum of Modern Art, 1992.

Schinz, Marina, and Gabrielle van Zuylen. *The Gardens of Russell Page.* New York: Stewart, Tabori & Chang, 1991.

Shirer, William L. *The Collapse of the Third Republic: An Inquiry into the Fall of France in 1940.* New York: Simon & Schuster, 1969.

Slesin, Suzanne. *Over the Top: Helena Rubinstein: Extraordinary Style, Beauty, Art, Fashion, Design.* New York: Pointed Leaf Press, 2003.

Smith, Jane S. *Elsie de Wolfe: A Life in the High Style: The Elegant Life and Remarkable Career of Elsie de Wolfe, Lady Mendl.* New York, Atheneum, 1982.

Smith, Sally Bedell. *Grace and Power: The Private World of the Kennedy White House.* New York: Random House, 2004.

———. *In All His Glory: The Life and Times of William S. Paley and the Birth of Modern Broadcasting.* New York: Touchstone, 1991.

———. *Reflected Glory: The Life of Pamela Churchill Harriman.* New York: Simon & Schuster, 1996.

Stadiem, William. *Too Rich: The High Life and Tragic Death of King Farouk.* New York: Carroll & Graf, 1991.

Stout, Nancy, and Jorge Rigau. *Havana.* New York: Rizzoli, 2003.

Thayer, Mary Van Rensselaer. *Jacqueline Kennedy: The White House Years.* Boston: Little, Brown, 1971.

Tweed, Katherine, ed. *The Finest Rooms by America's Great Decorators.* New York: Viking, 1964.

Veillon, Dominique. *Fashion under the Occupation.* Oxford, UK: Oxford International, 2002.

Vickers, Hugo. *The Private World of the Duke and Duchess of Windsor.* New York: Abbeville Press, 1995.

Walker, John. *Self-Portait with Donors: Confessions of an Art Collector.* Boston: Little, Brown, 1974.

West, J. B., with Mary Lynn Kotz. *Upstairs at the White House: My Life with the First Ladies.* New York: Coward, McCann & Geoghegan, 1973.

Wildenstein, George, et al., for Pavillon de la France, New York World's Fair. *Five Centuries of History Mirrored in Five Centuries of French Art.* France: Groupe de l'Art Ancien, 1939.

ARTICLES

Anthony, Carl Sferrazza. "Love, Jackie." *Forbes American Heritage* 45, no. 5 (September 1994): 90–101.

Brackner, Milton. "Parisian Assesses White House Decor." *The New York Times* (April 1, 1961): 1A.

Bernier, Rosamond. "Palm Beach Fable: The Private Wrightsman Rooms." *House & Garden* (May 1984), pp. 118-135.

Clifford, Marie J. "Helena Rubinstein's Beauty Salons, Fashion, and Modernist Display." *Winterthur Portfolio* 38, no. 2/3 (Summer/Autumn 2003), pp. 83-108.

Cornforth, John. "Boudin at Leeds Castle I." *Country Life* 1, no. 14 (April 1983), pp. 925-928.

———. "Boudin at Leeds Castle II." *Country Life* 1, no. 21 (May 1983), pp. 1018-1021.

"Decoration, Antiquités: Jansen." Unknown French publisher, dated 1922. [This article was included in the papers of Brigitte Boudin de Laage de Meux.]

Filler, Martin. "A Clash of Tastes at the White House." *The New York Times Magazine* (November 2, 1980): 89, pp. 90-93 and 146.

———. "Jackie, Queen of Arts." *House Beautiful* 136, no. 9 (September 1994).

Fowler, Glenn. "Wright Museum Is Among Winners." *The New York Times* (May 22, 1960): R1.

Franklin, Ruth. "A Life in Good Taste: The Fashions and Follies of Elsie de Wolfe." *The New Yorker* (September 27, 2004).

"Helena Rubinstein: In Her Paris home." *House & Garden* (January 1938), pp. 50-51.

"Historic Interiors: Lady Mendl, Her Beloved Villa Trianon." *Architectural Digest* (June 1982), pp. 66-73.

Jardel, Marguerite. "Tassinari and Châtel: 1762–1962." *La Revue Française* 137 (February 1962), supplement.

Lawford, Valentine. "The Duke and Duchess of Windsor in Paris." *Vogue* (April 1, 1964), pp. 176-187 and 190-194.

———. "The Leland Haywards of 'Haywire House.'" *Vogue* (February 15, 1964), pp. 124-127 and 130.

"L'Hotel de Chanaleilles Devient La Plus Somptueuse Demeure de Paris." *Connaissance des Arts* 105 (November 1960), pp. 74-113.

"Margaret Biddle Is Dead in Paris." *The New York Times* (June 9, 1956): 17.

Miers, Mary. "Leeds Castle: The Inside Story." *Country Life* (May 8, 2003), pp. 106-111.

"Mrs. Charles Wrightsman: A Collector's Pursuit of Art and Perfection." *Vogue* (October 1966), pp. 240-241.

"Mrs. Thompson Biddle's Two-Room Apartment." *Vogue* (August 1, 1952), pp. 74-77.

Nguyen, Khoi. "Gilt Complex." *Connoisseur* (September 1991).

O'Brien, Timothy L. "The Castro Collection: A Painting from Cuba offers a glimpse into the world of art smuggling." *The New York Times* (November 21, 2004), section 3, pp. 1, 10-11.

Reif, Rita. "Wrightsmans' Furniture Collection and Palm Beach Mansion to Be Sold." *The New York Times* (February 2, 1984): p. C1.

Robertson, Bryan. "Mrs. Wrightsman: The Enthusiasm of Collecting." *Vogue* (October 1, 1966), pp. 240-241.

Rosas, Carlos A. "When Louis Quinze Conquered New York." *Quest* (November 1996), pp. 64-70.

Russell, John. "Art: Rooms with A View to the Past." *The New York Times* (May 20, 1977): 72.

"Steuben Building on 5th Ave. Sold." *The New York Times* (March 20, 1959): 48.

Storey, Walter Rendell. "Hotel Decoration in the Grand Manner: Modern and Period Effects in Furnishings are Combined to Bring Charm and Comfort to the Waldorf-Astoria . . ." *The New York Times* (September 27, 1931): SM8.

"The Duke and Duchess of Windsor at La Cröe." *British Vogue* (September 21, 1938), pp. 74-79.

"The Party Line." *Time* 82, no. 21 (November 22, 1963), pp. 21-25.

Warren, Virginia Lee. "Baron's Daughter Finds Shop-keeping to Her Taste." *The New York Times* (July 28, 1965): 20.

ARCHIVES/LIBRARIES/PRIMARY SOURCES

Art Library of The Baltimore Museum of Art, Baltimore, Maryland.

The Mattie Edwards Hewitt and Richard A. Smith Photographic Collection, New York Historical Society, New York City.

Private collection of Arthur Bennett Kouwenhoven, Savannah, Georgia.

Private collection of Brigitte Boudin de Laage de Meux, Paris, France.

Private collection of Leon Amar, Palm Beach, Florida.

Private collection of Paul J. Manno, New York City.

Private collection of William Voss Elder III, Baltimore, Maryland.

INTERVIEWS

Amar, Leon, employee of Jansen, Inc., to James Abbott; interview held in Palm Beach, Florida, February 2003.

Châtel, Jean-Jacques, textile manufacturer, to James Abbott; interview held at Tassinari and Châtel offices, Paris, France, April 19, 1988.

de Laage de Meux, Brigitte, daughter of Stéphane Boudin, to James Abbott; interviews held in Paris, France, between 1999 and 2004.

Elder, William Voss, III, Curator of Decorative Arts, the Baltimore Museum of Art, to James Abbott; interview held at the BMA, Baltimore, Maryland, November 18, 1992.

Ernandez, Albert, employee of Jansen, S.A., to James Abbott; interview held in Paris, France, January 28, 2000.

Guest, Mrs. Winston, client, to James Abbott; interviews held in New York and by telephone, between 1998 and 2001.

Hadley, Albert, designer, to James Abbott; interviews held in New York and Maryland, between 1995 and 2003.

Kessel, Dr. Jerry, and Judith Kessel, relatives of Mrs. Charles Allen Jr., to James Abbott; interview held in New York, May 1, 2005.

Kouwenhoven, Arthur Bennett, employee of Jansen, Inc., to James Abbott; interviews held in New York and Savannah, between 1996 and 2005.

Mandron, Claude, employee of Jansen, S.A., and nephew of Stéphane Boudin, to James Abbott; interview held in Paris, France, February 5, 1999.

Manno, Paul J., onetime director of Jansen, Inc., to James Abbott; interviews held in New York, between 1996 and 2005.

Robin, Serge, employee of Jansen, S.A., to James Abbott, with Brigitte (Boudin) de Laage de Meux, January 28, 2000.

Sweeney, John A. H., Curator Emeritus, Winterthur, to James Abbott; interview held at Philipsburg Manor, North Tarrytown, New York, April 1987.

Wrightsman, Mrs. Charles B., client, to James Abbott; interview held in London, England, August 28, 2000.

PHOTOGRAPHS ON THE FOLLOWING PAGES ARE COURTESY OF AND USED BY PERMISSION OF THE FOLLOWING INSTITUTIONS OR INDIVIDUALS (ALL RIGHTS RESERVED).

2 courtesy of private collection.

8 collection of Brigitte Boudin de Laage de Meux, Paris, courtesy of Stephane de Laage.

10, 11 (left and right), 15, 16, 29, 36, 40, 42, 43 courtesy of Paul Manno, New York.

14 (top and bottom) courtesy of the Salisbury House Foundation.

17 courtesy of the Royal Archives, Windsor Castle, copyright HM The Queen.

12, 18, 22, 23, 34 courtesy of the collection of Brigitte Boudin de Laage de Meux, Paris.

21 courtesy of private collection.

25 Vogue, © 1937 Condé Nast Publications, Inc., New York.

27 courtesy of private collection.

30, 40 *Jansen Décoration*, Société d'Etudes et Les Publications Economiques, Paris, 1971.

31 Cecil Beaton/Vogue, © 1960 Condé Nast Publications, Inc., New York.

33 (top and bottom) courtesy of Gerald G. Stiebel and Steibel, Ltd., New York.

35 courtesy of private collection.

37 courtesy of private collection, photograph by Mark B. Letzer.

38 courtesy of private collection.

39 watercolor signed T. Hunlake from "The Estate of Pamela Harriman" sales catalogue, p. 349, courtesy of Sotheby's New York.

41 courtesy collection of Leon Amar.

44 courtesy of private collection.

46, 48–51, 53 courtesy of the Belgium Embassy, Washington, D.C.

54, 57–63 courtesy of Maria Carmen Gomez-Mena Beriro.

64, 66, 67, 69–71 archival photographs of original watercolors by Alexandre Serebriakoff, courtesy of the Ditchley Foundation, Oxfordshire, England.

65 courtesy of the Country Life Picture Gallery, London.

72, 74–79, 81 courtesy of HRH Crown Prince Alexander II.

82, 84–93 courtesy of private collection.

94, 96, 97, 99, and 101 courtesy of the Country Life Picture Gallery, London.

102, 104–111 courtesy of the Leeds Castle Foundation.

112, 114, 115, 117 © Getty Images, photography by William Vandivert/Time Life Pictures/Getty Images.

118 courtesy of Jean-Yves Brouard.

120–123 courtesy of the collection Chantiers de l'Atlantique, Cliché Economusée de Saint-Nazaire.

124, 126, and 127 courtesy of the Country Life Picture Gallery, London.

128, 130, 131, 132 courtesy of the Library of Congress, Gottscho-Schleisesner Collection.

134–137 collection of Paul Manno, New York.

138, 140–143 courtesy of the Library of Congress, Gottscho-Schleisesner Collection.

144, 146–151 collection of Paul Manno, New York.

152, 154–159 courtesy Caroline Palermo Schulze.

160, 162, 163, 165, 166 (top and bottom), 167 collection of Paul Manno, New York.

168 Horst/Vogue © 1956, Condé Nast Publications, Inc., New York.

170–173 Cecil Beaton ©, Sotheby's Picture Library, London.

174, 177–179 courtesy of the Lyndon B. Johnson Library, Austin, Texas.

180, 182–185, 187 courtesy of Christie's Images, Ltd., London.

188, 191–193 courtesy of the Metropolitan Museum of Art, New York.

194, 195 collection of Paul Manno, New York.

196, 199–203 *Argenteuil: Pour garder intacte la memoire du domaine royal,* courtesy of Alice Editions, Brussels, 2005.

206 (left) courtesy of Steuben Glass.

206 (right) courtesy of Harry Winston, Inc.

204, 207–209 collection of Paul Manno, New York.

210, 212, 216 courtesy of Judy and Jerry Kessel, New York.

218, 219 courtesy of Paul Manno, New York, photography by Robert B. Starr, III.

210, 213, 217 Sotheby's by permission of the estate of Mrs. Charles Allen, Jr., and Judith and Jerry Kessel, New York.

215 courtesy of Christie's, by permission of the estate of Mrs. Charles Allen, Jr., and Judith and Jerry Kessel, New York.

220, 222, 223, 225 *Jansen Décoration*, Société d'Etudes et Les Publications Economiques, Paris, 1971.

226, 228–230, 233 courtesy the Special Collections, University of Virginia Library, George Mason University, Charles Baptie Photograph Collection.

234 courtesy White House Historical Association.

236 courtesy of author's collection.

237 courtesy of collection of William Voss Elder, III.

238 courtesy of the John F. Kennedy Library, Boston, Massachusetts, photography by Jose Sanchez.

238 courtesy of Paul Manno, New York, photography by Robert B. Starr, III.

234, 239, 241 courtesy of the John F. Kennedy Library, Boston, Massachusetts.

240 courtesy of Tassinari & Chatel, photography by Jose Sanchez.

242, 244, 245 courtesy of Albert Hadley, Inc., photography by John Hall.

247–251 collection of Paul Manno, New York, photography by Robert B. Starr, III.

252-259, 262–269 collection of Paul Manno, New York.

260, 261 David Massey/House and Garden copyright 1972, Condé Nast Publications, Inc., New York.

268, 270, 272, 273, 275, 276, 277 courtesy of Alfonso Fierro March.

280–281(top and bottom), 282 (top), 283 (top and bottom), 284, 292 (left) courtesy of private collection.

282 (bottom), 285 (top and bottom), 290–295 collection of Paul Manno, New York. photography by Robert B. Starr, III.

292 (right) courtesy of Judith and Jerry Kessel, New York.

278, 286–289, 293 (top and bottom) courtesy of Christie's Images, Ltd., London.

T HIS BOOK WOULD NOT HAVE BEEN POSSIBLE WITHOUT THE initiative taken by the late Brigitte Boudin de Laage de Meux, daughter of Jansen's one-time president and creative genius, Stéphane Boudin. Whether through interviews in her beautiful Jansen-esque apartment or during somewhat spontaneous excursions through the streets of Paris, she invited me into the world of 'Boudin,' and thusly into the world of Jansen. I am indebted to her thoughtfulness, generosity, and passion to see her father's contributions to the world of design rightfully documented.

I thank the staff of Acanthus Press, specifically visionary Barry Cenower. I also acknowledge editor Mitchell Owens, whose personal passion for the topic was both challenging and encouraging.

The production of this book is equally enhanced by the generosity of time and consideration on the part of HIM Farah Pahlavi of Iran; HRH Princess Marie-Esmeralda of Belgium; HRH Prince Alexandre Emmanuel and Princess Léa of Belgium; HRH Prince Fayçal Bey of Tunisia; HRH Prince Alexander II of Yugoslavia; Maria Carmen Gomez-Mena Beriro; Mrs. Charles B. Wrightsman, iconic connoisseur and tastemaker; Stéphane de Laage de Meux, grandson of Stéphane Boudin; Leon Amar; Mr. and Mrs. Victor Barnett; Louis Bofferding; Benoist F. Drut; Albert Ernandes; Paul Ernandes; Augustin Batista-Falla; Pepe Fanjul; Alexis Gregory; Jamee and Peter S. Gregory; the late-C.Z. Guest; Albert Hadley; the late-Honorable Pamela Harriman; Judith and Jerry Kessel; Arthur Kouwenhoven; Marie-Cécile Levitte, wife of the French Ambassador to the United States; the late-Claude Mandron; Paul and Sheelagh Manno, two sources who have become good friends; Alfonso Fierro March, Pedro Girao and Emma Strouts; Suzy Menkes; Peter Nomikos; Liz O'Brien, and her staff at Liz O'Brien Gallery in New York; Caroline Palermo Schulze and her beautiful photography; the late-James Parker; Roger Prigent; Côme Remy; Serge Robin; Pierre-Marie Rudelle; Ronald Winston, Nina Giambelli, and Gerald G. Stiebel.

To author and researcher Gary Cohen, I owe my appreciation for all of his invaluable guidance. Sandra Stellman, Mark Letzer, Susanne Adams and Patrick Camus aided in translations, which were many. For information regarding the passenger liner 'Pasteur,' I wish to acknowledge the generosity of Thérèse Dumont, Chargée d'Information, Ecomusee de Saint-Nazaire, and historian Jean-Yves Brouard, whose own book on the history of this famous ship was recently published. I am equally indebted to: Michael Stier, Associate Permissions Manager, and Gretchen Fenston, Susan Train, and Sara Burch, Condé Nast Publications;

Leonora Trafford and Camilla Costello, Country Life Picture Library; Brigadier Christopher Galloway and The Ditchley Foundation, Oxfordshire; Alexia Bleathman, Archivist, Archive of Art and Design, Word & Image Department, Victoria and Albert Museum, who assisted in the research of Jansen of Paris, Ltd.; the late John Cornforth, who provided insight into Jansen's work in 1930s England; Katrien Timmers of Kasteel de Haar, the Netherlands; Caroline Shaw, Assistant Archivist, Rothschild Archive; Mary Lynn, Hotel Villa Magna, Madrid; Pauline C. Metcalf, who shared finds of early Jansen commissions; Scott Brunscheen, Director, Mary Beth Hill, and Chris Burch, Salisbury House Foundation, Des Moines, Iowa; Paula Mohr, Department of Architectural History, University of Virginia; Arlene Palmer-Schwind, curator extraordinaire, who shared valuable materials regarding Margaret Thompson Biddle's 'Les Embruns'; David A. H. Cleggett, friend, historian, and author of the "History of Leeds Castle and Its Families"; Andrea Murphy, Cultural Officer, and Raka Singh of the Belgian Embassy in Washington; art historian and new friend Françoise Arnaud; designer Andrew Virtue; Véronique Sacuto of Cartier, Paris; Nancy Porter of Albert Hadley, Inc.; Amy S. Wiggin, Hattie-Carnegie.com; Ruth Mitchell, The Maryland Historical Society; Harmony Haskins, White House Historical Association; and Michel de Grand Ry, Alice Editions.

I wish to thank my friends and former colleagues at The Baltimore Museum of Art, especially scholar Catherine Stewart Thomas, the former Assistant Curator of Decorative Arts. Equally important are: William Voss Elder, III; M. B. Munford; Anita Jones; Viola Holmes; Patricia Derus; Jose Sanchez; Arnold Lehman; Brenda Richardson; Constance Caplan; Anthony Deering; Charles Newhall; Suzanne Cohen; and the very generous and valuable Friends of the American Wing–loyal supporters of a most wonderful institution, one and all. Lastly, I want to acknowledge the support of Linda Tompkins-Baldwin, Librarian, and Emily Rafferty, Assistant Librarian; their assistance had no equal.

I also want to acknowledge the Washington County Museum of Fine Arts, Hagerstown, Maryland, and director Dr. Joseph Ruzicka. I am appreciative of this institution's Board of Trustees, which welcomed me to their mission of sharing an appreciation for art.

Finally, I thank friends Bud and Susanne Adams, Paul Barrett, Billie Conkling, Tom Cook, Dr. Susan Dackerman, Bill Elder, Dr. William L. Guyton, Patricia James, Ned and Dana Lewison, 'guardian angel' Mike Merson, Mary Meyer, Gregory Most, Mark Letzer, Elaine Rice-Bachmann, Dr. John Beverley Riggs, Freddie Saxon, John Shields and John Gilligan, Christopher Dean Shyer, Andrew van Styn, J. Scott Watkins, Paul and Karen Winicki, and my chief photographer and ever-protective big brother, Robert B. Starr, III. Added to this list is my friend and true mentor in the field of decorative arts, Joseph T. Butler; my fellow tassel-admirer and constant teacher with regards to the realities of interior decoration, the incomparable Mary Fagan of W. T. Barnes in Dobbs Ferry, New York; my sister and near-twin, Mary Abbott-Gillooly; my adopted family–'Mac' (1914-2005), Eleanor, Betsy, and Martha McIntyre; and lastly, Jonathan, whose gifts are too many to list, but all of which saved the day many times over.

–J. A. A.

BALTIMORE, MARYLAND

COLOPHON

ACANTHUS PRESS publishes fine books. We are interested in tracing—which often means rediscovering—the lineages of architectural and interior design. Just as we respect and are intrigued by building traditions, so we respect the traditions of good book design. Choices of type, paper, binding, and images, as well as printing production methods, are issues we consider and investigate with each Acanthus book. We see our mission as an enduring one— to create an Acanthus library of books thematically and visually related and reflecting variations on design themes that are elegant, subtle, and timeless.

The typefaces used throughout this book are digital versions of Monotype Garamond and Bernhard Modern. Many versions of Garamond exist. The Garamond we chose was originally cut in 1922 by the Monotype Corporation, which mistakenly called it Garamond after designs by the French designer, Claude Garamond (1480–1561). Later research revealed the face was closer to designs by another 16th-century French designer, Jean Jannon, who based his old-style designs on 15th-century Italian letterforms. Lucian Bernhard, a German art director who had emigrated to New York City in the early 1920s, designed Bernhard Modern in 1937 for American Type Founders, Inc. The face is his version of engravers' old-style type.

EDITING BY MITCHELL OWENS
COPYEDITING BY ANGELA BUCKLEY
LAYOUT BY POLLY FRANCHINI

JANSEN WAS PRINTED ON JAPANESE FINE ART MATTE PAPER
AND BOUND WITH T-SAIFU JAPANESE CLOTH
BY PHOENIX OFFSET, HONG KONG.

ACANTHUS PRESS

FINE BOOKS

   20TH CENTURY DECORATORS

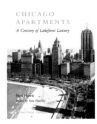   URBAN DOMESTIC ARCHITECTURE

 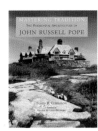  THE AMERICAN ARCHITECT

 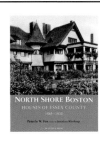 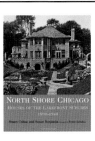 SUBURBAN DOMESTIC ARCHITECTURE

MAISON
JANSEN